MW00806128

TANF= Temporary Aid to Needy Families

Praise for *Women and Poverty*

"Bullock shines the light of her clear and bold analyses on such issues as discrimination, unpaid labor for motherhood and caregiving, labor market wage disparities, unaffordable housing, and violence. She examines the relationship between negative attitudes and beliefs about poor women and demeaning social policies. A 'must' for social and community psychologists, clinical and educational psychologists, and all other professionals and students who take seriously the mission of advancing human health and welfare."

Bernice Lott, *Department of Psychology,*
The University of Rhode Island

"With her book *Women and Poverty*, Heather Bullock continues her groundbreaking illumination of poverty and classism from a psychological perspective. Bringing her focus to the gendered construction of poverty, Bullock's compelling examination manages to be both expansive and particular – it encompasses the broad sociocultural trends and biases that perpetuate women's poverty, but also renders comprehensible the fluctuations and implications of recent welfare policies. Scholarly, passionate, and forceful, this book is a must-have resource for psychologists, educators, social service professionals, and policy-makers whose work interfaces with issues of social class and social justice."

Laura Smith, *Department of Counseling and Clinical Psychology,*
Teachers College, Columbia University

"In a time of obscene economic inequality, Heather Bullock's *Women and Poverty: Psychology, Public Policy and Social Justice* is essential reading. Scholarly and passionate, this book reveals the ways in which poverty is gendered, illuminates the costs of poverty to women and to our entire society, and gives us the tools to challenge class bias and advance just social policies."

Deborah Belle, *Department of Psychology, Boston University*

Contemporary Social Issues

Contemporary Social Issues, a book series authored by leading experts in the field, focuses on psychological inquiry and research relevant to social issues facing individuals, groups, communities, and society at large. Each volume is written for scholars, students, practitioners, and policy-makers.

Series Editor: Daniel Perlman

Multiculturalism and Diversity: A Social Psychological Perspective
Bernice Lott

The Psychological Wealth of Nations: Do Happy People Make a Happy Society?
Shigehiro Oishi

Women and Poverty: Psychology, Public Policy, and Social Justice
Heather Bullock

Forthcoming

Stalking and the Cultural Construction of Romance
H. Colleen Sinclair

Taking Moral Action
Chuck Huff

The Psychology of Helping Relations
Arie Nadler

Women and Poverty

Psychology, Public Policy, and Social Justice

Heather E. Bullock

WILEY Blackwell

This edition first published 2013
© 2013 Heather E. Bullock

Registered Office
John Wiley & Sons, Ltd, The Atrium, Southern Gate, Chichester, West Sussex, PO19 8SQ, UK

Editorial Offices
350 Main Street, Malden, MA 02148-5020, USA
9600 Garsington Road, Oxford, OX4 2DQ, UK
The Atrium, Southern Gate, Chichester, West Sussex, PO19 8SQ, UK

For details of our global editorial offices, for customer services, and for information about how to apply for permission to reuse the copyright material in this book please see our website at www.wiley.com/wiley-blackwell.

The right of Heather E. Bullock to be identified as the author of this work has been asserted in accordance with the UK Copyright, Designs and Patents Act 1988.

Library of Congress Cataloging-in-Publication Data

Bullock, Heather E.
  Women and poverty : psychology, public policy, and social justice / Heather E. Bullock.
    pages cm
  Includes bibliographical references and index.
    ISBN 978-1-4051-8351-2 (cloth) – ISBN 978-1-4051-8350-5 (pbk.)   1. Poor women–Social conditions.   2. Poverty.   3. Women – Economic conditions.   4. Women – Social conditions.   I. Title.
  HQ1381.B85 2013
  362.83'9857–dc23

                                                                    2013016704

A catalogue record for this book is available from the British Library.

Cover image: © photosmash / istockphoto
Cover design by Simon Levy Associates

Set in 10/12 pt Galliard by Toppan Best-set Premedia Limited
Printed in Malaysia by Ho Printing (M) Sdn Bhd

1   2013

This book is dedicated to Julian Fernald, my great love and friend. I am grate-ful to Harmony Reppond for her editorial assistance.

Contents

About the Author

Heather E. Bullock is Professor and Chair of the Psychology Department at the University of California, Santa Cruz (UCSC), USA, and served as Director of UCSC's Center for Justice, Tolerance, and Community. She studies the social psychological causes and consequences of economic injustice, with special attention to poverty among women. Much of her research focuses on identifying the attitudes and beliefs that predict support for antipoverty policies, and the impact of framing on policy preferences.

Professor Bullock has participated in initiatives to increase psychologists' attention to class-based discrimination and poverty. She was a member of the American Psychological Association's (APA) Task Force on Socioeconomic Status (SES) and chaired APA's Committee on SES. She received the Committee's 2013 Distinguished Leadership award for her contributions to understanding poverty and social class.

Before joining the faculty at UCSC, Professor Bullock served as an APA Congressional Fellow with the U.S. Senate Committee on Health, Education, Labor, and Pensions – Democratic Office. She worked for Senator Edward M. Kennedy on policies related to poverty, welfare reform, food insecurity, and early childhood education. She has also held faculty positions at Nebraska Wesleyan University and the Heller School for Social Policy and Management at Brandeis University.

Her co-authored book with Dr. Bernice Lott, *Psychology and Economic Injustice: Personal, Professional, and Political Intersections* (2007), was recognized by the American Library Association and the Association for Women in Psychology. Professor Bullock is the incoming editor of *Analyses of Social Issues and Public Policy*.

1

Women and Poverty:
An Ongoing Crisis

In the United States and around the world, women bear much of the brunt of poverty (Goldberg, 2010; International Labour Office (ILO), 2010; US Census Bureau, 2012a). Seventy percent of the world's poor are women (United Nations Women, n.d.), and despite tremendous differences in living standards, wealth, and opportunity, common root causes emerge around the world – discrimination, unequal sharing of family and household responsibilities, abusive relationships, lack of control and access to resources (e.g., education and land), and segregation into low-paid, low-status jobs (ILO, 2011). Substandard, dangerous living conditions, poor health and limited access to health care, lack of nutritious food, and the stress of financial insecurity are but a few of the devastating daily realities faced by poor women and their children.

In the United States, the richest nation in the world, the contrast between wealth and poverty is extreme, and women remain disproportionately poor despite progress toward gender equality. A staggering 40.9% of US female-headed households with children under the age of 18 were poor in 2011 (National Women's Law Center (NWLC), 2012). Although the Great Recession (December, 2007–June, 2009) has deepened women's economic hardship (Hayes & Hartmann, 2011), the history of women's poverty runs long and deep (Albelda & Tilly, 1997; Gordon, 1994; Piven & Cloward, 1993; Sidel, 1998).

This chapter provides an overview of contemporary rates of poverty and homelessness, illustrating the heavy burden of economic hardship on women. Emphasis is placed on understanding how poverty and homelessness are "counted" in the United States, and the consequences of different measurement strategies. Special attention is given to the shortcomings of official US poverty estimates, political controversies surrounding poverty measurement, and the role of social science research in addressing these challenges and bringing women's poverty to the forefront of public consciousness.

Women and Poverty: Psychology, Public Policy, and Social Justice, First Edition. Heather E. Bullock.
© 2013 Heather E. Bullock. Published 2013 by John Wiley and Sons, Ltd.

Women, Poverty, and Rising Economic Inequality

The Feminization of Poverty

Diana Pearce (1978) coined the term the "feminization of poverty" in the 1970s to describe disproportionately high rates of poverty among women in spite of seeming gains in gender equality and women's increased labor force participation. Lamenting this paradox, she observed, "Though many women have achieved economic independence from their spouses by their participation in the labor force (and in some cases, by divorce), for many the price of that independence has been their pauperization and dependence on welfare" (Pearce, 1978, p. 28). Of course, women are not a homogenous group, and the influx of white women into the paid labor force revealed what had long been a reality for women of color – work does not necessarily guarantee a life free from poverty. Feminist scholars are quick to point to variations in women's relationship to power, and the "feminization of poverty" has been criticized for failing to appreciate the diversity of women's experiences and for its relatively exclusive focus on income over other forms of deprivation and exclusion (Chant, 2007). With these caveats in mind, the "feminization of poverty" is an apt shorthand to describe women's overrepresentation among the poor in the United States and internationally (Brady & Kall, 2008; Goldberg, 2010).

The feminization of poverty is documented around the world, typically evidenced by women's greater lifetime risk of experiencing poverty and the higher rates of poverty found among women than men. In the mid-1980s, US women were 41% more likely to be poor than men (Casper, McLanahan, & Garfinkel, 1994), and these trends persist. In a study of mid-1990s poverty rates in eight industrialized nations, the United States had the largest gender poverty gap, with women's poverty rates outpacing men's by 38% (Christopher, England, Smeeding, & Phillips, 2002). Race and educational attainment intersect with gender to increase risk. Rank and Hirschl (2001) estimate that 98.3% of Black women between the ages of 25 and 75 with less than 12 years of education will experience poverty compared with 65.4% of similarly educated white men. Because women are at high risk of poverty during childhood, adulthood, and their senior years, the feminization of poverty is conceptualized using a life course perspective (Pearce & Moritz, 1988).

In the wake of the Great Recession and in the face of rising inequality (Hayes & Hartmann, 2011; Sherman & Stone, 2010), the US poverty rate in 2010 reached its second highest point since 1965, with 46.2 million people (15.1% of the population) or one in seven Americans living below official poverty thresholds ($22,314 for a family of four; US Census Bureau, 2011; Trisi, Sherman, & Broaddus, 2011). Deep poverty, defined as half of the poverty line (below $11,157 for a family of four), reached its highest point on record in 2010 with approximately 20.5 million people (6.7% of the population) falling below these levels (Trisi et al., 2011). There is little indication of improvement. In

2011, the official poverty rate (15%) and the number of people living below official poverty thresholds remained statistically unchanged from 2010 figures (US Census Bureau, 2012a). Likewise, "deep poverty" remained problematic, with 20.4 million people (6.6% of the population) falling below half of the poverty line.

Individuals and families hovering just above official poverty thresholds are not technically counted as poor, but are undoubtedly economically vulnerable. Their inclusion dramatically increases estimates of economic hardship. In 2010, the number of US residents with incomes below 200% of poverty thresholds rose from 33.0% in 2009 to 33.9% in 2010 ($44,226 for a family of four with two adults and two children; Trisi et al., 2011). Put another way, it can be argued that one-third of Americans are low income.

Delving deeper into these numbers reveals women's economic vulnerability. The poverty rate was 3.7 percentage points higher for women (14.6%) than men (10.9%) in 2011, and this gap grows wider when ethnicity and marital status are considered (NWLC, 2012). Across all racial and ethnic groups, women experience higher rates of poverty than white men (7.7%; NWLC, 2012). In 2011, 25.9% of Black women, 23.9% of Hispanic women, 27.1% of Native American women, 12.1% of Asian women, and 10.6% of white women lived below official poverty thresholds (NWLC, 2012). Marital status, particularly single motherhood, conveys further vulnerability. Nearly 41% of female-headed households lived below official poverty thresholds in 2011 compared with 21.9% of male-headed households with children and 8.8% of heterosexual married families with children (NWLC, 2012). Again, further insight into the feminization of poverty is gained by disaggregating these statistics by race and ethnicity. Approximately one in two Black female-headed families with children (47.3%), Hispanic female-headed families with children (49.1%), and Native American female-headed families with children (53.8%) live below official poverty thresholds (NWLC, 2012). White (33%) and Asian (26.3%) female-headed households with children fare relatively better, with approximately one in three or fewer of these families living in poverty.

Measuring Poverty: The Debates Behind the Numbers

These figures, as shocking as they are, likely underestimate the true extent of women's economic hardship. The scope of US poverty is highly contested, blunting the potential impact of high rates of poverty to impact social policy or spark significant public outrage. The definition and measurement of poverty lies at the heart of these debates.

Official Poverty Measurement. US poverty thresholds, or what we commonly call the "poverty line," were developed in the 1960s by Mollie Orshanksy, a research analyst with the Social Security Administration charged with constructing a measure of need to inform War on Poverty initiatives (Blank, 2008). Orshansky anchored her calculations to the US Department of Agriculture's "thrifty food" plan, an inexpensive "adequately nutritious" diet designed for temporary and/or emergency use. Based on data from the 1955 Household Food Consumption Survey indicating that about one-third of after-tax income was spent on food, poverty thresholds were constructed for families of different sizes by multiplying the cost of the economy food plan by three to determine minimal annual income needs (Willis, 2000). For instance, the poverty threshold in 1964 for a family of four with three children was $3100 ($1033 per year for food multiplied by three). Individuals and families whose incomes fall below their respective thresholds are considered "poor" (Willis, 2000). Orshansky's poverty thresholds were adopted in 1969 as a working definition of poverty (Fisher, 2008), and are updated annually to account for inflation, but the same basic formula continues to be used. The poverty threshold for a family of four in 1975 was $5,569, $10,989 in 1985, $15,569 in 1995, $19,971 in 2005, and $23,201 in 2011 (US Census Bureau, n.d.).

Criticism of US poverty thresholds is widespread (for comprehensive summaries, see Blank, 2008; Haveman, 2009), with both progressives and conservatives finding fault in how these figures are calculated and the validity of the poverty rates derived from them, albeit for different reasons. Continued reliance on the economy food plan as the foundation of poverty thresholds tops many lists. In 2010, US consumers spent approximately 35% of their income on housing compared with approximately 15% on food (US Bureau of Labor Statistics (BLS), 2011a). Progressives argue that meaningful poverty thresholds must reflect contemporary spending patterns, as well as a broad range of family expenses (e.g., child care, medical care, and housing), many of which are likely greater than food expenditures. Basing calculations on data that is so out of sync with contemporary realities and needs, it is argued, contributes to the gross underestimation of poverty and need. Conservatives also take issue with poverty measurement, particularly the fact that poverty rates are based solely on cash income before taxes. As such, it is claimed that poverty rates are inflated because the value of noncash benefits, such as food assistance (i.e., the Supplemental Nutrition Assistance Program, SNAP, formerly known as "food stamps") and housing subsidies, are not part of official poverty calculations (Rector & Sheffield, 2011).

Alternative Poverty Measures. Mounting criticism has resulted in the development of alternative poverty measures. The US Census Bureau (2012b) now reports a supplemental poverty measure (SPM) that takes into account common contemporary expenses (e.g., utilities and work-related transportation), receipt of in-kind benefits (e.g., subsidized housing, food assistance, and tax credits), and geographic differences in housing costs. SPM thresholds are slightly higher than official thresholds. In 2011, the official poverty threshold for a family with two adults and two children was $22,811, whereas SPM thresholds for a similar size family that owned a home with a with a mortgage was $25,703 and $25,222 for renters (US Census Bureau 2012b). Clearly, these thresholds still fall below what is needed to care adequately for a family.

The SPM paints a similarly bleak portrait of poverty. Under this alternative measure, the overall poverty rate jumps from the official rate of 15.0% in 2011 to 16.1% (US Census Bureau 2012b). Poverty rates for female-headed households remained statistically unchanged using the SPM; however, significantly higher poverty rates were found for senior citizens (15.1% vs. 8.7%), working age adults between 18 and 64 (15.5% vs. 13.7%), Asians (16.9% vs. 12.3%), Hispanics (28% vs. 25.4%), and whites (14.3% vs. 12.9%), and slightly lower rates of poverty for children under 18 (18.1% vs. 22.3%) and African Americans (25.7% vs. 27.8%; US Census Bureau, 2012b). These differences are largely attributed to government supports or lack thereof, with the small declines found for African Americans and children credited to safety net programs, and the higher poverty among senior citizens and working adults related to high medical and childcare expenses. SPM poverty rates highlight the crucial role of government programs in alleviating poverty, but contrary to conservative claims US poverty rates remain high even with the inclusion of benefits.

Although supplemental measures reflect progress, more holistic approaches to defining and measuring poverty are being explored. Multidimensional indices that conceptualize poverty in terms of tangible (e.g., health, education, and income) and less tangible (e.g., dignity, social inclusion, opportunity, political power, quality of work, physical safety, and psychological well-being) indicators have gained favor internationally (Alkire, Roche, Santos, & Seth, 2011; Oxford Poverty and Human Development Initiative, n.d.). For instance, the Multidimensional Poverty Index (MPI) developed by the Oxford Poverty and Human Development Initiative for the United Nations assesses acute poverty via deprivations in three areas: health (i.e., child mortality in family and nutrition), education (i.e., years of schooling and school attendance), and living standards (e.g., household electricity, drinking water, sanitation, and assets such as owning a refrigerator and having transportation; Alkire et al., 2011). Individuals and families are considered poor if deprivations are present in one-third or more of these dimensions. By assessing specific areas of need, social policies can be tailored to alleviate hardship in particular domains. This approach contrasts sharply from the singular focus on income that dominates US poverty measurement.

The United States stands apart even from other industrialized nations that rely on income-based measures. US poverty measurement is characterized as absolute because it is "fixed over time in real terms," meaning that poverty thresholds are "nonresponsive to economic growth or changes in living standards" (Blank, 2008, p. 234). Conversely, many of our industrialized counterparts use relative measures that compare "people on a distribution of resources and then defines the poor as those who fall below the average-income threshold for the economy" (Keister & Southgate, 2012, p. 174). The European Union, for example, sets risk of poverty at 60% of median income (Blank, 2008). Relative approaches tend to be viewed as more progressive and justice-oriented than absolute measures because deprivation is defined by societal living standards, anchoring poverty in real terms to the well-being of the larger population. When viewed through this lens, poverty is a measure of "social and economic distance" rather than a static absolute standard (Haveman & Mullikin, 1999, p. 6).

The Politics of Poverty Measurement. Relative conceptualizations have gained little traction in the United States, in part because reductions in poverty are difficult to gauge with relative measures. As Haveman (2009, p. 83) explains,

> Absolute poverty standards have the advantage of allowing citizens to judge the effectiveness of antipoverty programs by whether the programs move families above the fixed standard; in contrast, poverty will decline under relative measures only if the income of families in the bottom tail of the distribution increases more than that of the median family.

Conservative opposition is particularly strong, with well-known commentators such as Robert Rector (2010) likening relative poverty measures to a "built-in escalator clause" because poverty thresholds "rise automatically in direct proportion to any rise in the living standards of the average American" (para. 2). Consequently, relative conceptualizations are denounced as a "statistical trick to ensure that 'the poor will always be with you,' no matter how much better off they get in absolute terms" (Rector, 2010, para. 3). Conservative concerns, however, run far deeper than measurement. Discussing the possibility that President Obama would establish relative poverty thresholds, Rector (2010, para. 11, 12) lays bare the ideological stakes and feared political consequences:

> [it is] a public-relations Trojan horse, smuggling in a 'spread the wealth' agenda under the ruse of fighting real material privation – a condition that is rare in our [U.S.] society. . . . For the first time, the government is planning to define poverty as a problem that can never be solved by the American dream: a general rise of incomes of all Americans across society over time. By definition, poverty can now be solved only by the dream of the Left: massive taxes on the upper and middle classes and redistribution to the less affluent. In effect, the Obama poverty measure sets a new national goal of class warfare and income redistribution.

Although not overtly stated, the driving concern appears to be inequality, particularly the belief that relative measures, by connecting poverty to inequality, will generate momentum for redistributive policies. In problematizing inequality rather than poverty per se, relative measures shift attention to a larger set of questions about societal living conditions and the distribution of resources across society.

Of course, conservatives are not alone in their rejection of more progressive, sophisticated conceptualizations of poverty. Across the political spectrum, debates about poverty measurement tap into both ideological and practical considerations:

> Different measures imply a different size and composition of the target poverty population, different patterns of change in the extent of poverty over time, and thus a different set of antipoverty policies. Policymakers and citizens react to information on these patterns. Changes in poverty over time lead to questions about the direction of the nation, the effectiveness of its social policies, and the level of equality or inequality in the distribution of income. (Haveman, 2009, p. 81)

Ultimately, resistance to the adoption of more sophisticated, multifaceted official definitions of US poverty is as complex and multidimensional as poverty itself. Meaningful changes in how US poverty is operationalized would require not only expanding how we conceptualize poverty, whether it be via the adoption of a holistic set of indicators or tying poverty to broader societal well-being, but also the political will to face head on the classism, racism, sexism, and other structural inequities that privilege some groups over others and maintain poverty and inequality. It would also require breaking from deep-rooted beliefs in individualism and meritocracy that make social class and poverty taboo topics and situate responsibility for poverty on individual shortcomings (see Chapter 3).

Poor Women: Between a Rock and a Hard Place. Despite record-setting poverty rates in 2010, poverty remains largely off of the political "radar." Debates about poverty measurement show little sign of abating, and serious proposals to reduce poverty remain elusive. Cuts to welfare and unemployment benefits threaten to deepen hardship and push more families into poverty (Schott & Pavetti, 2011). In 2011, California reduced the cash aid it provides to poor families through CalWORKS, the state's Temporary Assistance for Needy Families (TANF) program, by 8%, dropping the average monthly grant from $694 in 2010 to $638 (Finch & Schott, 2011). When adjusted for inflation, TANF benefits in 34 states are now at least 20% below their 1996 purchasing power (Finch & Schott, 2011), and benefits are below 50% of the poverty line in all states (Sherman, 2012). One consequence of declining cash aid is that extreme poverty, defined as living on less than $2.00 a day, has risen dramatically. Between 1996, the year welfare reform was passed, and 2011, the number of US households living in "extreme poverty" more than doubled from 636,000 to 1.46 million, and nearly tripled for single female-headed households (Shaefer & Edin, 2012). The number of children in extremely poor households also doubled from 1.4 million to 2.8 million (Shaefer & Edin, 2012).

These highly disturbing trends elicit little attention in major political speeches. For example, President Obama's 2012 State of the Union address included only a passing reference to poverty (i.e., "A great teacher can offer an escape from poverty to the child who dreams beyond his circumstance" (Obama, 2012, para. 37). Instead, safety net programs credited for keeping millions of people out of poverty are constantly under attack and despite continued need, temporary expansions of these programs and other Great Recession initiatives are being permitted to expire (Sherman, 2011; Trisi et al., 2011). Indeed, Conservatives, including leading Republican candidates in the 2012 presidential race, targeted safety net programs, rather than poverty, as a root problem. This perspective is illustrated by former Massachusetts Governor Mitt Romney's (2011) foreboding warning of an encroaching "entitlement society," in which we are creating "a sizable contingent of long-term jobless, dependent on government benefits for survival. . . . Government dependency can only foster passivity and sloth" (para. 5, 10). This depiction has little grounding in reality. An analysis of 2010 federal budget and Census Bureau data conducted by the Center for Budget and Policy Priorities (CBPP) found that 91% of spending on entitlement and other programs (e.g., Social Security, SNAP, TANF, housing assistance, Medicaid, Medicare, Children's Health Insurance Program (CHIP), and the Earned Income Tax Credit (EITC)) assisted people who are elderly, seriously disabled, or members of working households, not people who choose not to work (Sherman, Greenstein, & Ruffing, 2012).

Poor women and their families are in the crosshairs of these methodological and political debates. Setting poverty thresholds arbitrarily low renders the millions of women and female-headed households hovering just above them invisible, and ultimately, underestimating the extent of hardship fuels a false sense of well-being that undercuts a strong safety net and the interrogation of disadvantage and privilege. As long as poverty and economic hardship are seemingly contained to a small portion of society, far-reaching major antipoverty initiatives can be framed as unnecessary and women's economic oppression ignored. Feminist and critical scholars bring these issues to the forefront, not only through scrutiny of the political consequences of different measurement techniques, but also through examination of the structural roots of the feminization of poverty. Doing so brings into clearer focus institutional sources of poverty, as well as the intergroup dynamics of inequality, particularly that some groups (e.g., whites and men) benefit from the poverty of others (e.g., women and people of color). These issues are explored in the following chapter.

The Feminization of Homelessness

The precariousness of women's economic status is further evidenced by homelessness among women and female-headed households. Although the majority of homeless adults are men, escalating rates of homelessness among women and families are indicative of systemic inequalities. Arangua, Andersen, and Gelberg (2005) report that in 1963, homeless women represented only 3% of the homeless population, but now comprise 32%. Homeless women and men in the United States face many of the same challenges – lack of affordable housing and widening gaps between earnings and rents – but for women, barriers to secure housing are intensified by the same factors that heighten vulnerability to poverty – low wages, the devaluation of women's work at home and in the workplace, single parenthood, a safety net that has failed to keep pace with expenses, and violent, abusive relationships (Bassuk, 1993). Biased banking practices also fuel housing insecurity. Higher interest subprime loans with unfavorable terms are disproportionately granted to women homeowners, in some instances, with interest rates that are higher than comparable US Treasury notes (Hertz, 2011). Low-income families and communities of color are also the frequent targets of predatory lending practices (Preserving the American Dream: Predatory Practices and Home Foreclosures, 2007).

whole fams going homeless

Estimates of Women's Homelessness. Families with children are the fastest growing segment of the homeless population, with many of these families headed by single mothers with young children under 5 years of age (American Psychological Association (APA) Presidential Task Force on Psychology's Contribution to End Homelessness, 2010; National Coalition for the Homeless, 2009). Disturbing rates of family homelessness are confirmed by point-in-time counts, which provide a snapshot of sheltered and unsheltered people on a single night, as well as period prevalence estimates of homelessness, which are based on reporting by a range of service providers over a 12-month period. On a single night in January 2011, 236,181 people in 77,186 family households were homeless (US Department of Housing and Urban Development (HUD), 2012a). Twenty-one of these families were unsheltered and living in places not intended for human habitation, such as cars, parks, or abandoned buildings (HUD, 2012a). The Great Recession has deepened family hardship. Between late 2007 and 2010, the number of families with children living in temporary shelters had risen by 28% to nearly 170,000 families, and approximately four times as many families were "doubled-up" with relatives and friends or living in other precarious situations (Rice, 2011). State-level data reveals similar trends. A survey of 29 US cities conducted between September 2009 and August 2010 found a 16% increase in the number of homeless families (US Conference of Mayors, 2011). Officials in 64% of surveyed cities expected family homelessness to continue to rise.

The vulnerability of single female-headed families is evident in HUD's (2012a) summary of shelter user demographics. In 2011, 1.5 million people spent at least one night in an emergency shelter or transitional housing unit, of which 35.8% were persons in families (HUD, 2012a). The gender dynamics of adults in families versus unaccompanied adults varies considerably. In 2011, approximately 72% of sheltered male adults were single men, while 28% were single unaccompanied women. This pattern reverses when families are considered: approximately 80% of sheltered adults in families were women, while just over 20% were men (HUD, 2012a). Between 2007 and 2010, the number of sheltered homeless individuals decreased by 6% from 1.15 million to 1.04 million, while during the same period of time, the number of sheltered homeless persons in families increased 20% from 473,541 to 567,334 (HUD, 2011a). Although the number of families in shelters declined by approximately 5% between 2010 and 2011, there were still 64,000 more people in families in a shelter in 2011 than there were in 2007, representing an increase of 13.5% (HUD, 2012a).

These trends are indicative of the feminization of homelessness, a phenomenon Richards, Garland, Bumphus, and Thompson (2010, p. 112) attribute to "decades of poor public policy decisions: ineffective state-based programs, a low minimum wage, lack of affordable housing, reduction in welfare benefits, deinstitutionalization, and the underlying violence that plagues the lives of women." Again, however, caution must be taken not to neglect differences in experiences and power among diverse groups of women. Race and racism are crucial to understanding women's experiences of homelessness. As Shinn and Gillespie (1994, p. 517) observe,

> Even among poor people, African-Americans and Latinos have less wealth than Whites and face more difficult housing conditions, in part due to ongoing racial discrimination, and these facts may account for the greater likelihood that they will become homeless.

In 2009, the median net worth of white households was $113,149 (assets minus debt) compared with $6325 for Hispanic and $5677 for Black households (Kochlar, Fry, & Taylor, 2011). Moreover, 35% of Black and 31% of Hispanic households had zero or negative net worth compared with just 15% of white households (Kochlar et al., 2011). This gross inequality underlies differential rates of homelessness across racial groups.

African Americans are overrepresented among people experiencing homelessness (Lee, Tyler, & Wright, 2010). In 2010, 42% of families residing in shelters or transitional housing programs were African American, 31% were white, 12% were Hispanic, 8.5% were multiracial, and 6.4% were other single races (HUD, 2011a). African American women without children in their care face elevated odds of experiencing chronic homelessness (Zlotnick, Tam, & Bradley, 2010), and alarming rates of homelessness are found among African American female veterans (US Government Accountability Office (GAO), 2011). Disproportionately high rates of homelessness among women of color underscore the importance of intersectional analyses and the need to critically interrogate systems of privilege and disadvantage.

Challenges to Accurate Measurement. As is the case with poverty, social scientists and policymakers contest the validity of various estimates of homelessness, the methodologies employed to calculate prevalence rates, and how homelessness is defined. The exclusion of people who are "doubled-up" with friends or relatives, staying at motels, or who do not seek emergency shelter or use other services, such as food pantries and soup kitchens, are major concerns. Rural homelessness may be less "visible" than urban homelessness, resulting in its neglect (Whitzman, 2006). The episodic nature of homelessness further compromises the accuracy of prevalence rates, and much of the research literature focuses on chronic homelessness rather than the larger population of people who are newly or temporarily unhoused (APA Presidential Task Force on Psychology's Contribution to End Homelessness, 2010). Consequently, the prevalence of homelessness and housing insecurity, more generally, are likely to be underestimated. Because women are more likely than men to "double-up," they are especially likely to be missed in official counts of US homelessness, but this is a global problem. Concerns for personal safety, the preponderance of shelters that serve men, and the cultural denial of homelessness as a problem affecting women all contribute to the undercounting of women in worldwide estimates of homelessness (Sikich, 2008).

How homelessness is defined influences both prevalence rates and eligibility for services and programs, with narrow definitions running the risk of excluding important subgroups (e.g., people in emergency shelters and people with housing vouchers). There is no single statutory definition of homelessness, but federal, state and local laws provide criteria for defining homelessness (APA Presidential Task Force on Psychology's Contribution to End Homelessness, 2010). Under the Stewart B. McKinney Act of 1987, a person is considered homeless if she or he:

> lacks a fixed, regular, and adequate nighttime residence; and . . . has a primary night time residency that is: (A) a supervised or publicly or privately operated shelter designed to provide temporary living accommodations . . . (B) An institution that provides a temporary residence for individuals intended to be institutionalized, or (C) a public or private place not designed for, or ordinarily used as, a regular sleeping accommodation for human beings. (42 U.S.C. §11302)

Some commonly overlooked groups are addressed by the Homeless Emergency Assistance and Rapid Transition to Housing (HEARTH) Act of 2009, which identifies people at imminent risk of losing their housing due to eviction, people in temporary institutional settings who lacked prior stable housing, unaccompanied youth, and people fleeing domestic violence or other life-threatening conditions as homeless (APA Presidential Task Force on Psychology's Contribution to End Homelessness, 2010). Nevertheless, concerns regarding the exclusion of some groups persist. APA's Presidential Task Force on Psychology's Contribution to End Homelessness (2010, p. 4) offers a definition designed to optimize inclusivity:

> Homelessness exists when people lack safe, stable and appropriate places to live. Sheltered and unsheltered people are homeless. People living doubled up or in overcrowded living situations or motels due to inadequate economic resources are included in this definition, as are those living in tents, or other temporary enclosures.

This broad conceptualization corresponds with common-sense understandings of homelessness and grounds my discussion of women's experiences, but such inclusive definitions are unlikely to be embraced by US policymakers who aim to reduce the scope of the problem simply by narrowing definitional parameters.

Organization of This Book

Overarching Goals

Alarming rates of economic hardship among women and female-headed households speak to the urgency of developing and adopting policies capable of real poverty alleviation. The economic and social exclusion of poor women and their families condemn millions to substandard housing and the threat of homelessness, limited access to education, health care, and nutritious food, and restricted opportunities for mobility. As Lott (2012, p. 655) observes, "Socioeconomic conditions and ideology are stacked against the health and welfare of low-income families and ensure diminished opportunities for a sizable segment of the U.S. population." Psychologists have a crucial role to play in documenting and challenging these hardships, revealing the complex dynamics of class-based oppression, designing effective policy interventions, and advocating for economic justice.

This book focuses on women's poverty, with the aim of drawing on social science research to both understand and challenge sources of women's poverty. Drawing on findings and insights from social psychology, policy studies, and critical and feminist scholarship, I examine the structural sources of women's poverty, low-income women's experiences and life chances, and policies that deepen women's economic hardship and those that promote greater economic equality.

This women-centered analysis is not intended to exclude men or to suggest that men are not also profoundly harmed by poverty or widening economic inequality more generally, but to bring into sharp relief the practices, structures, and policies affecting low-income women. The gendered construction of poverty means that although women and men "may find common ground and common interest in relation to employment and state policies, even in these areas their opportunities and losses differ" (Sutter, 1996, p. 419). In the face of rising poverty and homelessness, understanding these opportunities and losses is of utmost importance.

These trends are primarily examined in the context of the United States; however, parallels and contrasts with women's economic status in other developed and developing countries are made as appropriate. The United States is a particularly striking focal point, because as a nation of great wealth, significantly reducing, if not eliminating poverty, is an achievable goal. Yet US social policies are rarely designed with these objectives in mind. Instead, tax policies favoring the rich have widened the economic divide (Graetz & Shapiro, 2005; Kocieniewski, 2012), restrictive welfare policies have weakened the safety net (Handler & Hasenfeld, 2007; see Chapter 4), and declining investments in public goods, such as education (Newfield, 2008), have diminished opportunities for upward mobility. The failure to adopt policies and programs that would help "level the playing field" – universal health care, a generous welfare system that lifts families out of poverty, a commitment to a shared public good that invests in the development of human capital, self-sufficiency wages, a truly progressive tax system, and high quality, affordable child care – despite having the resources to dedicate to such initiatives, makes the United States an ideal site for studying the structural roots of poverty and the social psychology of inequality.

A guiding assumption throughout this book is that poverty is a socially constructed problem that could be greatly reduced if resources and opportunities were distributed equitably. For this reason, special attention is directed toward understanding the beliefs that justify poverty and class-based inequality and the structural, social, and cultural changes needed to reduce poverty among women and female-headed households. I draw heavily on political discourse surrounding poverty and welfare policy to illustrate the sociocultural tensions that allow poverty to persist in the midst of plenty. Doing so brings to the forefront how deeply embedded dominant understandings of poverty are in political rhetoric, and the role of policymakers and welfare policy itself in codifying classist attitudes and stereotypes of poor women, particularly "welfare recipients." As Schneider and Ingram (1997, p. 102) observe:

> Much of the public policy in the United States is produced in policy-making systems dominated by divisive social constructions that stigmatize some potential target populations and extol the virtues of others. These constructions interact with the political power of the target groups to establish the political agenda, focus the terms of the debate, and determine the characteristics of the policy design.

Classist stereotypes of welfare recipients as "dependent takers" and inferior mothers figure heavily into both political discourse and public perceptions of poor women, with damaging consequences for the formation of interclass alliances and support for antipoverty initiatives.

Social science research has much to offer both in terms of deconstructing these conceptualizations and offering evidence to move just policy initiatives forward. This book draws on diverse literatures to advance both goals. Social psychological research provides much needed insight into cross-class relations, the impact of classist attitudes on policy support, and collective action; feminist research reveals patriarchy's influence on social policy and the consequences of classed, raced, and gendered power relations; and critical scholarship makes salient how complex power dynamics inhibit progressive policy. Collectively, this work generates powerful insights into the causes and correlates of poverty and powerful ammunition to inform antipoverty efforts.

Remaining Chapters. The following chapter delves deeper into poverty and homelessness, examining the root causes of women's economic vulnerability. Emphasis is placed on structural sources of women's poverty and homelessness – wage disparities, family structure, discrimination, and lack of affordable housing. The role of weakened safety net programs in deepening hardship are also investigated, and in doing so, a compelling case for family-oriented, women-centered change is made. Contrasts and parallels between the United States and other industrialized countries illuminate policy choices and the undervaluing of women's labor both in and outside of the home.

Chapter 3 interrogates the oft-repeated claim that the United States is a "classless" society and the attitudes and beliefs that support this assertion. Public opinion and research examining US beliefs about poverty, wealth, class mobility, and economic inequality is reviewed and discussed in terms of their relationship to dominant US ideology (e.g., meritocracy, individualism, and equal opportunity), classist stereotypes, social psychological concepts and theories (e.g., system justification and fundamental attribution error), and their psychological and political functions. Implications of these beliefs are explored on both the individual and intergroup levels. Consequences for social policy are considered as well.

Chapter 4 offers a critical analysis of the Personal Responsibility and Work Opportunity Reconciliation Act of 1996 (PRWORA) and the impact of programmatic changes governing cash assistance to low-income families. Opinions differ sharply, with advocates citing declining caseloads as evidence of its success, while critics see continued poverty among welfare "leavers" as indicative of its failure. Working from the belief that women's economic and psychological well-being is the only true measure of "success," quantitative and qualitative studies evaluating welfare "reform" are reviewed with an eye toward the creation of a more just welfare system.

Chapter 5 draws on findings from focus groups with politically mobilized low-income women to explore some of the factors that facilitate welfare rights activism. Core facilitators of collective action included experiences of interpersonal and institutional classism in medical, educational, and social service settings; a strong structural critique of inequality and rejection of classist stereotypes; and a shared sense of responsibility for the plight of other poor women. Implications for social change and the formation of large-scale grassroots political movements are examined.

The final chapter explores pitfalls, possibilities, and promise in moving toward an economically just society. Barriers to economic justice are numerous and include both structural and attitudinal barriers to social change. Although formidable, these challenges are not insurmountable, and the widening gap between elites and the rest of the population may open new opportunities for poverty alleviation and asset building. The plight of the poor has largely been dismissed as a matter of questionable morals, limited discipline and motivation, and a weak work ethic (see Chapter 3), but as Frank (2010, para. 1) observes, income inequality may have finally grown "too big to ignore". The precipitous decline of the middle class (Littrell, Brooks, Ivery, & Ohmer, 2010) may reduce the levels of poverty and inequality that we, as a society, are willing to tolerate. Targeted policy recommendations for reducing women's poverty and inequality more broadly are offered, and potential roles for justice-oriented researchers in these movements are proposed.

2

Structural Sources of Women's Poverty and Homelessness

In the United States, stark contrasts in wealth and poverty are readily visible – high- and low-income neighborhoods border each other, and newspaper stories about economic hardship are reported alongside accounts of record earnings among elites. Nevertheless, the root causes of economic hardship receive short shrift. This chapter spotlights structural sources of women's poverty and homelessness. Demographic trends related to women's earnings and poverty are presented, attending closely to intersections of gender, race, and class and the impact of single motherhood, workplace discrimination, and the shortcomings of current safety net policies. Homelessness is also gendered and raced, and the second half of this chapter examines synergies in the causes of poverty, housing insecurity, and homelessness. Building on Wesely and Wright's (2005) observation that, "homeless women deserve consideration as a distinct group within the homeless population, a group that perhaps exhibits unique ways of becoming homeless, unique responses to the conditions of homelessness, and unique needs to prevent them from becoming homeless again" (p. 1083), the factors that contribute to the movement of women and female-headed households in and out of homelessness (e.g., poverty, lack of affordable housing, and violence) are discussed.

Sources of Women's Poverty

Discrimination is a root cause of women's poverty (Amnesty International, 2009). Unpaid caregiving and other domestic responsibilities, the devaluation of motherhood, particularly single motherhood, workplace segregation and exclusion, persistent earning gaps, and a weak safety net are born from sexism, racism, and classism, and their intersections. I introduce some key issues related to

Women and Poverty: Psychology, Public Policy, and Social Justice, First Edition. Heather E. Bullock.
© 2013 Heather E. Bullock. Published 2013 by John Wiley and Sons, Ltd.

caregiving responsibilities and women's work outside the home to illustrate some of the major structural sources of women's poverty.

Caregiving, Motherhood, and the Price of Unpaid Labor

Motherhood is touted as being among the most important "jobs," yet parenting and other caregiving responsibilities are largely uncompensated in the United States, at least in material terms. This is not the case in other industrialized countries such as Sweden, Germany, and France, in which individuals who care for dependent children or sick or elderly relatives receive caregiver credits and/or wages. Caregiver wages treat largely invisible work within the home as valued, paid labor, while caregiver credit bolsters public pension benefits by compensating for workforce separations due to caregiving responsibilities (Jankowski, 2011). Sweden, Germany, Australia, France, and the United Kingdom provide income-tested caregiver wages (British Columbia Law Institute & The Canadian Center for Elder Law, 2010). In Australia, separate initiatives provide caregiver allowances to low- and higher-income full-time caregivers. For a family of three, this support would be sufficient to cover the costs of rent, transportation, and groceries (British Columbia Law Institute & The Canadian Center for Elder Law, 2010). Many countries also have caregiver pension programs. In Germany, a parent with primary responsibility for caregiving is credited with the equivalent of one pension point (i.e., "equal to the pension entitlement a person with exactly the average income of all insured persons receives for contributions in 1 year") annually for the first 3 years of a child's life (Jankowski, 2011, p. 68). Parents who work outside the home while raising a child up to 10 years of age are also awarded pension credits (Jankowski, 2011). Time spent caregiving in Denmark is covered under a universal pension program that grants benefits based on years of residence (Jankowski, 2011). These family-friendly policies diverge dramatically from US treatment of caregiving work. The United States, Portugal, and Turkey share the unfortunate distinction of being the only members of the Organisation for Economic Co-operation and Development (OECD) with earning-based public pension programs that do not recognize years of unpaid caregiving (Jankowski, 2011).

Poverty and Unpaid Caregiving. As the primary caregivers in most families, women pay the price for the absence of these protections. Unpaid caregiving, whether full or part time, heightens women's risk of poverty across the lifespan. Gwendolyn Mink, a leading advocate for the adoption of a caregivers wage in the United States, observes that if mothers' unpaid labor were translated into its paid labor market responsibilities – "nursemaid, dietitian, cook, laundress, maintenance man, chauffeur, food buyer, dishwasher, seamstress, practical nurse, gardener" – women's incomes would be above poverty thresholds (Mink, 1998b, p. 149). This work, if compensated in 1972, would have amounted to earnings of $13,391.56 (Mink, 1998b), a figure higher than the median income of $11,120 that same year (US Census Bureau, 1973).

Women not only suffer immediate consequences in terms of lost wages, but also economic jeopardy later in life due to reduced contributions to Social Security. Social Security is intended to be gender neutral and treat female and male beneficiaries equivalently; however, women's caregiving responsibilities often translate into greater time spent out of the paid workforce, increased reliance on part-time work, and lower overall lifetime earnings (Meschede, Cronin, Sullivan, & Shapiro, 2011). In 2011, annual Social Security benefits to men 65 years of age and older averaged $15,795 compared with just $12,188 for women (Social Security Administration (SSA), 2013). Degree of reliance on Social Security varies by marital status, with unmarried women relying more heavily on Social Security benefits than unmarried men or heterosexual married couples. In 2011, Social Security benefits comprised 50% of the total income of unmarried women and widows aged 65 and older, but only 36% of unmarried elderly men's income and 31% of elderly heterosexual couples' income (SSA, 2013). In fact, Social Security is often the only source of income for many elderly single women, with 48% estimated to rely on Social Security for 90% or more of their income (SSA, 2013). In 2008, 44% of single senior women were left with a zero or negative budget balance after covering essentials (Meschede et al., 2011).

Feminist and poverty scholars have written extensively about the devaluation of caregiving and other unpaid labor within the home, connecting patriarchy and capitalism in order to increase attention not only to the devastating financial consequences for women, but also to broader social, political, and economic repercussions (Ferguson & Hennessy, 2010; Hochschild & Machung, 2003; Mink, 1998b; Primeau, 1992; Roesch, 2004). Women in the United States and around the world disproportionately perform unpaid labor, whether in the form of "housework" or caregiving for children or relatives (United Nations, 2010), and this skewed division of labor plays a crucial role in maintaining gender and economic inequality. Unpaid labor reinforces traditional gender roles that separate "work" and "family" and essentializes women as "natural" caregivers and men as "breadwinners." Viewed through this lens, only labor that occurs outside the home is defined as "work" and rewarded with pay, while caregiving and other labor within the home is seen as secondary, and subsequently caregiving responsibilities and caregivers are subordinated. As Ferguson and Hennessy (2010) explain, "This makes women dependent on men and devalued, since their work is outside the meaningful sphere of public economic production" (para. 12). Feminists also point to the pivotal role of unpaid labor in sustaining capitalism:

Women's labor within the family reveals that men, as capitalists and as husbands, benefit from women's unpaid household work. The social structures imposed by capitalism and patriarchy enable men to control women's domestic labor . . .

Capitalists benefit through the role women play in the reproduction of labor power, that is, the work necessary to support the lives of male workers for today's labor force and to shape children for tomorrow's labor force. (Primeau, 1992, p. 984)

Capitalism and patriarchy act in the service of each other with women's unpaid labor fueling economic production and economic growth. Men largely reap the benefits of women's unpaid labor at multiple levels – freedom from child care and other family responsibilities allows men greater time for work and other activities, and women's relative exclusion helps to ensure male dominance in the paid workforce and other spheres (Primeau, 1992). Ultimately, this affords power and control over women at home and in the paid labor market.

Shortchanging Caregiving: The Case of National Productivity. That unpaid labor contributes to national productivity but is excluded from calculations of gross domestic productivity (i.e., the total value of new goods and services produced within a country, GDP) is demonstrative of caregiving's devaluation. Estimates of the economic value of unpaid labor reveal the magnitude of these contributions. A 1995 analysis by the United Nations Development Programme (UNDP) values women's worldwide unpaid and underpaid labor at $11 trillion dollars. In nearly every country surveyed, women were found to work longer hours than men, with women carrying an average of 53% of total workload in developing countries and 51% in industrial countries (UNDP, 1995). In industrial countries, two-thirds of men's time was spent in paid work activities and one-third in unpaid activities; the reverse was true for women. More recent analyses provide further evidence of the tremendous economic value of unpaid labor leaving little doubt that others' prosper at women's expense. In India, women's unpaid work is estimated at upward of $612.8 billion (Evangelical Social Action Forum & Health Bridge, 2009). US estimates value total unpaid caregiving at $1.4 trillion (Roesch, 2004) and unpaid caregiving to people over 18 years of age with limited ability to perform daily activities at $354 billion (American Association of Retired Persons Public Policy Institute, 2007). And, even as more women work outside the home, it remains the case that mothers are more likely than fathers to reduce their paid work hours to accommodate childcare responsibilities (Bianchi, 2011) and to suffer losses in income related to domestic responsibilities (Kühhirt & Ludwig, 2012). It seems little progress has been made toward rendering the UNDP's 1995 conclusion that "men receive the lion's share of income and recognition for their economic contribution – while most of women's work remains unpaid, unrecognized and undervalued" (p. 88) no longer true.

Holistic alternatives to traditional GDP, which include the value of unpaid labor and other neglected facets of human welfare, offer a more comprehensive snapshot of national well-being. For example, the Genuine Progress Indicator (GPI) includes measures of household and volunteer work, pollution, crime and family breakdown, and income distribution to assess standard of living (Federal

Reserve Bank of Boston, n.d.). Such measures are an important step forward, but a fundamental shift in values is also needed. Feminists and antipoverty advocates use estimates of women's uncompensated labor to raise awareness of the magnitude of women's contributions to society and economic growth, and to lobby for fair compensation, but are quick to point out that an exclusively economic focus inadvertently risks reproducing the same flawed value system that equates "productivity" and progress with material gain and relegates relational and socioemotional work to secondary status. Ultimately, feminists call for a complete reordering of societal values that prioritizes nurturing and caregiving in its many forms, making it possible for women to care for their children and others without risk or fear of poverty.

Women in the Paid Labor Market: Progress, Pitfalls, and Poverty

Poverty and income are interrelated and although women have made considerable gains in the workforce, wage disparities continue to fuel disproportionately high poverty rates among women and racial and ethnic minorities. In 2011, an estimated 59.8% of paid working women and 71.3% of paid working men were full-time, year-round wage earners with respective median annual incomes of $37,118 and $48,202 (US Census Bureau, 2012a). This equates to a gendered wage gap of 77 cents for every dollar earned by men in 2011 (US Census Bureau, 2012a). The annual release of this widely anticipated aggregate figure reveals much about how women are faring in the paid labor market but only tells part of the story. Less publicized breakdowns of earnings by both race and gender reveal wider gaps, particularly for women of color. In 2011, full-time, year-round employed Hispanic women earned just 55% of white men's median earnings, Black women 64% of white men's median earnings, white women 77% of white men's median earnings, and Asian women 78% of white men's median earnings (National Women's Law Center (NWLC), 2012). These disparities persist across all educational levels, with Black and Hispanic women consistently earning less than white and Asian women (Mink, 2010).

Part-time work, which may allow for greater accommodation of caregiving responsibilities, offers little in the way of economic security. In 2010, 26.6% of women were part-time workers compared to just 13.4% of men (US Department of Labor, 2011). Women who work part-time or as seasonal laborers fare even worse than their full-time counterparts, with earnings a mere 72 cents for every dollar paid to a man in 2010 (Women of Color Policy Network, 2011). The inclusion of part-time and seasonal laborers drops Black and Hispanic women's earnings to 61 and 48 cents, respectively, for every dollar earned by white men (Women of Color Policy Network, 2011). Collectively, these figures make clear that whether working part- or full-time, women are economically disadvantaged in their ability to support a family or themselves.

Feminists identify sexist and racist wage disparities, coupled with low welfare benefits, as keeping women, particularly mothers, dependent on men. Indeed, marital status is strongly related to income (US Bureau of Labor Statistics (BLS), 2011a). Heterosexual married families in all racial groups outearn female-headed households; nevertheless, meaningful racial gaps exist. Among married families, Asian households have the highest median income ($85,082), followed by whites ($77,661), Blacks ($60,781), and Hispanics ($50,410). Incomes of female-headed households consistently lag behind their married counterparts with earnings of $46,179 (Asians), $38,131 (whites), $27,172 (Hispanics), and $25,563 (Blacks; Women of Color Policy Network, 2011).

Workplace Segregation. Women's lower earnings can be traced to an interconnected web of interpersonal and institutional bias and discrimination. The workplace is still highly gender segregated, with both horizontal (i.e., under/overrepresentation of women in certain occupations or sectors) and vertical segregation (i.e., underrepresentation of women at the top ranks of an occupation; "glass ceiling") contributing to lower earnings. Horizontal segregation is evident in women's overrepresentation in lower paying, lower status jobs (e.g., childcare workers, house cleaners, and food service) and underrepresentation in higher paying, higher status occupations, such as physician, lawyer, or executive (BLS, 2011a; Reskin & Hartmann, 1986). In 2008, approximately half of women worked in occupations in which they outnumbered men by at least two to one, whereas only one in six women worked in occupations in which men outnumbered them by at least two to one (Day & Rosenthal, 2009). On the other hand, two-thirds of men were employed in occupations populated by twice as many men as women (Day & Rosenthal, 2009).

Vertical segregation also remains a significant problem with gender segregation among managers increasing sharply in the 1990s after declining in the 1980s (Cohen, Huffman, & Knauer, 2009). Women's lower rates of promotion is one contributing factor (Blau & DeVaro, 2006). It is widely assumed that women's lack of advancement and lower earnings are related to intermittent work histories (e.g., taking time off or reduced hours to accommodate caregiving responsibilities) or less commitment to career advancement; however, Carter and Silva's (2011) longitudinal analysis of the career paths of 3,345 "high potential" female and male graduates of 12 MBA programs undermines such conclusions. Despite staying on a "traditional" masculine career path (i.e., consistent full-time employment, no self-employment or part-time work, no family, personal, or travel-related breaks in employment) and using the same full range of proactive advancement strategies (e.g., making achievements visible, blurring work–life boundaries, and searching for opportunities within and outside of the company) as their male counterparts, women advanced less and had slower pay growth than men (Carter & Silva, 2011). Thus, it appears that even when women "do 'all the right things,' they're unlikely to advance as far or earn as much as their male counterparts" (Carter & Silva, 2011, p. 13). This pattern also persists in female-dominated fields, such as nursing and elementary school teaching, with men advancing more quickly into leadership positions (Acker, 2009).

Sexist Stereotyping. Sexist stereotypes fuel the devaluation of women's workplace performance. An experiment by Alksnis, Desmarais, and Curtis (2008) illustrates the detrimental consequences of occupational stereotypes on women's earnings. Participants made a salary recommendation for one of three different jobs (i.e., department store clerk, magazine editor, or teacher) that were situated in either a traditionally "masculine" or "feminine" domain (i.e., sales clerk in a hardware vs. china/crystal department, editor for an automotive vs. gourmet food magazine, or industrial arts vs. home economics teacher). When asked to envision who worked in each position, respondents strongly associated "feminine" domains with women employees and "masculine" domains with men workers. Although participants rated "male" and "female" jobs similarly in terms of perceived responsibilities and skills, "male" jobs were consistently awarded higher salaries than parallel "female" jobs. Reflecting the insidiousness of contemporary sexism, positions were regarded as comparable and yet deemed as warranting less pay when associated with women (Alksnis et al., 2008).

The "Motherhood Penalty". Mothers and pregnant women are at heightened risk of workplace discrimination. Women with children pay a so-called motherhood penalty, earning less than childfree women, beyond what can be accounted for by human capital and occupational factors (Correll, Benard, & Paik, 2007). A two-part study by Correll et al. (2007) documents the high price of motherhood in the workplace. First, in an experiment, college student participants received a human resources memo, fact sheet, and resume of a hypothetical job candidate and were asked to make a series of employment-related decisions. Applicant materials were identical with the exception of gender, race, and parental status. Mothers were penalized in every arena. Compared with childfree women, mothers were judged as significantly less competent and committed, held to harsher performance and punctuality standards, recommended for lower starting salaries, and rated as less promotable and suitable for management (Correll et al., (2007). This is if they were "lucky" enough to get their foot in the door – despite identical qualifications, mothers (47%) were also less likely than childfree women (84%) to be recommended to be hired (Correll et al., (2007). Fathers, on the other hand, enjoyed a boost in their status, receiving ratings 5% higher than men without children.

To further test the "motherhood penalty," particularly whether mothers are less likely to be hired, Correll et al. (2007) moved from a controlled laboratory setting to real workplaces via a parallel audit study. Over an 18-month period, a total of 1,276 resumes were submitted to 638 employers hiring for entry- and mid-level marketing and business positions. For consistency with the laboratory study, similar materials were used and applicants were again varied in terms of gender and parental status. Analysis of callback rates revealed that childfree women received 2.1 times as many callbacks as equally qualified mothers (6.6% compared with 3.1%). Fathers did not receive a "boost" as they did in the laboratory study but were not penalized, leading the researchers to conclude that it is truly a "motherhood" not "parenthood" penalty (Correll et al., 2007).

Income Inequality: Contextualizing the "Wage Gap". The scope of workplace disparities has led Acker (2009) to question the efficacy of metaphors such as "glass ceiling" at capturing the depth and complexity of these inequities. Acker (2009) explains why "inequality regimes" may be a more appropriate, comprehensive term:

> All organizations have inequality regimes, defined as loosely interrelated practices, processes, actions, and meanings that result in and maintain class, gender and racial inequalities within particular organizations. . . . One common outcome of these inequality processes in the rich industrial nations of the North is that the persons at the top of most organizations are likely to be white men; they are very privileged and have great class power compared with most other people in the organization. The processes of exclusion that constitute a glass ceiling are class and race processes as well as gender processes. (pp. 201–202)

Acker's (2009) intersectional approach places the emphasis squarely on labor market inequities as (re)creating dominant power relations. From this vantage point, it is not simply a matter of gendered barriers to advancement but how wage and other workplace inequities serve dominant interests and maintain race, class, and gender privilege.

Trends in income and wealth inequality brings Acker's notion of inequality regimes into sharp relief and underscore the broader context in which women struggle to make ends meet. The portion of before-tax income going to the top 1% of households has risen dramatically since the late 1970s and now stands at levels last seen in the 1920s (Shaw & Stone, 2011). Since 1979, the before tax income of the top 1% increased 277% compared with only 38% for the middle 60% of the population and 18% for the bottom 20% (Shaw & Stone, 2011). The top 1% also rebounded more quickly than other groups in the wake of the Great Recession. In 2010, the richest 1% received a mind-blowing 93% or $288 billion of all income growth after adjusting for inflation (Rattner, 2012). From 2009 to 2010, their income increased nearly 12% or $105,000 with the very top 0.01 enjoying gains of 21.5% or $4.2 million (Rattner, 2012; Shaw & Stone, 2011). With an average income of $23.8 million, the 0.01%, or so-called super rich, have broken away from even the top 1% category to which they belong with those at the 99th to 99.5th percentile earning an average income of $418,000 (Shaw & Stone, 2011). Meanwhile, the average income of households in the bottom 90% remained at its lowest level since 1983 (Shaw & Stone, 2011). Put in more concrete terms, "the bottom 99% received a microscopic increase in pay per person of $80 in 2010, after adjusting for inflation" (Rattner, 2012, para. 4). It is unlikely that this would cover the cost of a monthly utility bill or supply of diapers.

Rising inequality stacks the odds against all but the very rich by eroding economic security and family well-being. For women, the widening income gap between the rich and everyone else further intensifies the effects of pervasive discrimination and longstanding wage differentials. And, the erosion of legal protections for women in the workplace leaves women with little recourse. The Supreme Court's 2011 decision to throw out a class-action suit against Wal-Mart struck a major blow to all women workers (Liptak, 2011) The suit, which claimed that Wal-Mart systematically pays women less than men and rewards women with smaller raises and fewer opportunities for advancement, sought billions of dollars of back pay and punitive damages on behalf of as many as 1.5 million female workers. Women hold 70% of hourly positions at Wal-Mart, but only 33% of managerial positions (Liptak, 2011). These statistics and other evidence of gendered gaps in pay and promotion were deemed insufficient to show common experiences among the plaintiffs, negating the necessary foundation for a class action suit (Liptak, 2011). Preventing this large-scale class action suit from moving forward sent a powerful probusiness message that "erects substantially higher barriers for women and men to vindicate rights to be free from employment discrimination" ("Wal-Mart wins legal victory in 'gender discrimination' case", 2011, para. 7).

State level assaults on workplace rights are also underway. In 2012, Wisconsin Governor Scott Walker recently repealed the state's 2009 Equal Pay Enforcement Act, which allowed targets of workplace discrimination based on gender, race, age, disability, religion, sexual orientation, and other factors, to seek damages in state courts (Goldberg, 2012). In 2009, Wisconsin ranked 36th nationally in terms of workplace gender parity but subsequently climbed to 24th in national parity rankings – an improvement that can be attributed to employers' observance of the new law (Goldberg, 2012). Complaints can still be pursued federally, but these claims tend to be more expensive and slower than at the state level. Much to the chagrin of all women, but particularly poor and working class women, Republican State Senator Glenn Grothman defended this decision in his assertion that money matters more to men than women:

> Take a hypothetical husband and wife who are both lawyers . . . but the husband is working 50 or 60 hours a week, going all out, making 200 grand a year. The woman takes time off, raises kids, is not go go go. Now they're 50 years old. The husband is making 200 grand a year, the woman is making 40 grand a year. It wasn't discrimination. There was a different sense of urgency in each person. . . . You could argue that money is more important for men. I think a guy in their first job, maybe because they expect to be a breadwinner someday, may be a little more money-conscious. To attribute everything to a so-called bias in the workplace is just not true. (Grothman, cited in Goldberg, 2012, para. 9, 13)

Underscoring the numerous challenges women face as they fight for fair earnings, these remarks make clear that reducing poverty will require both significant policy and attitudinal change.

Earning Power and Social Control: Restricting Women's Life Choices. It is important to note that the consequences of low earnings ripple far beyond obvious economic deprivation to restrict women's freedom in multiple spheres. Low earning potential can leave women with the difficult choice of economic dependence on a male partner or poverty. Not surprisingly, concerns related to economic survival are commonly cited barriers to leaving abusive relationships (Sanders & Schnabel, 2004). TANF provides much-needed cash aid, but the very low level of support coupled with restrictive regulations may discourage needy families from participating in the program. Strict work requirements and time limits on receipt may be particularly difficult for survivors of abuse to adhere too. Family violence waivers permit abuse survivors to be excluded from meeting program requirements for a specified period of time (e.g., "stopping the clock" to not count against lifetime benefit limits or to delay work requirements), but research suggests waivers are not evenly or effectively administered (Purvin, 2007). More to the point, it is difficult, if not ethically impossible, to assign a "time limit" to "recovery" from domestic violence. As Lindhorst, Oxford, and Gillmore (2007) note in their longitudinal analysis of the cumulative effects of domestic violence on adolescent mothers and welfare use before and after welfare reform, "It may be the case that the emphasis in the federal policy on moving women from welfare use into the labor force created increased hazards for battered women" (p. 823). Spanning 13 years, Lindhorst and her colleagues (2007, p. 823) found that women with histories of domestic violence "were no more likely to be on welfare, but after welfare reform they were more likely to be unemployed". The researchers posit that after being forced to exit the welfare rolls, domestic violence survivors, suffering from the long-term effects of their experiences, were unable to find and maintain paid work. It may also be the case that experiences of violence during the transition to adulthood are particularly detrimental to later employment. Based on these findings, they conclude that, "Cumulative domestic violence can have negative effects on economic capacity many years after the violence occurs, suggesting that policymakers recognize the long-term nature of the impact of domestic violence on women's capacity to be economically self-reliant" (Lindhorst et al., 2007, p. 812).

Penalizing Single Motherhood

Family structure plays a major role in the reproduction of poverty and inequality (McLanahan & Percheski, 2008), with single mothers and their children over-represented among the poor (US Census Bureau, 2012a). Half of single mother families have an annual income less than $25,000; two-fifths are "food insecure"; one-seventh rely on food pantries; and one-fifth have no health insurance (Legal Momentum, 2012). US poverty rates for female-headed households with children are nearly triple that of the general population (Legal Momentum, 2011b), and international comparisons reveal higher poverty rates for single mother families in the United States than other affluent nations, including Spain, Austria, Sweden, and the United Kingdom (Legal Momentum, 2011a). That US employment rates among single mothers also tend to be higher than comparison countries further confirms the degree to which low wages and lack of strong family support policies heighten the risk of poverty for US women.

Since the 1960s, rising rates of single motherhood, particularly among low-income women of color, has been the focus of considerably scrutiny. Approximately half of mothers are the sole custodial parent for some period of time; 45% of single mothers have never married, and approximately 55% are divorced, separated, or widowed (Legal Momentum, 2012). Women of color are more likely than white women to be single mothers with one-third of Black, one-quarter of Hispanic, and two-fifths of white women raising children on their own (Legal Momentum, 2012). Single motherhood is also more common among women that have completed fewer years of formal education. Single mothers account for nearly two in three births to mothers who did not complete high school, but only 9% of births to college-educated mothers (McLanahan & Percheski, 2008). McLanahan and Percheski (2008), discussing the convergence of these factors, observe:

> These educational differences in nonmarital birth rates combined with differences in divorce and remarriage rates produce a scenario in which children with mothers in the bottom educational quartile are almost twice as likely to live with a single mother at some point during childhood as children with a mother in the top quartile. (p. 259)

Family Structure and Class Mobility. Low-income status, family structure, and low educational attainment intersect to construct powerful barriers to upward mobility. Fifty-eight percent of children born to single mothers in the bottom third of the income distribution remain there, while only 10% move to the top third (DeLeire & Lopoo, 2010). Divorce also brings disadvantage and limited mobility. Children of divorced mothers in the bottom third of the income distribution are less mobile than children whose parents are continuously married; 74% of these children stay at the bottom of the income distribution compared with 50% of children of continuously married mothers. Economic status, in turn, shapes later educational opportunities (DeLeire & Lopoo, 2010). Adult children from families in the bottom income quintile are four times as likely to move to the top income quintile if they obtain a four-year college degree (Haskins, Holzer, & Lerman, 2009), but the benefits of postsecondary education are largely out of reach for low-income mothers and their children (see Chapter 4 for further discussion of education and welfare policy). Nearly 80% children in the top income quintile enroll in college compared with just 34% of children in the bottom income quintile, with graduation rates also favoring higher income students (53% vs. 11%; Haskins et al., 2009).

Stigma, the "Culture of Poverty," and the Politics of Single Motherhood. Single motherhood is highly stigmatized and public opinion regarding the impact of single motherhood on society is polarized (Morin, 2011). These tensions are play out in policymakers' interpretations of the sizeable body of social science research focusing on the pathways through which family structure is related to poverty. Social science research treats single motherhood as both a correlate and as a cause of poverty (McLanahan & Percheski, 2008), and not surprisingly, conservatives and progressives differ sharply in where responsibility for poverty is situated.

Conservatives attribute high rates of single motherhood and poverty, particularly in communities of color, to declining respect for the nuclear family, sexual promiscuity, and rejection of mainstream values. Poverty is seen as the consequence of weak work values, lack of discipline, and disrespect for education and the sanctity of marriage in communities with high concentrations of female-headed households. These concerns are perhaps most famously expressed in the US Department of Labor's 1965 report, *The Negro Family: The Case for National Action*, popularly known as the "Moynihan report," in which poor Black families were characterized as living in a "tangle of pathology" resulting from the legacy of slavery, poverty, and the absence of fathers and other male role models (p. 30). Family structure is also at the core of the "culture of poverty" hypothesis (Lewis, 1966), which posits that poverty is transferred from one generation to the next, from parent to child, through a shared culture of deficient values and behaviors (e.g., poor work ethic, disrespect for learning, and inability to defer gratification). Republican presidential candidate Newt Gingrich's proposal to lift "stupid" labor laws to permit poor children to work as janitors is aligned with this view of low-income families and communities:

> Start with the following two facts: Really poor children in really poor neighborhoods have no habits of working and have nobody around them who works. So they literally have no habit of showing up on Monday. They have no habit of staying all day. They have no habit of 'I do this and you give me cash' unless it's illegal. (Gingrich, cited in Blow, 2011, para. 3)

By equating poverty with criminal behavior and laziness, low-income families, themselves, become the source of poverty, but Gingrich's claims ignore two crucial realities. First, there is little evidence that poor families hold different values than middle-class families. Moreover, millions of poor parents work in the paid labor market, but their wages are too low to lift their families out of poverty. Single-mother households and women of color are particularly likely to be among the ranks of the "working poor" (US Department of Labor, 2012).

Policies derived from deficit perspectives seek to instill "appropriate" values (e.g., work requirements) and change family structure by encouraging the formation of married heterosexual households, discouraging "out-of-wedlock" births, and limiting access to or the size of welfare benefits as to not allow the state to "substitute" for a male partner or breadwinner. Feminist scholars see current attempts to limit childbearing among poor single mothers as a "resurrection of old-fashioned eugenics" (Thomas, 1998, p. 422), whether it be via "family cap" policies that deny further cash aid to welfare recipients after the birth of an "additional" child, coercive regulations that require recipients to identify a child's father so the state can pursue child support, or proposals to make welfare receipt contingent on the use of birth control. The forced sterilization of low-income women, particularly African American women, stands as one the most heinous examples of the state-sanctioned control of poor women's reproduction. In North Carolina, alone, an estimated 7,600 women and men were sterilized by "choice," force, or coercion between 1929 and 1974 to "keep welfare rolls small, stop poverty and improve the gene pool" (North Carolina Justice for Sterilization Victims Foundation, 2010; Severson, 2011, para. 7). Approximately 40% of those sterilized were people of color; 85% were and girls and women (Severson, 2011).

Instead of problematizing single motherhood, progressive scholars and policymakers focus on institutional sources of poverty that disproportionately impact single mothers – low pay, unemployment and underemployment, discrimination, occupational segregation, limited access to affordable, high-quality child care, child support delinquency, and lack of a family or caregiver wage (Legal Momentum, 2011b). Christopher's (2002) cross-national analysis of three potential sources of poverty – single motherhood, labor force participation, and public assistance programs – documents why this focus is well-placed. Her investigation revealed that poverty-level earnings and weak public assistance programs, not single motherhood per se, are responsible for greater poverty among US women. Even if single motherhood in the United States declined to levels found in comparison countries, Christopher (2002) found that US poverty rates would only slightly decline indicating that structural change is needed.

Single Motherhood and US Welfare Policy. Contemporary US welfare policies are especially harsh, providing benefits far below what it is needed to support a family (Finch & Schott, 2011; see Chapter 4 for an in-depth discussion of welfare reform and its consequences). Nevertheless, conservatives continue to claim that a generous welfare system encourages dependency. For example, Wisconsin Republican US Congressman Paul Ryan, in calling for cuts to Medicaid, food stamps, and TANF benefits, referred to current safety programs as "a hammock that lulls able-bodied people to lives of dependency and complacency" (Ryan, cited in Krugman, 2012, para. 2). In a similar but more pointed comment, Republican US Senate nominee Nebraska State Attorney Jon Bruning compared welfare recipients to raccoons while criticizing endangered species regulations (Associated Press, 2011). Bruning observed that biologists, in an effort to catch endangered beetles, place rat carcasses along the road but are thwarted by raccoons that come along and eat them. Drawing an analogy between the two, he explained, "They're not stupid". They're going to do the easy way, if we make it easy for them, just like welfare recipients all across America. If we don't incent them to work, they're going to take the easy route (Bruning, cited in Associated Press, 2011, para. 1).

Nothing could be further from the truth. Participation in US welfare programs, by design, is extraordinarily difficult. TANF benefits are set low as to not compete with low-wage jobs, work requirements compel participation in designated work activities, time limits restrict length of receipt, and surveillance and stigma make welfare receipt degrading (Handler & Hasenfeld, 2007; Mink, 1998b, 2001). Although two-fifths of all single mothers are poor, only one-tenth of all single mothers receive TANF benefits (Legal Momentum, 2012). International comparisons make clear that low public assistance benefits do more than punish recipients for being poor – they keep people poor, but not by robbing recipients of their motivation or making life easy as conservatives claim. In Kenworthy's (1999) analysis of 15 affluent countries between 1960 and 1991, social welfare policies helped reduce both absolute and relative poverty; however, the effects were smaller in the United States than in countries with more generous benefits (e.g., higher welfare payments, more extensive networks of programs that reach a wider range of groups, such as childfree adults). Scruggs and Allan's (2006) analysis of 16 OECD countries compliments these findings. More generous sickness benefits were consistently associated with lower relative and absolute poverty rates, while generous pensions were associated with lower absolute poverty rates. These findings implicate low benefits as the problem rather than the so-called welfare trap or single motherhood, underscoring the misguided nature of Republican Presidential nominee Mitt Romney's assertion "I'm not concerned about the very poor; we have a safety net there" (Romney, cited in Cohn, 2012, para. 4).

Discrimination against Single Mothers in the Workplace. Discrimination against poor single mothers also contributes to high rates of poverty. Single motherhood carries the same pejorative assumptions about work commitment and unreliability that motherhood more generally conveys, as well as classist, racist, and sexist stereotypes that associate single motherhood with immorality. Bornstein's (2011) analysis of 2,600 cases of family responsibilities discrimination (FRD) involving low-wage workers, many of whom were single mothers, illustrates this contempt and hostility. The most common type of FRD lawsuits involved harassment and discrimination against pregnant, low-income women. Cases involving pregnant workers included being fired after announcing their pregnancy, banned from certain positions regardless of their capabilities, denied minor, cost-effective accommodations, harassed about birth control practices, and encouraged by supervisors to have abortions (Bornstein, 2011). Single mothers described being the target of inappropriate sexual comments, name calling, derogatory graffiti, and being asked insulting questions about their children's ancestry

(Bornstein, 2011). These biases likely play a role in the failure of women's employment to rebound in the wake of the Great Recession. The unemployment rate among single mothers in 2010 was 14.6%, up from 8.0% in 2007 (US Department of Labor, 2011).

Given these trends and women's high poverty rates, more generally, it comes as little surprise that rates of homelessness among women and families are equally troubling. I now turn to this specific facet of poverty with the aim of highlighting connections among poverty and homelessness in women's lives.

Sources of Women's Homelessness and Housing Instability: Intersections and Insights

The term "the homeless" falsely conveys the impression of a homogenous group, but this is far from the case. Women's life histories and experiences vary considerably, as do their pathways in and out of homelessness. Nevertheless, homelessness, like poverty, is at its core a structural problem and both share many of the same root causes. In the US Conference of Mayors 2011 survey of 29 cities, unemployment, lack of affordable housing, and poverty were the most commonly cited causes of homelessness among households with children. Domestic violence, eviction, and low-paying jobs were less frequent but also mentioned. For many women, these and other factors, such as discrimination, limited educational attainment, sole-parenting responsibilities, and the absence of a strong safety net, intersect to intensify vulnerability.

A Volatile Combination: Low Earnings and Unaffordable Housing

Low earnings and high rates of poverty make finding affordable housing especially difficult for women, particularly single female-headed households with children. It is recommended that no more 30% of a household's gross income be spent on housing; households paying over 30% of their income are considered "cost burdened," and those paying more than 50% are "severely cost burdened." Fewer and fewer households can secure affordable housing. An estimated 12 million renters and homeowners pay more than 50% of their incomes for housing, and it is impossible for a family in any state with one full-time minimum wage earner to afford a two-bedroom fair-market rental apartment (i.e., fair-market is defined as the 40th percentile of rents in an area; US Department of Housing and Urban Development (HUD), 2012b). An analysis by the National Low Income Housing Coalition (NLIHC) documents the depth of the gap between earnings and rental costs (Bravve, Bolton, Couch, & Crowley, 2012). To afford the 2012 national monthly fair market rent of $949 for a two-bedroom apartment, a family would need an annual income of $37,690 or a year round, full-time hourly wage of $18.25 (Bravve et al., 2012). These earnings are $4.00 higher than the wages earned by the average renter and are nearly three times the minimum wage (Bravve et al., 2012). These gaps are even wider in expensive states, such as California and New Jersey, where a year-round full-time hourly wage of $26.02 and $25.04, respectively, are required to afford fair market rents.

The scarcity of low-income housing further limits prospects of finding an affordable place to live. Between 2007 and 2010, the number of rental units for $500 a month or less declined by 1 million, while rentals priced at $1,250 or more grew by two million (Bravve et al., 2012). The shrinking supply of affordable housing is aptly compared to a game of musical chairs, in which fewer and fewer units are available to an increasingly desperate, growing pool of renters (Rollins, Saris, & Johnston-Robledo, 2001; Shinn & Gillespie, 1994). Extremely low-income renters, defined as households with earnings less than 30% of the area median income, are particularly hard hit. In 2010, there were only 5.5 million affordable rental units but 9.8 million extremely low-income renters (NLIHC, 2012). Put another way, for every 100 of these renters, there were only 56 potential units that did not exceed spending more than 30% of household income on housing and utilities (NLIHC, 2012). When both affordability and availability are considered, the situation grows increasingly dire – only 30 units met both criteria per 100 extremely low-income renters.

Stretched to the limit, poor families have few choices but to take on unaffordable rents, leaving little left for other necessities, or accept unsafe, substandard housing because nothing suitable is available. Clampet-Lundquist's (2003) interviewed 18 poor African American and Puerto Rican single mothers living in two Philadelphia neighborhoods to learn how women negotiate the affordable housing crisis. All respondents were receiving TANF or had earnings below $8.50 an hour; none were receiving formal housing assistance (e.g., housing vouchers). To stay housed, women shared crowded, difficult living conditions with mothers, partners, and friends, "rehabbed" abandoned properties, lived in substandard, dangerous conditions, and remained in unsafe neighborhoods. This is a high price paid daily by millions of low-income women across the United States.

Lack of affordable housing also heightens women's vulnerability to abuse and harassment treatment by landlords. Reed, Collinsworth, and Fitzgerald's (2005) examination of approximately 3,500 pages of testimony by 39 victim-witnesses in three separate federal lawsuits filed against landlords and property owners in Texas, Georgia, and Ohio lends much needed insight into this under-studied form of harassment. Low-income women renters experienced harassing behaviors that ranged from crude comments to threats against their significant others to home invasions to unwanted physical contact by landlords. Although some commonalities with workplace harassment were observed, harassment in housing was often characterized by a male "possessiveness" uncharacteristic of workplace harassment. Explaining this distinction, Reed and her colleagues (2005, p. 458) state:

In the workplace, feelings of hostility or attitudes that women 'do not belong' are common, whereas in housing, these types of attitudes are less common than is the desire to possess the tenant sexually and the sense of entitlement by the landlord to consider his tenants as part of his 'property.' The similarities to the traditional distinction between the public and private spheres are striking.

These disturbing findings underscore the invisible consequences of unaffordable housing and that home is not necessarily a "safe haven" for poor women.

Subsidized Housing: High Demand, Limited Supply. Greater availability of housing vouchers and other forms of federal rental assistance would increase women's housing options, but due to limited funding, only 1 in 4 eligible low-income families receives housing assistance (Rice, 2011). The Section 8 Housing Choice Voucher program has served as the primary federal housing program for low-income households, senior citizens, and disabled people since 1974, with recipients paying 30% of their income for rent and utilities, and vouchers covering remaining rental expenses up to a specified limit (Katel, 2009). Vouchers are typically used to find housing in the private rental market, but in some cases can be used toward purchasing a home. Approximately 2.1 million low-income households receive housing subsidies (Katel, 2009), and among them, families with children (54%), many headed by single mothers, comprise the largest share of voucher recipients (Center on Budget and Policy Priorities (CBPP), 2009; Katel, 2009). Because demand for vouchers far outpaces supply, many cities maintain long waiting lists for the program, opening their lists only briefly every few years to new applicants. Applicants can wait years to receive a voucher. When the Chicago Housing Authority opened its Section 8 waiting list in 2008, about 232,000 people applied for just 40,000 slots (Burnette, 2010). Khadduri (2008) projects that even if the program grew by 100,000 units a year, the supply of affordable housing would be insufficient to prevent all needy families from sleeping in a shelter or somewhere not intended for habitation.

Some states are experimenting with "rapid reentry" programs to address this tremendous shortfall. The general goal of these programs is to get families out of shelters and off of long waiting lists by providing them with relatively immediate short-term vouchers. In a Massachusetts pilot program, families received 1-year vouchers with an option for those in good standing to reapply for two consecutive 6-month vouchers. An evaluation of the program by Meschede, Chaganti, and Mann (2012) revealed both strengths and weaknesses of the rapid reentry model. Strengths included greater family housing autonomy and the cost effectiveness of vouchers over shelters, but the time-limited nature of the program created significant problems and stress. Families worried about whether their extensions would be granted and if they would be forced to return to shelters, and some families struggled after receiving extensions because their landlords refused to accept a 6-month lease. Of 60 families who exited the program, only 25% were able to retain their housing without a subsidy, 23% transitioned to a permanent subsidy (i.e., Section 8, public housing), 20% disappeared, 18% doubled up with families or friends, and 4% returned to a shelter (Meschede et al., 2012).

Although the current situation is terrible, housing programs have long been under assault (see Shinn & Gillespie, 1994). Funding cuts, landlords' withdrawal of rental units, and resistance to low-income housing in middle-class neighborhoods all translate into shrinking rental assistance and public housing for poor families (Duke, 2010; Rollins et al., 2001). The 2009 Recovery Act provided $1.5 billion for homelessness prevention, and despite its likely role in preventing sharper spikes in family homelessness during the Great Recession, support is once again on the chopping block (Rice, 2011). In fiscal year 2012, total funding for HUD programs will fall 9% below their 2011 level, and as a result, it is estimated that 12,000–24,000 vouchers may not be renewed (Rice, 2011).

Research findings support the expansion, not the contraction, of subsidized housing programs. Homelessness is less prevalent in areas with larger percentages of subsidized rentals for very poor households, and housing subsidies play an important role in lifting families out of poverty (Khadduri, 2008). An experiment found that housing vouchers decreased homelessness by 74% among families receiving welfare benefits (Khadduri, 2008). Five years into the study, 12.5% of families in the comparison group had spent time on the street or in a shelter during the previous year compared with 3.3% of families who were granted vouchers at the time of random assignment (Khadduri, 2008). These findings illustrate the lifeline that housing support provides and the shortsightedness of cutting housing programs.

The Impact of Welfare "Reform" on Affordable Housing. The shortage of affordable housing is compounded by the dismantling of the welfare system and other public income supports (see Chapter 4 for a comprehensive discussion of welfare reform's impact). Cash aid has never been generous, but state reductions in the size of TANF grants and the failure of benefits to increase with inflation have dramatically reduced "buying power" (Page & Nooe, 2002). Moreover, complying with work requirements and other TANF regulations may be particularly difficult for homeless mothers, putting them at high risk of losing their benefits (Roschelle, 2008).

While TANF's relationship to increased hardship and homelessness has garnered some attention, other benefits have disappeared entirely with little public scrutiny. Under the Personal Responsibility and Work Opportunity Reconciliation Act of 1996 (PRWORA), commonly known as "welfare reform," Supplemental Security Income (SSI) stopped being granted to individuals who are disabled solely on the basis of alcohol and drug abuse (Anderson, Shannon, Schyb, & Goldstein, 2002). This policy change meant not only the loss of cash assistance but also the potential loss of medical care, because Medicaid eligibility was tied to SSI disability status for many of these individuals. This is a devastating combination but especially so for those already struggling with financial and health issues. The majority of women and men interviewed about the impact of losing addiction disability benefits reported that their benefits had been primarily used to pay rent (Anderson et al., 2002). Termination of benefits disrupted their housing arrangements and resulted in losing housing independence. Doubling-up with friends and relatives was a common strategy, with the threat of homelessness omnipresent. A 31-year-old woman who moved in with her mother describes the tension that resulted from no longer being able to contribute to household expenses:

> My Mom talks about getting food and talking about kicking me out cause I don't have no kind of money coming in. Sometimes she gets mad at me cause we don't have money and don't have nothing to eat and she says I'll have to go stay at shelters from time to time. . . . She's use to getting that money from Social Security and paying the rent and now she don't get any. And now that she don't get any, she's telling me she can't take care of me and my kids. (Anderson et al., 2002, p. 281)

This friction not only threatens social and family networks, but also prospects for substance abuse recovery and health, more generally. Homelessness, itself, can trigger episodes of depression and exacerbate heath problems. Moreover, in a study by Page and Nooe's (2002) of homeless women with and without children in their care, substance abuse, a history of mental illness, health problems, chronic homelessness, and crime victimization clustered together, pointing to the need for holistic approaches to well-being and pathways out of homelessness.

Health and Homelessness. Although substance abuse and mental illness are risk factors for becoming homeless and can make exiting homelessness all the more difficult, the majority of people who experience homelessness are neither mentally ill nor drug or alcohol dependent (American Psychological Association (APA) Presidential Task Force on Psychology's Contribution to End Homelessness, 2010). According to a 2010 point-in-time estimate, 26.2% of sheltered adults experienced serious mental illness, and 34.7% had substance abuse issues (HUD, 2011a). Higher rates of substance abuse and mental illness have been found among homeless adults unaccompanied by children than homeless adults with children in their care (Robertson, 1996). The stereotype that the vast majority of people who are homeless are mentally ill and/or substance abusers is inaccurate and diverts attention away from the economic roots of homelessness and compounds the stigma associated with it. Shinn and Gillespie (1994) powerfully argue that these individual-level factors "contribute little to overall rates of homelessness" (p. 505), and that our efforts should be directed toward increasing the supply of affordable housing and income supports that make it possible for low-income groups to compete for middle income housing.

Homeless women's ability to "compete" in the housing market and the workplace is further compromised by poor physical health. Compared with people who are housed, people who are homeless have higher rates of tuberculosis, hypertension, peripheral vascular disease, hepatitis, asthma, diabetes, HIV/AIDS, nutritional deficiencies, and other chronic conditions (APA Presidential Task Force on Psychology's Contribution to End Homelessness, 2010; Lee, Tyler, & Wright, 2010). Among women, more severe histories of homelessness are associated with giving birth to low-weight babies, a greater number of gynecological symptoms, and rape (Arangua, Andersen, & Gelberg, 2005). Differential mortality rates reveal the devastating consequences – the risk of death among homeless women in Toronto under 45 years of age is 5 to 30 times higher than in their housed counterparts (Whitzman, 2006).

Lack of health care is a major barrier to medical treatment, and people who are homeless may face even greater challenges to accessing care than other low-income groups. In a study of the health circumstances of 974 homeless women between the ages of 15 and 44, 37% of participants reported not receiving needed medical care within the past 12 months (Arangua et al., 2005). Commonly cited barriers included long wait and travel times, high costs, fear of receiving bad news, and being seen by different doctors at each visit, whereas facilitators of care included free transportation, being treated for diverse issues at one location, living in a house or apartment, weekend or evening clinic hours, and assistance finding providers from shelters and soup kitchens (Arangua et al., 2005).

Unfortunately, these positive conditions are the exception, not the norm, and limited healthcare resources are compounded by feeling unwelcome and discriminated against by healthcare providers (Wen, Hudak, & Hwang, 2007). Highly publicized cases of "patient dumping," such as the release of a 63-year-old disoriented, homeless woman without her clothes and shoes from Kaiser Permanente's Bellflower hospital to a park despite being in poor health, stand out as particularly egregious (Winton & DiMassa, 2006), but other more subtle interpersonal forms of discrimination can be equally damaging. Feeling talking down to, lack of eye contact, and stereotyping by healthcare professionals can deter homeless women from seeking care. Price, Desmond, and Eoff (1989) found that 58% of a sample of 192 nurses believed that poor women deliberately get pregnant to collect welfare benefits. In a more recent study, student nurses tended to express neutral attitudes toward working with homeless clients, but also reported that they would decline care under certain conditions (Zrinyi & Balogh, 2004). Even shelter staff charged with assisting clients with healthcare needs may be ambivalent toward doing so. Focus groups with shelter staff highlight these complexities (Hatton, Kleffel, Bennett, & Gaffrey, 2001). Staff described helping residents navigate the laborious, confusing paperwork associated with Medi-Cal, California's Medicaid program, and voiced their own frustration with a system they perceived as deliberately keeping needy people out, but still characterized residents as lacking the "assertive communication skills" needed to access health care (Hatton et al., 2001, p. 28).

Violence and Homelessness. Violence is consistently identified as a source of women's housing instability and homelessness (Bassuk, 1993; US Conference of Mayors, 2011). According to the National Alliance to End Homelessness (n.d.), survivors of domestic violence comprise approximately 12% of the sheltered homeless population. Prevalence rates range across studies but are consistently alarming. It is estimated that two-thirds of homeless mothers have histories of domestic violence (Substance Abuse and Mental Health Services Administration, 2011) and childhood sexual and/or physical abuse is associated with chronic homelessness (Zlotnick, Tam, & Bradley, 2010). A Massachusetts study found that 92% of homeless women had experienced physical or sexual assault during their lives, 63% were survivors of violence by an intimate partner, and 32% had been assaulted by their most recent partner (National Alliance to End Homelessness, n.d.). The strong association between violence and women's homelessness is not unique to the United States (Sikich, 2008). In Australia, for example, half of homeless women attribute their situation to violence (Murray, 2011). Abuse often continues if partners are able to locate women at shelters or on the streets (Murray, 2011; Roschelle, 2008).

Homelessness itself leaves women exposed and increases their vulnerability to violence. Homeless women experience rape, assault, and robbery more often than do housed women (Bassuk, 1993). In D'Ercole and Struening's (1990) predominantly African American sample of 141 women living in a New York City homeless shelter, residents were approximately 106 times more likely to be raped, 41 times more likely to be robbed, and 15 times more likely to be assaulted than their housed African American counterparts. Further evidence comes from Wenzel, Leake, and Gelberg's (2001) study of 974 homeless women in Los Angeles County. One-third of respondents reported being "kicked, bitten, hit with a fist or object, beaten up, choked, burned, or threatened or harmed with a knife or gun" in the past 12 months (Wenzel et al., 2001, p. 740). Unhoused women adopt a wide range of strategies to try to keep safe, including riding public transportation overnight (Nichols & Cazares, 2011), isolating themselves from others, seeking male protectors or companions, wearing baggy clothes to downplay their bodies, and trying to appear tough (Huey & Berndt, 2008).

The relationship of domestic violence to housing instability and homelessness is complex, and ending or "leaving" an abusive relationship should not be equated with either a residential move or a direct pathway to homelessness (Ponic et al., 2011). Women may, for example, try to remain in their homes after ending an abusive relationship, but loss of a partner's income may erode housing stability. To better understand these patterns, Ponic and her colleagues (2011) investigated the housing arrangements of 304 Canadian women who left abusive relationships. Approximately one-third of women moved in the 6 months prior to leaving an abusive relationship, and in the one year period of time around leaving (i.e., 6 months before and after leaving), 35.5% did not move, 30.9% moved once, and 33.6% moved two or more times. "Movers" typically transitioned from private market housing to doubling-up with family and friends, and not surprisingly, those who moved multiple times had lower incomes, higher rates of unemployment and public assistance receipt than nonmovers. They also were more likely to live in unaffordable housing and to have experienced greater levels of violence. These findings speak to the need for enhanced housing and economic supports before and after leaving abusive relationships.

Shelters: Refuge and Risk. Homeless shelters are characterized by their own risks and dangers. Women not only voice concerns for their own safety but also for their children. Fear of being judged as a "bad mother" also looms large. Poor, single, homeless mothers, regardless of their actual parenting skills or love for their children, diverge from idealized images of middle-class motherhood. Mothers living in family shelters describe feeling monitored by shelter staff and as if they are "walking on eggshells" when interacting with their children (Cosgrove & Flynn, 2005, p. 134). These sentiments are deepened by mandatory participation in parenting classes common to many shelters and the general loss of autonomy that comes with institutional living (Cosgrove & Flynn, 2005; DeWard & Moe, 2010). Shelter rules may interfere with mothers' ability to set and uphold their own parenting practices. For example, Averitt (2003) found that shelter residents felt their parental authority was undermined when staff gave their children instructions that differed from their own.

Although such actions are invasive and humiliating in their own right, perhaps the greatest concern is that increased surveillance by social service professionals will result in being separated from their children (Whitzman, 2006). This is cited as a powerful deterrent to entering a shelter, and with no clear standard for assessing risks to children's health and safety related to housing issues, child welfare professional wield considerable power and have a wide margin of discretion in decision making (Shdaimah, 2009). In their study of mother–child separation, Cowal, Shinn, Weitzman, Stojanovic, and Labay (2002) found that 44% of mothers who entered shelters became separated from one or more of their children under the age of 17 compared with 8% of the housed mothers who received public assistance and had never been in a shelter.

Housing Discrimination. Women, particularly those who are mothers, are at high risk of experiencing housing discrimination. Moreover, other marginalized identities (e.g., disability, mental health issues, racial and ethnic minority status) intersect to heighten jeopardy. Housing discrimination is typically equated with landlords' refusal to rent to an individual or a family on the basis of group characteristics, but housing discrimination can take many forms. Hertz (2011) reports that US women have brought forth over 200 cases in which mortgage applications were turned down due to pregnancy or maternity leave; cases have also been filed by expecting and new mothers who were advised by bank officers not to apply for mortgages once they were known to be pregnant. Bias against families is also evident in the lack of housing assistance for homeless female veterans. A US Government Accountability Office (GAO, 2011) study found that more than 60% of grant and per diem housing programs serving homeless women veterans do not accommodate children, and among those that do, restrictions on the age and number of children are common. Compared with other forms of housing discrimination (e.g., disability access, race, and religion), the public appears to be less aware and supportive of fair housing laws that protect families with children. Only 38% of 1,001 survey respondents knew that it was illegal to treat households with children differently than households without children and 59% supported landlords' differential treatment of families with children (Abravanel, 2002).

Being a "battered" woman brings its own risk of housing discrimination. In a study by Barata and Stewart (2010), landlords were almost 10 times less likely to relay that a rental unit was available to a caller who identified herself as staying at a battered women's shelter than a woman who did not reveal her current housing arrangement. In a related survey, 35% of 31 landlords perceived renting to battered women as risky, and 23% overtly admitted that they would not rent to battered women (Barata & Stewart, 2010).

Survivors of abuse are also at high risk of eviction. The so-called one-strike policy allows public housing agencies to include lease provisions which:

> provide that any criminal activity that threatens the health, safety, or right to peaceful enjoyment of the premises by other tenants, or any drug related criminal activity on or off such premises, engaged in by a public housing tenant, any member of the tenant's household, or any guest or other person under the tenant's control, shall be cause for termination of tenancy. (42 U.S.C. §1437d (1)(6) cited in King, 2010, p. 48)

In practice, this means that women can be evicted from public housing for the behavior of a relative, partner, or friend even if they are unaware of their actions. In one highly publicized case, a Tampa woman was served with an eviction notice because her son was accused (but not yet convicted) of drug possession (King, 2010). Feminist scholars argue that poor African American women are disproportionately targeted by one-strike evictions and that this policy, along with welfare reform, are indicative of the long arm of the state to marginalize and discipline Black women and their families (King, 2010). Concerns have also surfaced that landlords use complaints from neighbors and/or other evidence of fighting as grounds for safety-related evictions. This claim appears to be well substantiated. A HUD (2011b, p. 6) memo on this issue notes that, "Victims are often served with eviction notices following violent incidents. Landlords cite the danger posed to other tenants by the abuser, property damage by the abuser, or other reasons for eviction." It is possible, in some cases, for these evictions to been challenged as violating the Violence Against Women Act and/or the Fair Housing Act (HUD, 2011b). Nevertheless, discrimination in its many forms continues to undermine women's ability to secure and maintain safe, adequate, affordable housing.

Structural Inequality Demands Structural Solutions

The US government recently concurred with recommendations made by the United Nations Human Rights Council that steps be taken to protect the rights of people who are homeless in the US and that further efforts be undertaken to reduce US homelessness (National Law Center on Homelessness & Poverty, 2011). US support for these recommendations is an important step forward because doing so positions the reduction of homelessness as a "human rights obligation" (National Law Center on Homelessness & Poverty, 2011, para. 2). Whether this expressed support will translate into meaningful action remains to be seen, but will certainly require reversing the current direction of US social policy. Reducing poverty and homelessness will require rejecting austerity policies that starve state and federal governments, restoring and strengthening the safety net, investing in asset building programs, overturning policies that criminalize people who are poor and/or homeless, and the adoption of policies that reduce income and wealth inequality. It will also require a commitment not yet seen to full economic, social, and political equality for all women and their families.

3

Beliefs about Poverty, Wealth, and Social Class: Implications for Intergroup Relations and Social Policy

Persistent poverty and deep economic inequality belie the oft-repeated claim that the United States is a "classless" society. Aversion to confronting social class divisions extends from the unspoken mandate to avoid finances in "polite" everyday conversation to political discourse that emphasizes opportunities for upward mobility while glossing over barriers that limit such movement. Yet even when left unspoken, interclass differences in power and prestige are an ever-present aspect of life in the United States, as are dominant cultural values that equate prosperity with hard work and virtue, and poverty with laziness and vice. Assumptions about the root causes of poverty, wealth, and class status pervade popular media, ranging from rags-to-riches storylines in daytime dramas and blockbuster films, to classic and contemporary works of fiction, to coverage of "self-made" millionaires, such as Donald Trump and Bill Gates (Bullock, Wyche, & Williams, 2001). "Morality" tales of descent into poverty convey equally powerful messages about causality, deservingness, and worth. These highly meaningful narratives, which both reflect and reinforce the widening gap between the rich and everyone else, go largely unquestioned and uninterrupted.

This chapter explores perceptions of poverty, wealth, and social class in the United States through an examination of public opinion polls and research investigating beliefs about economic opportunity and class mobility. Particular attention is also given to stereotypes about low-income women and attributions for poverty and wealth among diverse socioeconomic groups. These beliefs are considered in terms of their relationship to dominant US ideology (e.g., meritocracy and individualism), social psychological concepts and theories (e.g., system justification, belief in a just world, and the fundamental attribution error), and the psychological and political functions they serve. The implications of accepting or rejecting these beliefs among different socioeconomic groups are explored. Individual and intergroup consequences of social distancing (e.g., "My family will never be poor"; "Low-income people hold values and beliefs that are

Women and Poverty: Psychology, Public Policy, and Social Justice, First Edition. Heather E. Bullock.
© 2013 Heather E. Bullock. Published 2013 by John Wiley and Sons, Ltd.

at odds with the middle class"; "I am not like other welfare recipients") are discussed, and on the macro-level, consequences for social policy are examined.

The Ideology and Reality of the "American Dream"

The "American dream" posits that through hard work and initiative, anyone regardless of her or his socioeconomic status, race, ethnicity, or citizenship, can succeed in the United States (Hochschild, 1995). Describing his own trajectory via the American dream, President Barack Obama (2007, para. 6) explains:

> These are dreams that drove my mother. A single mom – even while relying on food stamps as she finished her education, she followed her passion for helping others, and raised my sister and me to believe that in America there are no barriers to success – no matter what color you are, no matter where you're from, no matter how much money you have.

At its foundation, the American dream is predicated on the belief in un-bounded, limitless opportunity, available for the "taking" through a combination of innovation, dogged perseverance, and risk-taking, and while individual goals may vary, "success" is often conceptualized in terms of economic reward and social mobility. Core themes of the American dream also include "freedom to accomplish anything you want with hard work, freedom to say or do what you want, and that one's children will be financially better off" (Economic Mobility Project, 2009, p. 5). Modern-day American dream stories are embodied in the incredible ascent of Barack Obama and Bill Clinton, both men from families of limited means, to the US presidency or entrepreneurs such as Sam Walton, who rose from Depression-era poverty to become one of the richest entrepreneurs in the world through his chain of Wal-Mart stores. Although these individual, or some might say "token" successes, are largely credited to the unique character-istics and drive of those involved, these "successes" are also taken as evidence of the fluidity of class boundaries and equality of opportunity.

Real prospects for class mobility diverge sharply from the promise of the American dream. Economic mobility is lower in the United States than other industrialized countries, including France, Germany, Sweden, Denmark, and Canada, with children's economic, educational, and socioemotional outcomes more closely associated parental education and income in the United States than other nations (Economic Mobility Project, 2011b; Isaacs, Sawhill, & Haskins, 2008). Only 6% of US children born to parents in the bottom fifth of the income distribution make it to the top fifth in adulthood, yet a sizeable percentage of Americans (39%) believe that it is common to start out poor, work hard, and become rich in the United States (Economic Mobility Project, 2009). Governor Mitch Daniels' (2012, para. 7) highly publicized assertion during the Republican response to President Obama's State of the Union address that "We do not accept that ours will ever be a nation of haves and have nots; we must always be a nation of haves and soon to haves" speaks to the notion of unbounded opportunity and the possibility that a windfall is waiting "just around the corner."

Belief in the American dream is a mainstay of public opinion (Hanson & Zogby, 2010). Even in the wake of the Great Recession, 68% of 2,000 poll respondents said they have or will achieve the American dream, and the same percentage reported feeling in control of their economic situation (Economic Mobility Project, 2011a). Although some weakening of belief in the American dream has been observed (Bostrom, 2002; Hanson & Zogby, 2010), Hanson and Zogby (2010) note continued "resistance to questioning the American dream regardless of inequalities" in their comprehensive review of polling data (p. 581). This observation is supported by the relatively strong, albeit lower belief in the American dream that is found among people of color and other marginalized groups than those who are white and affluent (Hochschild, 1995).

Core Tenets of the American Dream

The American dream's cultural stronghold is derived from its fusion of core tenets of US ideology: individualism, meritocracy, and the Protestant work ethic.

Individualism. Individualism refers to "a cluster of beliefs emphasizing independence, the pursuit of self-fulfillment, and individual responsibility for achievement" (Bullock, 2008, p. 53). Cross-cultural studies document the prominence of individualism over collectivism in US political thought and national identity. Individualism pervades many aspects of daily life, ranging from advertising (e.g., "just do it"; "an army of one"), to popular wisdom to be "true to yourself" and to "follow your dreams," to the primacy of the nuclear family over community and other affiliations, to educational and workplace emphasis on individual contributions, skills, and performance.

Individualism is also evident in US political rhetoric that lauds individuals who are described as "pulling themselves up by their bootstraps" rather than relying on government assistance. Attitudes toward assisting struggling homeowners in the wake of the Great Recession offers but one illustration. In a national telephone poll of 979 adults, 53% of respondents believed that the federal government should help people who are having trouble paying their mortgages, while 40% disagreed (Condon, 2011). While there are likely many sources of this objection, deep-rooted belief in individual responsibility is likely a core cause. Of course, psychology itself is not immune to the influence of individualism. Individualism is also charged as undergirding mainstream US psychology's choice of the individual as the preferred unit of study, reliance on positivist methods, and analysis of complex behavior that is devoid of sociocultural context (Becker & Marecek, 2008).

Meritocracy. Meritocracy, that individuals "get ahead and earn rewards in direct proportion to their individual efforts and abilities" (McNamee & Miller, 2009,

p. 2), complements individualism by promoting the belief that excellence rises to the "top." Merit is typically equated with "intelligence, industriousness, educational attainment, creativity, and competency" (Edsall, 2012, para. 4). By this same measure, failure to excel is seen as a reflection of lackluster effort because position is derived from individual qualifications rather than being born into a privileged family (Edsall, 2012). Republican Presidential candidate Mitt Romney's (cited in Edsall, 2012, para. 3) campaign statement illustrates how deeply ingrained meritocracy is in US society:

> . . . people achieve success and rewards through hard work, education, risk taking, and even a little luck. The founders . . . called it the 'pursuit of happiness.' We call it opportunity, or . . . the freedom to choose our course in life. A merit-based, opportunity society gathers and creates a citizenry that pioneers, that invents, that builds and creates. And as these people exert the effort and take the risks inherent in invention and creation, they employ and lift the rest of us, creating prosperity for us all. The rewards they earn do not make the rest of us poorer, they make us better off.

This statement is particularly noteworthy because it moves beyond associating merit with individual reward to making the case that meritorious individuals also contribute to wealth and well-being of others. This belief is evident in portrayals of economic elites as "job creators" and as "engines of economic growth" and undergirds arguments against progressive taxation (e.g., "high tax rates on the rich will undermine economic growth") and "trickle down" economics (e.g., "income and wealth will filter down from elites to other socioeconomic groups and spur economic growth").

So strong is US belief in meritocracy that hard work and perseverance are widely seen as primary determinants of "success." For instance, a 2009 survey found that respondents believed that personal characteristics (e.g., hard work and drive) are more important contributors to economic mobility than external factors (e.g., economic conditions and economic circumstances growing up) by a 71 to 21 margin (Economic Mobility Project, 2009). This is particularly striking given that 94% of respondents also described the current economic condition of the US negatively (Economic Mobility Project, 2009). Optimism about prospects for getting ahead remained strong even among lower-income, less-educated, and unemployed respondents. These findings are echoed in an Economic Mobility Project (2011a) poll in which respondents were asked to identify which of two statements best reflected their position: "Whether or not a person gets ahead economically in this country depends on drive, hard work and obtaining the right skills" or "Circumstances beyond any person's control like the state of the economy or competition for jobs can severely limit a person's ability to get ahead economically." Approximately 46% of respondents strongly identified with the first statement, while just 26.9% strongly supported the second statement.

Denial of structural realities is also evident in long-term polling trends that show respondents as more than twice as likely to choose the statement "Blacks who can't get ahead in this country are mostly responsible for their own condition" as consistent with their beliefs than, "Racial discrimination is the main reason why many Black people can't get ahead these days" (Hanson & Zogby, 2010, pp. 578–579). Rejection of racial discrimination as a barrier to mobility for people of color is a stable finding among a majority of white respondents and is evident not only in direct statements minimizing racism as a source of inequality but also in limited support for policies that promote racial equality (e.g., affirmative action and school desegregation) or that redistribute resources to the poor such as welfare policy (Hochschild, 2006).

The Protestant Work Ethic. The high value placed on hard work is consistent with the Protestant work ethic, "an orientation towards work which emphasizes dedication to hard work, deferment of immediate rewards, conservation of resources, the saving of surplus wealth, and the avoidance of idleness and waste in any form" (Beit-Hallahmi, 1979, p. 263). Offering moral and religious justification for capitalism and the accumulation of wealth, the Protestant work ethic is heavily influenced by the Calvinist belief that earthly success is indicative of God's favor (Christopher, Zabel, Jones, & Marek, 2008; McNamee & Miller, 2009; Uhlmann, Poehlman, & Bargh, 2009). Over time, the association with religion and frugality has faded (Christopher & Jones, 2004; McNamee & Miller, 2009), but the emphasis on hard work and the association of wealth with virtue has remained. Describing the history of the transformation of the Protestant work ethic and its importance to capitalism, McNamee and Miller (2009, p. 6) observe:

> The asceticism part of the ethic, while good for savings, depresses the demand for goods. This hard work/no play combination eventually results in an imbalance for supply and demand. . . . People need either to produce less or to consume more. Americans chose to consume more. . . . Consumption was redefined, not as an evil of self-indulgence but as a just reward for hard work. . . . Americans no longer worked hard simply for the glory of God but increasingly for self-enhancement.

They conclude that secularized remnants of the Protestant work ethic are also evident in the high value placed on independence and personal responsibility (McNamee & Miller, 2009).

The Protestant work ethic not only fuels the "American dream" it also plays a pivotal role in justifying inequality and prejudice toward poor and low-income groups, and perceptions of class status more generally. The Protestant work ethic is correlated with a network of hierarchy enhancing beliefs, including belief in a just world (i.e., that the world is a fair, predictable place in which people get what they deserve), right-wing authoritarianism, and social dominance (i.e., preference for group-based hierarchy and inequality; Christopher, Zabel, Jones, & Marek, 2008). As Uhlmann et al. (2009, p. 36) observe, ". . . the legacy of the Protestant faith in earthly punishments and rewards has multifold effects, not all of which are welcome. The (often implicit) belief that bad people are punished on earth contributes to ideologies that justify social inequality." Rosenthal, Levy, and Moyer's (2011) meta-analysis of published and unpublished studies illustrates this point. Support for the Protestant work ethic was associated with greater prejudice toward marginalized groups (e.g., people of color, people who are homeless, poor, or unemployed, and people who are gay) and lack of support for policies and programs that assist disadvantaged people. These relationships were significantly stronger among Western samples, leading the researchers to speculate that in countries such as Canada, England, New Zealand, and the United States, the Protestant work ethic is more closely aligned with individualism and personal responsibility than in other countries (Rosenthal et al., 2011).

Complicating the "American Dream": Implications for Leveling the Playing Field and Social Policy

Together, individualism, meritocratic beliefs, and the Protestant work ethic contribute to a culture in which economic status is largely perceived as the result of individual effort and merit, and poverty as the consequence of lesser skill and drive. Viewed through this lens, inequality is seen as an inevitable byproduct of personal characteristics rather than structural inequity. Despite these "victim blaming" leanings, it is inaccurate to characterize the United States only in terms of its insensitivity to inequality. Rather, Page and Jacobs (2009, p. 97) see the competing values of individualism, meritocracy, and egalitarianism as resulting in

> blends or compromises among three pairs of inclinations that push in different directions: belief in individual self-reliance but dislike of extreme economic inequality; skepticism about government but pragmatic willingness to turn to government when needed; and hostility to taxes but realistic acceptance of the need for tax revenue.

Indeed, this "conservative egalitarianism" is crucial in making sense of seemingly contradictory public attitudes. For instance, support for policies to assist vulnerable groups is greater than might be assumed given the strength of US belief in individualism and meritocracy. Nearly two-thirds of poll respondents agreed with the statement, "The government should guarantee every citizen enough to eat and a place to sleep" (Bostrom, 2002, p. 13), and in another survey, the majority of respondents believed that economic mobility could be enhanced by government policies that would make college more affordable (75%), reduce healthcare costs (67%), promote early childhood education (61%), and support job training (60%; Economic Mobility Project, 2009). A nationally representative sample of 608 respondents found that 80% favored having their tax dollars used to pay for programs for people whose jobs had been eliminated, and 78% supported having their taxes used for food stamps and other programs for people who are poor (Page & Jacobs, 2009).

There are, however, limits and restrictions to this seeming largesse. Public opinion data make clear that Americans are more concerned with equality of opportunity than equality of outcomes (Bostrom, 2002). US respondents, in one survey, believed by a margin of 71 to 21 that giving people a fair chance to succeed is more important than reducing inequality (Economic Mobility Project, 2009). This same pattern of beliefs emerged across demographic groups, even among respondents with annual incomes less than $20,000. Acceptance, or at least comfort, with differential outcomes is also evident in the relative lack of concern with elites and their economic stronghold. Specifically, polls find that "stickiness" at the top of the class hierarchy is typically not viewed as a significant national problem even though "stickiness" at the bottom often is (Economic Mobility Project, 2011a). Yet, true concern with inequality requires careful attendance to the distribution of wealth as well as poverty, and the problematizing of both great wealth and deep poverty. Although some evidence suggests that concern with inequality has grown alongside the widening income and wealth gaps, it remains unclear as to whether this will translate into meaningful redistribution efforts (McCall & Kenworthy, 2009).

Skepticism about the efficacy of government intervention further tempers public outcry for expanded programs and services. An Economic Mobility Project (2011a) survey found that 36.5% of 2,000 respondents strongly believed that the government does more to hurt than help people move up the economic ladder. These reservations, although disheartening, are not ungrounded. In Gilens' (2005) analysis of the correspondence between public preferences and policy outcomes between 1981 and 2002, a moderately strong relationship between public wants and government action was found, but when diverse income groups supported different policies, policy outcomes strongly reflected the preferences of high-income Americans and bore little resemblance those of the poor and middle class. Gilens (2005, p. 778) concludes that this vast discrepancy in responsiveness to different income groups "stands in sharp contrast to the ideal of political equality that Americans hold dear" and "call into question the very democratic nature" of the United States.

Collectively, public opinion polls reveal a complex and at times contradictory desire for increased "opportunities for economic success" and wanting "individuals to take care of themselves when possible" (Page & Jacobs, 2009, p. 99). Tropman (1998) proposes that these seemingly oppositional beliefs are perhaps better conceptualized as reflecting "value dimensions" that encompass both dominant and subdominant beliefs (Tropman, 1998). For instance, the dominant values of achievement, individualism, and fair play contrast with the subdominant values of equality, collectivity, and fair share, respectively (Tropman, 1998). These values coexist alongside each other in everyday living. As Tropman (1998) explains, "We encourage and celebrate achievement, on the one hand, yet trumpet equality, on the other; we espouse competition, yet laud cooperation; we feel fair play is the way to go, yet we long for fair share as well" (p. 6). Nevertheless, a significant dilemma remains. Support for the poor and progressive antipoverty initiatives are associated with subdominant beliefs, and while enjoying some support, as a nation, we appear to be less committed to collectivism than individualism and other subdominant beliefs (Tropman, 1998). Social psychological research examining attributions for poverty and wealth and their relationship to welfare and other safety net programs brings these leanings and their consequences into sharper focus.

Attributions for Poverty and Wealth

The seemingly simple but inevitably complex questions, "Why are some people poor? Why are some people rich?" are the core of social psychological examinations of beliefs about economic inequality.

Types of Causal Explanations

Three primary causal attributions for poverty were identified in Feagin's (1975) landmark study of US beliefs about poverty: individualistic explanations, which focus on the deficient behaviors and characteristics of poor people, themselves (e.g., lack of thrift, lack of effort, and lack of ability and talent); structural attributions, which emphasize the role of societal factors (e.g., prejudice and discrimination, poorly funded schools, low wages, and being taken advantage of by the rich), and fatalistic causes, which emphasize the importance of luck, fate, and illness. These groupings, although subject to criticism (see Lepianka, van Oorschot, & Gelissen, 2009), remain foundational. Attributions for wealth fall into the same general categories, with distinctions drawn between individualistic (e.g., personal drive, ability, willingness to take risks, and careful money management), structural (e.g., inequality embedded in the economic system, ruthlessness, political influence, and family privilege), and fatalistic explanations (e.g., winning the lottery and good luck; Furnham, 1983; Smith, 1985; Smith & Stone, 1989).

Despite their shared three-factor typology, the contrast between individualistic attributions for poverty and wealth is stark and indicative of larger societal biases; wealth accumulation is typically associated with valued personal characteristics, whereas undesirable qualities and vice are connected to poverty. As a consequence, individualistic attributions for wealth are largely complimentary (e.g., "Her hard work and perseverance paid off"), while parallel attributions for poverty are derogatory (e.g., "She is lazy; she has no work ethic"). Because classist stereotypes (e.g., laziness, lack of interest in education, devaluation of work, and sexual availability) are so deeply embedded within individualistic explanations for poverty, they serve "double duty," acting as both descriptors and explanations of group status.

The centrality of individualism is evident in dominant US attributional patterns that show greater support for individualistic than structural attributions. Fatalistic explanations typically garner the least support, a finding that further illustrates the extent to which poverty and economic status, more generally, are seen as being under personal control in the United States (Feagin, 1975; Furnham, 2003). In Kluegel and Smith's (1986, p. 78) national survey of beliefs about inequality, individual causes of poverty were rated as more important than structural factors, with the top five reasons being "lack of thrift and proper money management skills"; "lack of effort"; "lack of ability and talent"; "attitudes that prevent advancement"; and "failure of society to provide good schools for many Americans." Only the last of these five explanations is structural in nature.

Attributions for wealth are the focus of considerably less research than explanations for poverty, perhaps reflecting the societal tendency to view poverty as problematic and wealth as desirable and beneficial. Attributions for wealth are are less well understood than those for poverty; nevertheless, the same overall patterns persists with individualistic explanations enjoying stronger support than other causal attributions (Hunt, 2004). Three individualistic causes were rated as "very important" (i.e., "personal drive, willingness to take risks"; "hard work and initiative"; and "great ability or talent") by 57% of Kluegel and Smith's (1986, p. 77) respondents compared with 42% who rated four structural causes as "very important" (i.e., "money inherited from families"; "political influence or 'pull'"; "the American economic system allows them to take unfair advantage of the poor"; and "dishonesty and willingness to take what they can get"). These findings led Kluegel and Smith (1986, p. 77) to conclude, "The general public picture seems to be that the wealthy attain their position (if not through inheritance) by their hard work and willingness to take risks." Similarly, at least 90% of respondents in Smith and Stone's (1989) survey of 200 Southeastern Texas residents believed that hard work, risk-taking, talent, and perseverance were important sources of wealth. Nevertheless, structural causes such as better schools, inheritance, and contacts were also viewed as important.

Additional Conceptualizations

More recent research builds on these basic attributional groupings, testing the importance of additional explanations, and contributing additional layers of complexity (e.g., Bullock, 1999; Bobbio, Canova, & Manganelli, 2010; Hunt, 1996, 2004, 2007; Robinson, 2009). Cultural explanations for poverty, as embodied in the "culture of poverty hypothesis," have emerged as figuring significantly into lay understandings of poverty (Bullock, Williams, & Limbert, 2003; Cozzarelli, Wilkinson, & Tagler, 2001). Accordingly, poor whites and people of color are believed to endorse values that clash with mainstream "middle-class" culture (e.g., devaluing education, preferring to make "easy money" through illegal activities rather than via hard work). The transmission of these values from low-income parents to their children is seen as perpetuating an inescapable cycle of poverty. Traditional individualistic attributions and culture of poverty explanations share a focus on personal responsibility, but cultural deficit explanations may be a more covert, socially acceptable way to blame the poor for their status because emphasis is placed on family and psychological shortcomings rather than "harsher," more overtly biased explanations, such as lack of intelligence (Bullock et al., 2003). This seemingly benign but equally damaging form of classism parallels modern racism and benevolent sexism.

Other research suggests that structural attributions are more multifaceted than originally conceptualized (Lepianka et al., 2009). Two distinct sets of structural attributions for poverty were found in Bullock's (2004) study of social worker and welfare recipient beliefs with one set focusing on economic factors (e.g., low wages and corporate downsizing) and another emphasizing the importance of prejudice (e.g., being taken advantage of by the rich and discrimination against ethnic minorities and the poor). These findings underscore the importance of updating measures to ensure that a full range of contemporary explanations is considered.

Implications of Attributions for Low-Income Women and their Families

Findings in three domains directly speak to the relevance of causal attributions for poverty and wealth to the treatment and well-being of poor women and their families.

Intergroup Differences in Attributions

Differential patterns of support across demographic groups are often aligned with and reinforce broader power differences. In Feagin's (1975) study, white Protestants and Catholics, middle-income earners, and those with moderate levels of education favored individualistic explanations for poverty, while African Americans, low-income earners, and those with less education preferred structural attributions. Gender, political affiliation, and direct experience with poverty and/or public assistance are also important, with stronger support for structural attributions found among women, liberals, and welfare recipients than men, conservatives, and people who have not received public assistance (Bullock, 1999; Cozzarelli et al., 2001; Grossman & Varnum, 2011; Hunt, 1996, 2004, 2007; Robinson, 2009; Zucker & Weiner, 1993). The relationship of higher education to attributions for poverty is complex, with differences found between students in diverse major areas of study. For instance, McWha and Carr (2009) found that business students were more supportive of individualistic attributions for poverty than social science students.

Stronger support for structural attributions for wealth is found among low-income groups, African American and Latinos/as (Hunt, 2004; Kluegel & Smith, 1986); stronger support for individualistic attributions tends to be found among European Americans and political conservatives (Furnham, 1983; Kluegel & Smith, 1986). Emphasis on individual responsibility for poverty among powerful groups is consistent with a "pull yourself up by your bootstraps" mentality that negates structural disadvantage. Likewise, seeing merit and skill as primary sources of wealth may fuel an ideological "blind spot" toward the role of privilege. As a consequence, groups with the most power to affect change may be least likely to see its necessity, and generating support for poor women will likely mean reaching across gender as well as racial and political lines.

Beliefs among Service Providers and Recipients. Large-scale survey findings are complimented by focused analyses examining beliefs among specific subgroups. Of particular importance is research examining how social workers and other professionals who work with low-income women and their families view poverty. Some research indicates that social workers are more structurally oriented than the general population (e.g., Reeser & Epstein, 1987), however, recent research suggests that this may not be the case. In Robinson's (2011, p. 2386) study of social workers and inner-city teachers' attributions for poverty and attitudes toward welfare reform, both groups favored psychological/medical (i.e., "sickness and physical handicaps"; "psychological and emotional handicaps"; "poor self-esteem") and family/moral (i.e., "out-of-wedlock childbirth"; "lack of family values"; "divorce"; "drug abuse") explanations over traditional structural and individualistic attributions. Discussing the potential impact of these findings on interclass relations, Robinson (2011, p. 2399) observes,

> Interpretations rooted in psychological and family dynamics may inflict a less moralistic, but no less pathologizing version of poverty on poor children. Seeing poverty as the result of divorce or lack of self-esteem is better than attributing it to alcoholism or laziness, but is hardly a motivation to change an oppressive economic situation. This view of poverty calls for the interventions of professionals, not the organization of masses. It confronts economic deprivation with family therapy and mothering classes.

This assertion points to the importance of moving beyond documentation to examining how about attributions for poverty play out in caseworker–client interactions, and because social workers are not a homogenous group, considering the impact of a wide range of factors including educational level, political orientation, years of experience, and administrative versus frontline status is necessary (Rehner, Ishee, Salloum, & Velasques, 1997; Reingold & Liu, 2009).

Although social workers and welfare recipients share a working and/or lived knowledge of poverty and interact within the same institutional structure, they occupy different social and economic locations and hold different levels of authority and power (Bullock, 2004; Strier, 2008). In Bullock's (2004) comparison of social worker and welfare recipient attitudes, both groups endorsed economic/structural attributions for poverty more strongly than other explanations; however, welfare recipients perceived prejudice as playing a greater role in causing poverty than did social workers. Welfare recipients also supported increased welfare funding and progressive welfare polices more strongly than did social workers. Weiss-Gal, Benyamini, Ginzburg, Savaya, and Peled (2009) report complimentary findings in their study of social works and service users in Israel. Both groups expressed similar levels of support for individualistic and psychological explanations (e.g., "People are poor because they have emotional problems"), but service users attributed greater importance to structural and fatalistic causes than social workers (Weiss-Gal et al., 2009, p. 129). Further evidence comes from Strier's (2008) finding that frontline Jerusalem social workers communicated support for culture of poverty explanations, whereas clients favored structural attributions. Disparate group status intensifies the significance and potential impact of these differences.

Explanations for Attributional Patterns

Basic social psychological principles offer insight into attributional patterns, particularly support for individualistic versus structural explanations, and their potential implications for intergroup relations.

The Fundamental Attribution Error and the Actor-Observer Effect. The fundamental attribution error, which refers to the tendency to "underestimate the impact of situational factors and to overestimate the role of dispositional factors in controlling behavior" (Ross, 1977, p. 183), helps makes sense of the general bias toward dispositional explanations. The fundamental attribution error has been found to be more pervasive in western than eastern countries (Choi, Nisbett, & Norenzayan, 1999), with the overall preference for individualistic attributions for poverty in the United States indicative of this cross-cultural difference. Generating situational explanations for negative outcomes may also require more effort than constructing personal causes for success, meaning that a greater "cognitive load" is associated with situational than individualistic attributions (Skitka, Mullen, Griffin, Hutchinson, & Chamberlin, 2002).

The actor–observer effect – the tendency of individuals to attribute their own setbacks to situational factors but the negative outcomes of others to personal causes – provides further insight into attributional differences, particularly across social class groupings (Jones & Nisbett, 1972). This insider/outsider difference is evident in the preference for structural attributions among the poor (actors) and personal causes by the nonpoor (observers). While offering much needed insight, differential group patterns cannot be reduced solely to cognitive biases. The alignment of beliefs about poverty and wealth with broader power differences is indicative of the need to also consider how beliefs contribute to and justify the distribution of resources (Bullock, 2008).

Dual Consciousness. Although groups tend to differentially endorse one type of attribution over another, it would be misleading to characterize attributions for poverty and wealth as unidimensional or to portray individuals or groups as adhering to "neat" discrete categories of beliefs. Individualistic and structural attributions are not mutually exclusive and multiple, even seemingly contradictory beliefs, may be simultaneously endorsed. The tendency of marginalized groups to endorse both structural and individualistic attributions is described as a form of "dual consciousness" (Bullock & Waugh, 2005; Hunt, 1996, 2004), in which the "relative success and the importance of beliefs in internal, individual sources of advancement" are emphasized along with "minorities' relative disadvantage and the continuing significance of external, environmental barriers to equality" (Hunt, 1996, pp. 310–311).

This phenomenon is well-documented among marginalized groups (Bullock & Waugh, 2005; Hunt, 1996, 2004; Seccombe, 2011). In Bullock and Waugh's (2005) study of low-income Mexican American farmworkers, structural attributions for poverty were favored over individualistic explanations, but support for individualism was also relatively strong. Similarly, Hunt (2004) found that African Americans and Latinos/as were more structural than individualistic in their understandings of poverty, but support for personal attributions was also prominent, with respondents of color more likely than European Americans to hold the poor responsible for their economic status. Likewise, women receiving public assistance convey support for individualistic beliefs despite offering primarily structural analyses of poverty (Seccombe, 2011). These findings are illustrative of the "argument that structuralist beliefs are most popular among disadvantaged strata and are 'layered onto,' but are not replacing of (in a zero-sum manner) an existing individualistic base" (Hunt, 2004, p. 849).

Psychological research has focused almost exclusively on the relationship between individual-level characteristics and beliefs, but dual consciousness may also be fostered by contextual and community-level factors. Merolla, Hunt, and Serpe (2011) found that people living in areas with higher rates of poverty and concentrated disadvantage endorsed significantly higher levels of both individualistic and structural beliefs about poverty, suggesting that experiences with, as well as experiences of, economic disadvantage may shape causal attributions. Relationships among personal economic status (i.e., whether respondents were above or below the poverty line), concentrated neighborhood disadvantage, and beliefs about poverty could not be fully disentangled due to data limitations, but the inverse association found between household income and structural attributions was weaker in areas of concentrated disadvantage. The researchers speculate that support for both individualistic and structural beliefs among people living in areas of concentrated disadvantage may result from being "afforded more opportunities both for (1) relatively intimate/nonthreatening contact with the poor (e.g., friendships) and (2) myriad undesirable and anonymous behaviors such as aggressive panhandling" (Merolla et al., 2011, p. 219).

For people of color and low-income groups, endorsement of structural and individualistic attributions is likely grounded in coming up against pervasive obstacles to upward mobility, pride in personal achievements, and hope that individual agency "pays off." Findings from Bullock and Limbert's (2003) study of women receiving public assistance who were enrolled in a community college program support this interpretation. Structural understandings of wealth, poverty, and income inequality were favored over individualistic attributions, yet respondents also believed in the American dream and perceived class boundaries as permeable. Acknowledging structural obstacles, it seems, does not necessarily diminish belief in personally "beating the odds" through hard work and perseverance (Bullock & Limbert, 2003).

"Dual consciousness" has important consequences for women and their families. Belief in individualistic attributions and class permeability, particularly the potential for upward mobility, may nurture optimism in the face of severe economic hardship, but may also may neutralize potentially radicalizing aspects of poverty and act as a powerful disincentive to class-based action (Bullock & Limbert, 2003). When group boundaries are perceived as permeable, members of disadvantaged groups are less likely to engage in collective action (Wright & Taylor, 1998). Moreover, individualistic beliefs may contribute to scapegoating and social distancing from other low-income groups and public assistance programs (e.g., seeing oneself as different from other low-income women; see Chapter 5; Seccombe, 2011). Low-income participants in Hirschl, Rank, and Kusi-Appouh's (2011) focus groups, for instance, described individualistic attributions as unfairly imposed upon them and as contributing to frustration and isolation, but still viewed other poor people through an individualistic lens.

Nevertheless, groups with greater power tend to be more individualistic and less structural in their understanding of poverty and wealth than less powerful groups. The alignment of group advantage with beliefs about poverty and wealth come into sharper focus when relationships to other beliefs are considered.

Attributions for Poverty and Wealth as One Dimension of a Network of Legitimizing Beliefs. Attributions for poverty and wealth operate within a broader system of hierarchy enhancing or attenuating beliefs. Individualistic attributions for poverty are correlated with belief in the Protestant work ethic (Cozzarelli et al., 2001; Wagstaff, 1983), belief in a just world (Cozzarelli et al., 2001), authoritarianism (Cozzarelli et al., 2001), social dominance (Lemieux & Pratto, 2003), political conservatism (Kluegel & Smith, 1986; Robinson, 2009; Weiner, Osborne, & Rudolph, 2010; Zucker & Weiner, 1993), economic conservatism (Bobbio et al., 2010), and stereotypes about poor people and welfare recipients (Bullock, 1999; Cozzarelli et al., 2001; Henry, Renya, & Weiner, 2004). Conversely, structural explanations are positively correlated with political liberalism (Kluegel & Smith, 1986; Robinson, 2009; Weiner et al., 2010; Zucker & Weiner, 1993) and the belief that poverty is difficult (Reutter et al., 2005), and negatively correlated with social dominance (Bobbio et al., 2010), economic conservatism (Bobbio et al., 2010), just world beliefs, (Cozzarelli et al., 2001), and authoritarianism (Cozzarelli et al., 2001). Attributions for wealth, although less researched, appear to follow the same general pattern, with individualistic attributions positively associated with economic conservatism and structural attributions for wealth negatively correlated with authoritarianism (Bobbio et al., 2010).

The system justifying function of attributions for poverty and wealth become clear when viewed through this wider vantage point. Individualistic attributions fit squarely into what Sidanius, Devereux, and Pratto (1992, pp. 380–381) refer to as legitimizing myths as a "coherent set of socially accepted attitudes, beliefs, values, and opinions that provide moral and intellectual legitimacy to the unequal distribution of social value." If poverty is the result of personal failings, then it is the individual who must change, not broader systems. Similarly, if wealth is perceived as a reflection of individual merit, then the fairness of the "playing field" goes unquestioned. Structural attributions, on the other hand, challenge the legitimacy of institutions by situating class status as the result of privilege, discrimination, and unfair (dis)advantage. As part of a broader network of beliefs, attributions for wealth and poverty gain strength and power, in part, through their relationship to other legitimizing beliefs. Identifying these interconnections yields insight into the constellation of beliefs that undergird interclass relations.

Power-Based Explanations for Attributional Patterns. Focusing on the legitimizing functions of attributions moves away from traditional social psychological conceptualizations of stereotypes and attributions as benign cognitive shortcuts or individual-level attitudes to considering how ideology maintains and justifies inequality (Bullock, 2008). Critical race theory (CRT) and critical race feminism (CRF) further advance this line of analysis by considering how race and gender, but also other identities, such as class, are socially constructed and reproduced to maintain dominant power relations (Delgado & Stefancic, 2012; Limbert & Bullock, 2005, 2009; Wing, 2003). Dominant ideology serves as one mechanism through which class status and the unequal distribution of resources are legitimized. Research examining how attributions for poverty and wealth are related to support for social and economic policies reveals the full-force of legitimizing beliefs and their profound consequences for low-income women and their families.

Attributions and Social Policy: The Justification of Economic Inequality

The importance of attributions for poverty and wealth to the well-being of poor women and their families is most directly demonstrated by research examining support for welfare and other antipoverty programs (Appelbaum, 2001; Feagin, 1975; Kluegel & Smith, 1986). Bradley and Cole (2002, p. 381) succinctly summarize, "Internal attributions towards causation of poverty predict individual solutions to poverty; conversely, external attributions towards causation predict external solutions for poverty."

Causal Attributions and Welfare Policy. These relationships are illustrated by Bullock et al.'s (2003) finding that progressive welfare policies (e.g., "Welfare benefits should be adjusted each year to keep up with increases in the cost of living"; "Welfare recipients should be able to access education and job training free of charge") were predicted by structural attributions for poverty, dissatisfaction with income inequality, and attributing wealth to privilege, whereas restrictive welfare policies (e.g., "If welfare recipients receive 3 warnings or sanctions for not following the rules or taking their case worker's advice, they should be removed from the welfare rolls"; "Fingerprinting welfare recipients is a good idea because it might help reduce fraud") were predicted by individualistic attributions for both poverty and wealth (pp. 50–51). Working with an Australian sample of respondents, Hastie (2010) found that structural attributions for poverty predicted support for three different types of poverty alleviation pro-grams: proposals to provide families with a minimum income (most similar to current welfare programs); a guaranteed job initiative; and a more radical plan to equalize household income.

The connection of attributions for poverty to policy initiatives is also illustrated by Guetzkow's (2010) insightful historical analysis of US congressional discourse from the "Great Society" period of 1964–1968 and the "neoliberal" era of 1981–1996. Policymakers' framing of the causes of poverty and the characteristics of the poor shaped the antipoverty policies that were adopted in each timeframe. In the 1960s, congressional discourse framed poverty as resulting from community breakdown, which was seen as stemming from discrimination and limited opportunities, whereas in the 1980s and 1990s, poverty was attributed to family breakdown and framed as resulting from the alleged generosity of the welfare system (Guetzkow 2010). As Guetzkow (2010, p. 191) surmises:

> The poor in the 1960s were framed as hopeless, helpless victims of discrimination and economic transformations; in the 1980s and 1990s, the poor were viewed as rational actors who lacked the values that would guide them to make the right choices.

In alignment with these understandings, initiatives such as Job Corps and Community Action Programs rose to the forefront in the 1960s, while the 1980s and 1990s saw the rise of "reform" initiatives focused on work, personal responsibility, and benefit restrictions (Guetzkow, 2010).

Causal Attributions and Policies Targeting the Wealthy. Equally crucial is the role that attributions play in supporting policies that increase the economic divide by privileging elites. Favorable attitudes toward entrepreneurs and other groups perceived as creating their own affluence (Christopher et al., 2005) may translate into support for policies that benefit elites. Attributing wealth to personal initiative and "warm" feelings toward the wealthy, for instance, have been found to predict support for eliminating taxes on dividend earnings, the income that corporations pay to their stockholders (Bullock & Fernald, 2005). Perceiving wealth as the outcome of privilege, a structural attribution, is associated with support for progressive welfare policies, whereas individualistic attributions for wealth are related to endorsement of restrictive welfare policies (Bullock et al., 2003).

Beyond Attributions: Other Relevant Beliefs. Many other beliefs are also important to understanding policy attitudes, both in conjunction with causal attributions and independently. Perceived wastefulness and government inefficiency (Smith, 1987), just world beliefs (Appelbaum, Lennon, & Aber, 2006; Hafer & Choma, 2009), conservatism (Zucker & Weiner, 1993), perceived "undeservingness" (Appelbaum, 2001), classist stereotypes (Bullock, 1999; Henry et al., 2004), and racist beliefs (Dyck & Hussey, 2008; Fox, 2005; Gilens, 1999; Gilliam, 1999; Neubeck & Cazenave, 2001) are associated with policy preferences.

Gilens' (1999) analysis of national survey data shows the relative impact of some of these beliefs. Stereotyping African Americans as lazy and poor people as "undeserving" emerged as the strongest predictors of white opposition to welfare followed by conservatism and individualism. The significance of race is also evident in Gilens' (1999) finding that negative stereotypes about Black welfare mothers were nearly twice as strong in predicting antiwelfare attitudes than stereotypes of white welfare mothers. These findings are supported by historical and contemporary analyses of the welfare system that systematically document racism as a central driver not only of antiwelfare sentiment, but also a force behind the adoption of punitive welfare policies (see Chapter 4; Neubeck & Cazenave, 2001; Soss, Fording, & Schram, 2011; Soss, Schram, Vartanian, & O'Brien, 2001).

Intersections of Racism, Classism, and Sexism and Welfare Policy. Although claimed to be a race-neutral policy, "welfare" is a racially charged codeword that activates images of people of color, particularly African American and other so-called "undeserving" poor (Katz, 1989), even when not explicitly mentioned. "Welfare racism" – "racialized attitudes, policies, and practices" (Neubeck & Cazenave, 2001, p. viii) and judgments of "undeservingness," more generally, appear to be largely driven by the belief that poverty is a matter of personal control whether via "poor" life choices (e.g., single motherhood and dropping out of high school), a deliberate rejection of hard work and other mainstream values, or in the case of ethnic minority status, a desire to "play the race card" rather than seize available opportunities. As Henry et al. (2004, pp. 52–53) observe:

> Stereotypes of those on welfare portray them as lazy people who are capable of working, but instead choose to engage in morally questionable strategies in order to increase their monthly welfare checks. This stereotype stands in opposition to American values that those who work hard should get the rewards that society has to offer, and those who do not work hard do not deserve such rewards. Through the propagation of these stereotypes via the media and political rhetoric, the image of the welfare recipient has developed into that of a person who epitomizes laziness and yet is reaping the benefits of our social system.

Shorthand terms, such as "welfare queen," draw their power from these beliefs and intersecting racist, sexist, and classist characterizations of welfare recipients as lazy, sexually promiscuous, and disinterested in education, work, or obeying the law. So great is the stigma of welfare receipt that in a study examining responses to 17 stereotyped groups, ranging from housewives to migrant workers to people with developmental disabilities, Fiske, Xu, Cuddy, and Glick (1999) found that only welfare recipients were both disliked and disrespected, and were uniquely perceived as lacking both warmth and competence.

In further social mapping of stereotyped groups, Fiske (2012, p. 35) reports that "poor people," "immigrants (all over the world)," "homeless people," and "drug addicts (in the United States)" share welfare recipients' extreme outgroup status. Explaining the devaluation that accompanies being stereotyped as incompetent and lacking warmth, Fiske (2012, p. 35) explains:

> Triggering disgust and contempt, they are viewed as extremely low-status and as undermining the values of society . . . note that poor blacks and poor whites, as well as welfare recipients, land here. They allegedly lack both typically human qualities such as sociability and uniquely human qualities such as autonomy, so people effectively dehumanize them.

This marginalized status places welfare recipients and poor people, more generally, outside of the scope of justice, or as Opotow (1990) explains, "when individuals or groups are perceived as outside the boundary in which moral values, rules, and considerations of fairness apply" (p. 1).

The consequences of these beliefs for policy attitudes are evident in the drop in support that occurs when the term "the poor" is replaced with "welfare" in public opinion polls (Smith, 1987; Weaver, Shapiro, & Jacobs, 1995). In a study by Henry and his colleagues (2004) investigating the origins of this split, welfare recipients and welfare policies elicited more negative emotional reactions than did poor people and policies to assist the poor. Anti-Black attitudes predicted these differential emotional reactions to welfare recipients versus the poor. Further analyses revealed that attitudes toward welfare were mediated by belief that welfare recipients are more in control of and more responsible for their situation than poor people (Henry et al., 2004). The importance of perceived control and/or responsibility is also evident in Appelbaum's (2001) finding that liberal welfare policies receive greater support when described as assisting "deserving" (e.g., people with disabilities) rather than "undeserving" groups (e.g., able-bodied men). Beliefs about group "deservingness" are also central to support for other social policies such as affirmative action (Renya, Henry, Korfmacher, & Tucker, 2005).

Summary

The consequences of beliefs about poverty and wealth for the treatment of poor women and societal change are far-reaching. Attributional patterns are aligned such that those with greater power to advocate for economic equality are less likely to see the need for it. Moreover, causal attributions, independently and through their association with other legitimizing beliefs and core US ideology, are closely connected with support for policy initiatives that can close or widen the economic gap. Attributions for poverty and wealth also have consequences for help-giving and other interpersonal and institutional responses to poverty. Belle's (2006) analysis of contested responses to economic inequality following Hurricane Katrina provides one illustration of how beliefs about economic and racial inequality can inform action (or lack of it).

The Tenacity of Classist Attitudes and Beliefs

Individualism and meritocracy, so much a part of the "American dream" and so embedded in US culture, contribute to a social, political, and economic climate in which classism can flourish. Indeed, these beliefs, which emphasize the potential for upward mobility and situate failure to "climb the class ladder" on lack of individual effort, are themselves classist. Classism is "the systematic oppression of subordinated class groups to advantage and strengthen the dominant class groups. It's the systematic assignment of characteristics of worth and ability based on social class" (Class Action, n.d., para. 1). As Lott (2002, p. 102) explains,

> Treating poor people as other and lesser than oneself is central to the concept and practice of classism. Through cognitive distancing and institutional and interpersonal discrimination, the nonpoor succeed in separating from the poor and in excluding, discounting, discrediting, and disenabling them.

Unpacking Classism

Social psychologists approach classism as being comprised of three independent but related constructs: classist prejudice refers to negative attitudes toward poor and working-class people; classist stereotypes describe widely endorsed, socially sanctioned beliefs about the poor and working classes; and classist discrimination refers to interpersonal behaviors and institutional policies and practices that distance, marginalize, and/or penalize poor and working-class people (Bullock, 1995).

Understanding Classist Stereotypes. Many classist stereotypes – that low-income women and men are lazy, irresponsible parents, and disinterested in work and education – are embedded in individualistic attributions for poverty, but classist stereotypes are far more pervasive in their reach and extend beyond dispositional explanations for poverty. Classist stereotypes connect low-income status with a broad spectrum of negative characteristics including criminality and disrespect for "mainstream" values. Smith, Allen, and Bowen (2010) illustrate the association of criminality and inappropriate behavior, more generally with low-income status. Participants were presented with 174 serious but nonviolent infractions that included illegal offenses (e.g., lying under oath and embezzling money) and "rude" behaviors (e.g., cutting in line at the cash register and participating in excessive public displays of affection), and then asked to identify which, if any, class grouping (i.e., "poor/low-income," "working class," "middle class," "wealthy/upper class," or "could be any of these") these behaviors are most closely associated with. Selected by respondents for 125 out of 174 infractions, the category "could be any of these" received the highest number of endorsements, but among the four class categories, "poor/low-income" was the most frequently selected group with 27 participant endorsements (Smith et al., 2010). Eight of these items were "class tagged," in that references to welfare and poverty were explicit (e.g., "Someone who sells his/her food stamps to merchants for cash"; "Having additional children to increase one's welfare payments"), making their identification with poor people highly likely and expected (Smith et al., 2010, p. 42). However, for the other 19 items, poor/low-income people were identified as the likeliest perpetrators despite any overt references to a particular social class group. For instance, low-income/poor people were identified as least likely to bathe and most likely to steal change out of a parking meter, paint graffiti, steal wallets from a department store and sell them, and use a stolen credit card (Smith et al., 2010). Although other social classes were also associated with infractions, the poor were unique in that they were more likely than other groups to be linked to offenses that a person from any social class could potentially commit (Smith et al., 2010).

Intersections with Racism and Sexism. Perceptions of deviance are classed, raced, and gendered. Cozzarelli and her colleagues (2002) found that poor men were more likely than poor women to be labeled as dirty, criminal, and alcoholic, whereas poor women were viewed as more hardworking, proud, family-oriented, friendly, responsible, loving, nice, and healthy than poor men. However, poor women were also more likely to be described as having too many children. These findings illustrate the adherence of classist stereotypes to traditional gender roles, with poor women perceived as "acting out" through their sexuality, one of the few spheres in which women have historically been perceived as exercising "power," and poor men through their participation in traditionally masculine forms of destructive behavior such as criminality. Warning against the conclusion that poor women are viewed more positively than poor men, Cozzarelli et al. (2002) point to the importance of evaluating stereotypes of marginalized groups (e.g., the poor) in relation to more powerful reference groups (e.g., the middle class) rather than their subordinate peers, and in fact, poor women are consistently viewed less favorably than their middle-class counterparts (Bullock et al., 2001; Lott & Saxon, 2002).

Classist beliefs are intertwined with both racist and sexist stereotypes. Thus, stereotypes surrounding sexual availability, single motherhood, and irresponsible parenting are more likely to be applied to poor women of color than poor white women. Indeed, terms such as the "underclass," which dominated popular discourse and public imagination in the 1980s through the mid 1990s, are grounded in racist stereotypes of poor African American men as drug dealers and poor Black women as lazy welfare cheats and irresponsible "baby factories" (Bensonsmith, 2005; Gans, 1995). So fused are terms such as "welfare" and "underclass" with race and gender that they act as "codewords," activating racist, classist, and sexist assumptions without explicit mention of these dynamics.

Republican presidential candidate Mitt Romney's television ads about the Obama administration "dropping the work requirement from welfare" – an assertion with no grounding in reality – is but one indication that racist stereotypes about poor women of color are alive and well (Romey, cited in Toure,

2012, para. 3). These ads continued to run even after being discredited, leading Toure (2012, para. 3) to conclude that their purpose is to update the "old 'welfare queen' meme" and "[re]create racial resentment around entitlements." Such strategies may have helped garner support for Romney's presidential campaign. One poll found that 57% of Republicans believed that people are poor because they do not work hard, and in another poll, in which respondents were asked "Why do most Black voters so consistently support Democrats?", the second most commonly cited reason given by Republicans was that "black voters are dependent on government or seeking a government handout" while for Democrats it was that "their party addresses issues of poverty" (Toure, 2012, para. 3). Both parties gave "don't know" as their number one response.

Classist stereotypes operate independently and in conjunction with racist and sexist beliefs and other legitimizing beliefs (e.g., the Protestant work ethic) – a point that is not lost on politicians and policymakers or anyone who has used or been the target of a classist slur (e.g., "redneck"; "welfare queen"; or "white trash"). These intersections amplify potential for harm, underscoring the need to attend closely to multiple identities in the construction, impact, and dismantling of stereotypes.

Classism and Its Consequences for Everyday Interactions

The Early Sting of Classism. Children are aware of social class and classist stereotypes at a young age (Chafel, 1997; Neitzel & Chafel, 2010). In Woods, Kurtz-Costes, and Rowley (2005) study of fourth, sixth, and eigth graders, all groups viewed the poor as less academically competent than the rich. Classist stereotyping grows more common with age, with descriptions of the rich and poor shifting from physical characteristics (e.g., appearance and possessions) to differences in personal abilities and traits (Chafel, 1997; Leahy, 2003). Individualistic attributions for poverty and wealth also increase as children grow older (Leahy, 2003), and paralleling adult demographic patterns, socioeconomic and racial differences among children are documented. In Chafel and Neitzel's (2005) study of 64 racially and socioeconomically diverse 8-year-olds, descriptions of material and physical aspects of poverty were more commonly provided by children from lower than higher socioeconomic status (SES) families. Lower SES children were also more likely than their higher SES peers to discuss needs that went beyond basic necessities, such as lacking a strong social network; Black and biracial children were more likely than white children to speak about the need for more humane treatment of the poor, but lower SES children were equally likely to discuss more humane treatment of the poor regardless of race (Chafel & Neitzel, 2005). Similar to adults, poor children and children of color, tend to express greater sensitivity toward poverty and economic inequality and have a more complex, nuanced understanding of it.

Unfortunately, nonpoor schoolmates, teachers, and other important groups in young people's lives may lack this sensitivity, making low-income youth the targets of classist humiliation and discrimination (Darley & Gross, 1983; Kozol, 1991; Lott, 2001). Narratives of growing up poor often include discussions of the shame of poverty and the desire to "pass" as middle class (Kurth, 2012). The sting of class stigma is evident in Kurth's (2012) refusal to eat free lunch in middle and high school so that she could be perceived as middle class. In Weinger's (1998) interviews in which poor children described poverty in terms of crisis and hardship and middle-class status as relatively worry-free, and in Kozol's (1991) reports from students about what it means to attend schools without running water, operating toilets, or basic supplies.

The Not-So Hidden Injuries of Classism in Adulthood. Class stigma and discrimination also figures prominently into the experiences of poor adults. The pain that is felt by the targets of welfare stigma is vividly described by program recipients (see Chapter 5; Seccombe, 2011; Soss, 2005; Williams, 2009) and in historical analyses documenting the deliberate stigmatization of welfare recipients through onerous policies and procedures designed to cause humiliation and deter participation (Gordon, 1994; Katz, 1989; Piven & Cloward, 1993). The ongoing use of these tactics to intimidate and deter women, particularly women of color, from applying for and/or receiving benefits is documented in feminist and critical analyses of contemporary welfare policy (Fisher & Reese, 2011; Limbert & Bullock, 2005; Mink, 2001; Smith, 2007; Soss et al., 2011). It is also evident in the distance that some recipients place between themselves and other public assistance recipients and programs even when personally receiving aid (Appelbaum & Gebeloff, 2012; Fine & Weis, 1998; Seccombe, 2011).

Class stigma has important implications for personal well-being. Discrimination and economic inequality is associated with depression and poor mental health (Belle & Doucet, 2003). Working with a sample of 210 low-income women, Mickelson and Williams (2008) found that internalized class stigma (i.e., negative feelings about being poor) was related to lower self-esteem, whereas experienced stigma (i.e., beliefs about being stigmatized by others) was related to perceiving less available support from members of one's network. Both types of stigma were associated with greater fear that requests for support would be rejected and depression.

Isolation and Avoidance. Efforts to avoid stigmatizing interactions may intensify low-income women's isolation and deepen hardship. In Solomon's (2007) ethnographic study of welfare recipients living in a small city in upstate New York, women described steering clear of neighbors because they feared being scrutinized or having their parenting skills questioned. Although this strategy may succeed in reducing opportunities for negative interactions to occur, it also means passing up potential support (e.g., rides to the supermarket and help with child care). Describing this double bind, Solomon (2007, p. 46) observes:

> Welfare practices suggest that poor women need to develop skills toward self sufficiency and not depend on others who may compromise their ability to find and

keep a job, antagonize welfare, or otherwise draw the attention of authorities . . . Discerning trouble and scrutiny from help is commonly difficult but necessary work for these women. On the one hand, they need social support to overcome obstacles to work. On the other hand, they need social distance to protect themselves from public scrutiny and possible sanctions and suffering.

Cross-class interactions may be particularly stressful, and poor and working class groups may protect themselves from hostility by modifying their behavior. In a series of studies examining cross-class interactions by Garcia, Hallahan, and Rosenthal (2007), working class students reported greater discomfort when interacting with higher-income students than with other working class students and were less expressive in these interactions. Working-class students reported that they would intentionally change their behavior when interacting with a wealthy stranger but not with a working-class stranger; higher income students said their behavior would stay the same regardless of the class status of whom they interacted with.

Experimental research suggests that this caution is warranted. Power, Cole, and Fredrickson (2010) found that a female target who expressed anger about being poor elicited angry responses from class-privileged respondents, whereas a female target who conveyed shame elicited pity. Participants also preferred donating money to the female target who was ashamed rather than angry about being poor. The researchers conclude,

> From the perspective of poor women, it is more dangerous to be the recipient of anger than pity, so it may behoove them to stay in their shameful, emotionally subordinate place. The poor are only able to avoid anger and gain pity from those with power by expressing emotions that suggest they accept the blame for poverty. In doing this, those with class privilege are able to feel pride about their 'accomplished' higher standing, thus justifying inequities in the class system. (Power et al., 2010, p. 194)

Classism and the Reproduction of Class-Based Power Relations. Ultimately, classism reproduces class privilege and disadvantage. While class-reproducing aspects of cuts to public school funding or tax breaks for the wealthy are fairly evident, the impact of interpersonal classism may be less obvious but equally detrimental. Streib's (2011) ethnography of 4-year-old preschoolers illustrates how even if not consciously or deliberately acted upon, classist norms and biases reproduce class privilege. About half of the preschoolers were from working class families and received scholarships to attend, while the other half were from upper middle class families with parents paying up to the equivalent of a year of in-state college tuition. Students worked with the same teachers, played with the same toys, and participated in the same activities. Nevertheless, Streib (2011) soon noticed that class differences in the children's linguistic patterns resulted in very different treatment in the classroom. Upper middle-class children tended to know more words and call out more frequently, which prevented working class children, who typically raised their hands before speaking up, from being heard (Streib, 2011). Upper middle-class children also interrupted, asked for attention, and requested help more often (Streib, 2011). Consequently, teachers gave more attention to these assertive children. This not only gave upper-middle-class children greater control, it also provided them with more opportunities to improve their speaking skills (Streib, 2011). These same skills also served upper-middle-class children well in their disputes with working class children over toys.

According to Streib (2011), working class children were not purposefully excluded, but in favoring the linguistic style of middle class students, teachers inadvertently reproduced class privilege and disadvantage. Streib (2011, p. 350) concludes:

> Working-class students may be learning, as young as age four, that school is not a place for them. They see the teachers' attention drifting to their peers of a different class, they see their own needs going unmet as their peers receive more help, and they come to find out that when they argue with an upper-middle-class peer in school it is unlikely they will win.

Schools are just one of the contexts in which these powerful lessons are learned. These same lessons are repeated across the lifespan in a broad range of contexts.

Initiatives to Reduce Classist Bias: Barriers to Attitude Change

Initiatives to reduce classist bias reveal how difficult it is to change attitudes and beliefs. Educational programs, which seek to increase structural understandings of poverty via course curriculum (e.g., books, films, and activities) and/or service learning activities, represent one important line of attack on classist beliefs. Underlying both approaches is the belief that exposure to the structural roots of poverty – whether through course content or interpersonal interactions – can reduce classist bias.

The Limited Effectiveness of Service Learning and Other Interventions. Evaluations of anti-bias efforts provide evidence that change is possible but also difficult. Mistry, Brown, Chow, and Collins (2012) assessed the impact of a one-week eighth-grade social studies program designed to increase sensitivity to poverty and economic inequality. Students' beliefs were measured one week before the curriculum, one week post-instruction, and again six months later. After the intervention, students were more likely to emphasize fatalistic attributions and less apt to focus on individualistic causes for poverty than they were beforehand, but rarely cited structural sources of poverty and continued to rate individual effort as the most influential factor in determining success (Mistry et. al., 2012). The researchers attribute the program's limited success to its brevity, noting that a week-long intervention is likely far too brief to challenge bias as deeply entrenched as classism. The fact that students' were overheard referring to poor people as "hobos," "beggars," and "dumpster divers" early in the study, that high rates of Black poverty were attributed to having "a lot of babies," and that references were made to "living off welfare" and "not looking for a job" is indicative of the degree to which participants were familiar with and comfortable voicing classist stereotypes (Mistry et al., 2012, pp. 312–313). Such beliefs are unlikely to fade quickly.

Longer interventions with college students do not necessarily fare much better. Sanders and Mahalingam's (2012) content analysis of final papers in a semester long course on intergroup dialogue revealed continued difficulty openly discussing social class and class privilege. The researchers' attribute these difficulties to the conflation of class with race, strong societal taboos against discussing social class, and the endorsement of classist stereotypes (Sanders & Mahalingam, 2012). Service-learning courses and community service units embedded in general classes encourage more than intergroup classroom dialogue by requiring students to work with diverse groups in nonprofit agencies or other community settings. Seider, Gillmor, and Rabinowicz's (2011) study of a one-year college course "Individual and Social Responsibility" documents the potential of community service to facilitate attitude change. Firsthand encounters with low-income children, women, and men increased the salience of structural sources of poverty; however, these effects were uneven across business and non-business majors (Seider et al., 2011). Although business students developed a deeper appreciation of structural privilege, their faith in the US economic system appeared unaltered as evidenced by a slight increase in just world beliefs. The researchers see their findings as illustrating Kluegel and Smith's (1986) notion of "compromised images" by which people append "their newfound understanding of inequality to existing beliefs about the justness of America's opportunity structure, rather than allowing this new understanding of inequality to *supplant* or *re-shape* their existing worldviews" (Seider et al., 2011, p. 499).

A similar pattern of "compromised images" emerged in Seider's (2011) mixed-method study of high school students' beliefs about homelessness, opportunity, and inequality. After completing a justice-oriented literature curriculum, participants expressed more complex understandings of the causes of homelessness; however, their beliefs about opportunity remained largely unchanged, and respondents' invoked legitimizing and naturalizing beliefs to justify their own class position (Seider, 2011). These seemingly contradictory ideas are revealed in one respondent's remarks about the unfairness of a hardworking "single mom working two jobs who still lives in an apartment in like a ghetto," but still lags behind "some big business guy . . . just because it's not as high up of a job" (Seider, 2011, p. 351). However, this structural assessment was subsequently naturalized by her assertion that, "But I guess that's just the way the world works because someone has got to work those jobs" (Seider, 2011, p. 351). Later in the interview, she explained her own family's affluence and class position by characterizing her father as a more motivated, harder worker than his peers in the low-income neighborhood where he grew up.

Even when intergroup contact reduces classist stereotypes, policy attitudes may remain unchanged. Knecht and Martinez (2009) examined the impact of intergroup contact on volunteers for Project Homeless Connect, a one-day event that provides an array of social services to people who are homeless at one location. After volunteering, respondents were less likely to make individualistic attributions for homelessness (e.g., substance abuse and laziness), and reported feeling more comfortable around people who are homeless, but their policy preferences remained consistent. Although support for coercive policies (e.g., forcibly removing homeless people from public areas) declined modestly after volunteering, the majority of respondents were unchanged in their attitudes toward restrictive (i.e., restrictions on the right to sleep in public spaces or panhandle) and preventative (e.g., transitional housing, substance abuse treatment, and job training) policies (Knecht & Martinez, 2009). Among respondents whose opinions changed, attitudes were evenly divided between moving in a positive and negative direction. Knecht and Martinez (2009) conclude that attributions for homelessness may not correspond as closely with policy preferences as is commonly believed. It may also be the case that the seeming inflexibility of policy attitudes versus perceptions of homeless individuals is, in fact, a consequence of social desirability demands, with respondents feeling greater pressure to express positive attitudes toward people who are homeless than homeless policy (Knecht & Martinez, 2009).

The More Things Change, the More They Stay the Same: Attitudes toward Welfare Policy in the Wake of "Reform". The durability of stereotypes is further illustrated by research examining attitudes toward welfare policy. Prior to major reform in 1996, welfare was among the most unpopular social programs (Weaver et al., 1995), and Dyck and Hussey's (2008) tracking of opposition to welfare spending using American National Election Studies data from 1992, 1996, 2000, and 2004 shows the resistance of these beliefs to change. Despite dramatic changes to the welfare system and post-reform discourse – notably the decreased salience of poverty and welfare in major news magazines and more accurate racial pictorial representations of poor people – attitudes toward welfare remained as strongly racialized in 2004 as they were a decade earlier, with the stereotyping of Blacks as lazy figuring prominently in welfare opposition. Dyck and Hussey (2008) conclude that welfare-related stereotypes run so deep that greater sustained exposure to counter-stereotypical information would be needed to challenge them, but also note the difficulty of reaching "such a threshold of dramatic, salient, and sustained change" given the sweeping changes that occurred during the time period studied (p. 611).

Why Is Attitude Change so Difficult? Basic social psychological processes play a role in making stereotypes resistant to change. People are likely to remember information that is consistent with their preexisting beliefs and may even misremember information to maintain consistency. For instance, after viewing a videotaped vignette, Gilliam (1999) found that white respondents were less likely to remember seeing a white than an African American welfare recipient. Hindsight bias, when people believe that they knew the outcome of an event before it happened, also reinforces preexisting beliefs. In Hölzl and Kirchler's (2005) analysis of attitudes toward the euro, hindsight bias was stronger for negative economic developments when individuals held negative attitudes toward the euro and stronger for positive developments when attitudes toward the euro were positive. For better or worse, economic events that were causally linked with respondents' beliefs about the euro created a "closed" feedback loop and stable understandings of the economy (Hölzl & Kirchler, 2005).

Cognitive biases can help us understand why individual level attitude change is so difficult, but these micro-level processes only provide partial insight into the maintenance of classist beliefs. The sheer pervasiveness of individualism and meritocratic beliefs in the mainstream media and political discourse make it very difficult for counterhegemonic information to take hold. Even charitable messages may convey subtle classist biases that inadvertently encourage distancing from the poor. In Bishop's (2008) review of 20 Goodwill advertisements, she found that middle-class donors were commonly depicted making contributions safely from their homes without interacting with low-income women and men, or doing so from a safe distance via a uniformed Goodwill truck driver who picked up their contributions. Bishop (2008) argues that these representations reaffirm already entrenched perceptions of the middle class as "caring" and "good," while also communicating the acceptability of keeping one's distance from the poor.

Even when media portrayals of poor and working class people are neutral or relatively positive, structural sources of inequality are rarely presented and this lack of contextual framing negates institutional sources of poverty and wealth. This is the case in post-reform newspaper coverage of poverty and welfare reform (Bullock et al., 2001) and analyses of the media framing of the Bush administration's TANF reauthorization proposal and the 2003 dividend tax cuts, which dramatically reduced the rates at which income from stock holdings is taxed (Limbert & Bullock, 2009). Limbert and Bullock (2009) found that news coverage of welfare reauthorization and dividend taxation reduction, two redistributive policies with very different beneficiaries, differed sharply. Even though wealthy stockholders are the primary beneficiaries of lowering tax rates on dividend earnings, these initiatives were described as socially just tax code corrections that would benefit individuals across the socioeconomic spectrum, particularly "senior citizens." On the other hand, welfare reauthorization coverage honed in on "welfare recipients" and the importance of "tough love" programs to incentivize work and marriage (Limbert & Bullock, 2009). Implicit in discussions of both sets of policies was the notion that poverty and wealth are earned, with "seniors" (e.g., hard working, white, middle class) and "welfare recipients" (e.g., poor, lazy, African American single mothers) acting as codewords to activate beliefs about "deservingness."

Putting Theory into Practice. The bottom line is that initiatives to challenge classist beliefs and frames must compete against a relentless barrage of messages, both overt and covert, that scapegoat the poor and valorize the wealthy (Kendall, 2011). Even when structural explanations for poverty and wealth are supported, difficulty fully rejecting dominant constructions of class as an earned status remains. This is as true of politics as it is of everyday interactions and discourse. As Lowe (2008) observed in her interviews with urban adolescent parents, young women often discussed their life experiences using a structural lens, but their articulation of these stories was frequently overshadowed by mainstream conceptualizations of welfare recipients as lazy and restrictive policies as necessary and beneficial.

Breaking free of these dominant constructions would require what Stryker and Wald (2009) refer to as "value redefinition." Drawing on political rhetoric from congressional floor debates of welfare reform, they demonstrate how conservatives successfully redefined traditional understandings of "compassion" in relation to welfare policy. In this context, "compassion" has historically meant shared responsibility for the well-being of the poor and support for safety net programs, but was redefined during debates about welfare reform to mean personal responsibility and freedom from "dependence," including from the very programs designed to assist low-income groups (Stryker & Wald, 2009). This redefinition is dramatically illustrated in Representative Jack Kingston's (R-GA) response to the claim that that those voting for PRWORA lacked compassion:

> Nothing is more cruel than having a welfare system that traps children in poverty, that makes children and families break up, that makes them live in housing projects where the dad cannot be at home, where there is a high drug use, where there are teenage dropout rates and teenage drug abuse. I do not see why they think that is compassion. (Kingston, cited in Stryker & Wald, 2009, p. 546)

Reducing classism will ultimately require not only redefining "compassion" but also dominant constructions of "success," "wealth," and "poverty" and reordering our value system to put interdependence above independence and shared well-being above competition. It will also require dismantling classist stereotypes so that it is no longer the case that "processes of symbolic and moral differentiation, along with claims about pollution and stigma, are at the cultural foundation of U.S. welfare policy" (Steensland, 2006, p. 1286). Resistance to such efforts will be great, not only because these beliefs are central to US ideology, but also because they legitimize capitalism, a system in which great fortunes are made at the expense of others' labor and subordination. This is not to diminish the need for greater empathy (Segal, 2007) or to suggest that micro- and macro-level change efforts are not worth pursuing or are inevitably doomed to failure, but rather to underscore why such initiatives must vigilantly attend to the broader political, economic, historical, and social context of wealth, poverty, and inequality.

Concluding Thoughts

At the 2012 Republican and Democratic Conventions, Ann Romney and Michelle Obama discussed the financial hardships they experienced early in their relationships with presidential candidate Mitt Romney and President Barack Obama, respectively. Ann Romney recounted that as newly married college students, they frequently ate pasta and tuna fish, worked on a desk they created by putting a door on sawhorses, and ate dinner on an ironing board (Cohen, 2012). Michelle Obama discussed her husband retrieving a coffee table from a dumpster and driving a dangerously rusted out car (Cohen, 2012). Ann Romney's claims, in particular, drew considerable scrutiny given that Mitt Romney's father was CEO of an automobile company, governor of Michigan, and ran for US President (Cohen, 2012). Ann Romney, herself also came from a well-off family. Barack and Michelle Obama, on the other hand, came from far more humble socioeconomic origins.

The overarching message of these "rags-to-riches" stories – "Anyone can move up the socioeconomic ladder regardless of where they start" and "There are no limits to upward mobility" – resonate with deeply entrenched beliefs in meritocracy, class permeability, individualism and the American dream. Indeed, it seems de rigueur for political candidates to recount stories of poverty or economic hardship to gain legitimacy with voters, but the reality is most political elites are also economic elites. Nearly half of members of the US Congress are millionaires, with US senators registering an estimated median net worth of $2.63 million and their counterparts in the US House of Representatives a median net worth of $756,765 (Brush, 2012). Tellingly, between 1984 and 2009, the median net worth of House members almost tripled, while the net worth of the people they represent declined slightly during this time (Brush, 2012). Given what we know about the real prospects for upward mobility in the United States, apart from the mythology of "rising to the top," the odds are tilted toward policymakers having privileged roots. Rags-to-riches narratives downplay such privilege, rendering invisible the policies and practices that distribute wealth and power upward and maintain the position of elites. Dominant US beliefs about poverty and wealth are the ideological "glue" that legitimizes class position.

No system of inequality can exist without an ideology to nurture, protect, and advance it. The social science research discussed in this chapter documents how dispositional attributions for poverty and wealth along with belief in meritocracy, individualism, and the Protestant work ethic contribute to the acceptance of tremendous economic disparities in the richest nation in the world, and support for policies that both create and perpetuate wealth and poverty. Neither generous welfare benefits nor strong safety net programs are likely to be supported if beneficiaries are perceived as responsible for their own hardship. Intersecting classist, racist, and sexist stereotypes paint a portrait of dependency, irresponsibility, and undeservingness.

Derogation of the poor stems from a wide range of motivations – a sense of powerlessness to affect change (Fine, 1982), a desire to distance oneself from a negatively stereotyped group (Appelbaum & Gebeloff, 2012; Seccombe, 2011), fear of ending up in a similarly precarious situation, or a genuine sense of superiority and entitlement – nevertheless, the bottom line is the same: resources could be distributed differently, but we choose not to do so. Political pundit Stephen Colbert (2010) reaches a similar conclusion in his searing commentary of the hypocrisy of US Republicans who claim to closely follow Christian teachings of compassion but also argue for restricted benefits for low-income groups:

> If this is going to be a Christian nation that doesn't help the poor, either we have to pretend that Jesus is just as selfish as we are or we have to acknowledge that he commanded us to love the poor and serve the needy without condition and then admit that we just don't want to do it.

Dominant beliefs about poverty and wealth buffer such realizations by focusing attention on deservingness and shifting responsibility for poverty on the poor themselves.

For poor women and their families, debates about the causes of poverty, actual or perceived, are not academic or abstract. Classist beliefs and their intersections with racism and sexism are borne out in policies that govern much-needed benefits, such as cash assistance and health care, in interactions with teachers, neighbors, and caseworkers, and in our own self-understandings. Until economic disparity is widely understood as undeserved and unjust, support for progressive social policies and widespread change will remain elusive.

says attitude before policy but how?

4

Welfare Reform at 15 and Beyond: How Are Low-Income Women and Families Faring?

It has been more than 15 years since the Personal Responsibility and Work Opportunity Reconciliation Act of 1996 (PRWORA, P.L. 104-193) changed the structure of public assistance in the United States. Ending welfare's status as an entitlement program, PRWORA's passage fulfilled former President Clinton's 1992 campaign promise to "end welfare as we know it" by ushering in a new era of social policy for poor women and families. PRWORA replaced the unpopular cash assistance program Aid to Families with Dependent Children (AFDC) with the Temporary Assistance for Needy Families (TANF), a cash support program that includes time limits and work requirements for families receiving aid. TANF was reauthorized in 2005 as part of the Deficit Reduction Act (DRA, P.L. 190-171) and since October 2010, Congress has extended TANF several times, authorizing it through March 2013.

. At welfare reform's 10th anniversary in 2006, caseloads had dropped by 54% from 12.2 million in 1996 to 4.5 million (Clinton, 2006). Both policymakers and social scientists passionately debate the impact and meaning of this decline. In this highly politicized arena, proponents of "reform" equate declining caseloads as evidence of its success, while critics cite high poverty rates, particularly among welfare "leavers," as indicative of its failure. In the wake of the Great Recession, the meaning of low welfare rolls have come under even greater scrutiny with, in some cases, both advocates and critics of reform expressing concern that the program no longer reaches a sufficient number of eligible families. Despite significant increases in poverty and unemployment, TANF receipt only increased 12% between December 2007 and September 2009, the first 22 months of the recession (Legal Momentum, 2010a). During this same time period, recipients in the Supplemental Nutritional Assistance Program (SNAP, commonly referred to as "food stamps") increased by 35%, and the unemployment rate increased by 96% from 5.0% to 9.8% (Legal Momentum, 2010a). According to the Center on Budget and Policy Priorities (CBPP, 2012a), in 1996, 68 families received

Women and Poverty: Psychology, Public Policy, and Social Justice, First Edition. Heather E. Bullock.
© 2013 Heather E. Bullock. Published 2013 by John Wiley and Sons, Ltd.

TANF for every 100 poor families but in 2011, this number had dropped to only 27 families receiving TANF for every 100 poor families.

This chapter draws on quantitative and qualitative research to explore debates about declining welfare rolls and evaluate the impact and success of welfare "reform." The scope of welfare reform is broad and only selected key features are reviewed with emphasis placed on the understanding the consequences of current policy on women's financial and psychological well-being. Contemporary welfare reform and the historical foundations of cash assistance in the United States are analyzed using a critical lens to deconstruct underlying racism, sexism, and classism in federal law and state programs. Feminist and critical analyses of the history of the US welfare system reveal longstanding bias, competing beliefs about the limits of social responsibility and understandings of "citizenship," and conflicting attitudes toward women's paid employment outside the home (see Gordon, 1994; Katz, 1986, 1989, 2001; Piven & Cloward, 1993). These tensions and biases continue to define US welfare policy, particularly public support for restrictive reform regulations (e.g., time limits on aid, work requirements, sanctions, "family caps," and restrictions on immigrant applicants), and the discourse that surrounds cash assistance.

Welfare Reform: Temporary Assistance for Needy Families

In August 1996, Congress passed welfare reform legislation that replaced AFDC with TANF. TANF differs markedly from the AFDC program. PRWORA ended welfare's status as an entitlement – a shift that is of great philosophical and practical significance (for a summary of policy changes and trends, see Martin & Caminada, 2011; Schott, 2012). PRWORA ended the "guarantee" of cash aid to eligible low-income families. As such, states may turn away needy families even if they meet eligibility criteria. Moreover, spending on the program is no longer automatically associated with the number of recipients but is instead subject to annual appropriation via block grant funding (Martin & Caminada, 2011). Progressive poverty scholars consider the loss of federal entitlement status as a fundamental blow to the safety net and a severing of the social contract because need no longer ensures support. During an economic recession (or any time of increased need), the practical implications of this change would be acutely felt if the welfare rolls were to rise but federal block grant funds did not increase to meet current demand (Zedlewski, 2008).

Under the TANF system, states receive block grant funds from the federal government to design and operate their own cash assistance programs for low-income families. TANF funds must be spent in ways that are consistent with the primary goals of the federal law to:

(1) provide assistance to needy families so that children may be cared for in their own homes or in the homes of relatives; (2) end the dependence of needy parents

on government benefits by promoting job preparation, work, and marriage; (3) prevent and reduce the incidence of out-of-wedlock pregnancies and establish annual numerical goals for preventing and reducing the incidence of these pregnancies; and (4) encourage the formation and maintenance of two-parent families. (PRWORA, 1997, SEC 601)

Notably, poverty alleviation is not identified as a program objective.

In terms of concrete programmatic changes, PRWORA expanded welfare-to-work programs and imposed time limits on welfare receipt (2 consecutive years or a lifetime limit of 5 years). States have the authority to set shorter time limits if they choose to, and 8 states have time limits between 21 and 48 months (Danziger, 2010). Thirty-five states maintain the federal standard of 60 months, and six states have no time limits (state funds can be used to provide benefits beyond the federal limit) (Danziger, 2010). However, states continue to change their policies. For instance, as of July 1, 2011 an adult caregiver (e.g., parent) can only receive 48 months of cash aid through CalWORKs, California's TANF program. Other changes include the denial of federal public assistance to most legal immigrants during their first 5 years in the United States; and allotted federal funds for marriage promotion and sexual abstinence programs (Reese, 2007).

To discourage TANF recipients from having additional children while on assistance, "family cap" regulations permit states to maintain a family's current cash benefit levels rather than increasing them when a new child is born to the family (US General Accounting Office (GAO), 2001). Incentives for states to reduce "out-of-wedlock" births were also built into the law through the establishment of so-called illegitimacy reduction bonuses to high performing states. For four years beginning in 1999, a cash award was granted to states with the largest decline in births to single parents and abortion rates that fell below 1995 levels.

TANF is a "work first" program, favoring work requirements over investment in human capital through education and job training. Despite requiring that TANF recipients meet strict work requirements to receive benefits, work programs were not funded under the law. After 24 months of assistance (or earlier at a state's discretion), recipients must engage in an acceptable "work activity" to continue to receive their benefits. PRWORA designated the following activities as eligible to count toward meeting work requirements: unsubsidized employment, subsidized public or private sector employment, work experience, on-the-job training, job search and job readiness assistance, participation in community service programs, vocational education training (not to exceed 12 months), job skills training directly related to employment, attendance at a secondary school or a program leading to an equivalency certificate, education directly related to employment, or the provision of childcare services to individuals participating in a community service program (CBPP, 2012a). Many states rejected English literacy, basic education, and citizenship preparation as work participation activities (Western Interstate Commission for Higher Educa-

⭐ *punishes girls only*

tion (WICHE), 1998). Single teen parents are required to attend school, obtain a high school diploma or GED, or be enrolled in an approved alternative education program.

these

Not only must recipients work outside the home, but a specified number of work hours must also be met. In 1997 and 1998, recipients were required to work outside the home at least 20 hours per week (WICHE, 1998). This requirement increased to 25 and 30 hours per week in 1999 and 2000, respectively. Two-parent families were required to work 35 hours per week in 2000 and thereafter (WICHE, 1998). Parents of children up to 1 year of age and disabled adults are exempt from work requirements. Recognizing that workforce participation requires child care, PRWORA established the Child Care and Development Block Grant to support childcare programs (GAO, 1998).

accessibility rules → also accessibility

PRWORA sets state goals for work participation by making receipt of federal funds contingent on increased work participation rates over time. One-half of all single-parent families were required to work by 2002, and 90% of two-parent families by 1999. No more than 30 percent of the TANF families that a state counts toward meeting its federal work rates can do so through vocational education (Schott, 2012).

PRWORA allows states to sanction recipients who fail to meet work requirements or other program regulations (e.g., missed appointments with caseworkers and noncompliance with state requirements, such as children's immunization and school attendance, cooperating with establishing paternity, and obtaining substance abuse treatment). Sanction policies vary from state to state and entail a partial or full family loss of TANF benefits and potentially other forms of assistance. Under TANF, all states have policies requiring sanctions when a family does not comply with work requirements (GAO, 2000). Thirty-six states call for a partial sanction (i.e., a reduction in family cash benefits) the first time a family does not meet program requirements, with 37 states requiring a full-family sanction (i.e., the loss of cash benefits) for repeated "noncompliance" (GAO, 2000). The length of sanctions varies considerably, with first sanctions lasting up to 1 month or until the family member begins to comply with work requirements (GAO, 2000). For repeated infractions, sanctions last for at least 3 months, even if the family comes back into line with program requirements (GAO, 2000). In addition to sanctioning access to TANF, approximately one-quarter of states disqualify adults from receiving Medicaid and one-third of states disqualify the entire family from the Food Stamp program when the head of the household does not meet TANF work requirements (GAO, 2000).

These policy changes were, for the most part, supported by a broad range of stakeholders, including Democrats and Republicans, employers, and conservative corporations and organizations albeit for different reasons (Reese, 2007). As Reese (2007) observes:

Large sectors of the business community supported welfare reform as part of a broad neoliberal agenda intended to minimize labor costs and taxes; politicians viewed it as a way to compete for corporate campaign contributions and the votes of traditional white voters; conservative Christians promoted welfare reform as part of a broad agenda for promoting Christian churches and traditional 'family values,' while anti-immigrant groups viewed restrictions on legal immigrants' welfare use as a way to reduce future immigration into the country. (p. 50)

When assessing TANF's impact, "success" meeting both overt policy goals and the potentially less overt objectives of various stakeholders is important.

Contextualizing Welfare Reform Evaluation Research

Has welfare "reform" succeeded? Longstanding debates about the root causes of poverty and the function and impact of public assistance make this seemingly simple question far more complex than it may appear at first glance. Welfare policy has long been a heavily politicized "hot-button" issue defined by liberal and conservative ideological boundaries (e.g., the merits of bigger versus smaller government and comprehensive versus minimal social programs). These tensions as well those that transcend traditional partisan lines pervade research in this area. As historian Michael Katz (1989) aptly observes, "Three major issues have dominated both conservative and liberal poverty discourse for centuries: the categorization of the poor; the impact of poor relief (welfare) on work motivation, labor supply, and family life; and the limits of social obligation" (p. 4). Since the end of the nineteenth century, social scientists in industrial societies, including psychologists, have amassed a large body of research addressing these core areas (O'Connor, 2001; Zuckerman & Kalil, 2000). In PRWORA's wake, researchers continue to be guided by these same age-old concerns but with even greater urgency, given the establishment of time limits and welfare reform's work-first philosophy. These areas of study and the research questions derived from them are of considerable import but also may often carry with them unarticulated assumptions and values (e.g., judgments of deservingness and implicit beliefs about social responsibility).

These concerns are not the only factors that inform the evaluation of welfare reform or research in this area. As with all research endeavors, investigators bring their own values and assumptions to the process, and the methodologies employed also possess strengths and shortcomings. Researchers inevitably face tradeoffs in their attempts "to balance theory, substance, and method" but these aspects of the research process are typically left unacknowledged (Soss, Condon, Holleque, & Wichowsky, 2006, p. 798). Feminist scholars have persuasively argued for greater self-reflexivity among researchers (e.g., considering the impact of differential status among participants and investigators and identifying one's own political viewpoint and social location), however, such practices have yet to become normative (Hesse-Biber & Leavy, 2007). Equally important is the acknowledgment of the important role that social scientists play in assessing welfare reform and whether it is judged a "success" or a "failure." And, although rarely made explicit by mainstream researchers, social scientists have the power to identify and define both "problems" and "solutions" via the questions they chose to ask, the hypotheses they test, and the interpretations they advance (Steinitz & Mishler, 2001).

Some critical scholars assert that the underlying design of welfare reform evaluation research, itself, may carry with it particular interpretations and biases. Nelson's (2002) analysis of the Manpower Demonstration Research Corporation's (MDRC) of Vermont's Welfare Restructuring Project (WRP) highlights the subtle and not-so-subtle biases embedded in the larger welfare reform literature. Among the overt biases Nelson (2002) identifies is an overreliance on experimental methods in welfare reform research. Experimental research, while powerful, is not without its limitations, especially when used to the exclusion of other approaches. The power of experiments is their ability to potentially identify cause and effect relationships through random assignment and the control of confounding variables. Yet it is the interplay of intersecting variables that is crucial to understanding welfare reform and its impact. Recipient characteristics associated with difficulty securing employment and exiting the welfare system (e.g., domestic violence and mental health) and key contextual variables (e.g., economic conditions) are frequently stripped from experimental analysis because random assignment is believed to control for their effects (Nelson, 2002). This was the case in MDRC's analyses of Vermont's reform efforts, in which time limits were credited for reduced caseloads, while the role of a strong economy was dismissed (Nelson, 2002).

A less overt but equally troubling issue is the direct translation of dominant "reform" discourse into empirically tested variables without identifying or considering the possibility of alternative research questions, measures, or constructs (Steinitz & Mishler, 2001). Language is a powerful symbolic tool, and the association of welfare with "dependency" evokes images of long-term, intergenerational welfare receipt and ineffective policy (Bartle, 1998; Fraser & Gordon, 1994; Stryker & Wald, 2009). Mainstream constructions not only seep into everyday understandings of the welfare system but also evaluation efforts. For example, by defining "dependence" solely in terms of welfare receipt and "success" as reduced caseloads, researchers grant credibility to these constructions and the research questions derived from them (Steinitz & Mishler, 2001). The failure to propose and test alternative interpretations restricts how we think about the "causes" and "solutions" to poverty. Describing this problem as well as the limitations of strict adherence to experimental methods, Nelson (2002) explains:

> In a world where only one kind of dependency is bad, poor people can become the objects of experimentation rather than the subjects of their own lives. And in a world where the concern of those who evaluate welfare reform is the (statistically significant) differences among those receiving different mixes of triggers and incentives, the only kind of applied research that will be acceptable will be that which

fits within the boundaries of 'conventional wisdom or common sense of the moment.' (p. 23)

Collectively, these critiques underscore the importance of attending not only to the research questions posed but those that remain unasked or unexamined. In the case of welfare reform, this also means considering progress toward the stated goals of the 1996 legislation and potentially worthy aims that were not part of the legislation. Critical scholars argue for careful analysis of what narratives are left untold, whose voices are rendered invisible, and the power inequities maintained by the inclusion of some perspectives and exclusion of others (Limbert & Bullock, 2009). People of color and women, especially women of color, are likely to be excluded or presented in ways that support race, class, and gender inequities (Delgado & Stefancic, 2012; Wing, 2003). Building on these concerns, the remainder of this chapter synthesizes what we do and do not know about the impact of welfare "reform," with a critical eye toward exposing implicit values and unspoken assumptions in social science research and the role of these biases in maintaining class, gender, and race-based power inequities.

Is Welfare Reform a Success?

Providing for Needy Families?

Among TANF's four stated goals is the provision of support to needy families so that children can stay in their own homes or with relatives (PRWORA, 1997). Economic hardship is a tremendous stressor on family well-being. Poverty and financial difficulties are related to family stress and dissolution (see Conger et al., 1990; Papp, Cummings, & Goeke-Morey, 2009). TANF provides much needed cash aid to poor families, but the minimal level of support falls far below the true costs of raising children and caring for a family.

Relative to other programs that assist low-income families (e.g., food stamps, Medicaid), the proportion of funds spent on cash assistance has decreased over time. Federal and state TANF spending on assistance dropped from $13.9 billion in 1997 to $9.6 billion in 2011 (CBPP, 2012b). To document the decline of cash welfare, Danziger (2010) contrasts how spending on low-income families has shifted over time. She notes that in 1987, 29% of such spending was dedicated to cash aid, 29% to medical care, 11% to food assistance, and 11% to work/training programs. In 2002, the proportion spent on cash assistance had dropped to 20% and the proportion spent on medical services had grown to 54% (Danziger, 2010). Only 1.5% was spent on work/training programs. Poor families now receive proportionally less of their income from public benefits than in previous decades, with public cash benefits contributing about half as much as was previously the case (Danziger, 2010). In 1979, 25.4% of the post-tax income of single-parent families came from government sources (e.g., cash assistance, food stamps, disability, and Earned Income Tax Credit); this figure dropped to

13% by 2006 (Danziger, 2010). And states are making due with less. The annual $16.6 billion annual federal TANF block grant allocation has not been adjusted for inflation, and states now receive 30% less in real dollars than they did in 1997 (CBPP, 2012b).

Cash benefits vary considerably across the United States, with assistance lagging far behind inflation. TANF cash benefits are below half the poverty line in all states (CBPP, 2012b). For example, in Alabama, a low benefit state, a single-parent family of three was eligible for a cash grant of $164 in 1996, $215 in 2008, and $215 in 2010. A similar family in a higher benefit state, such as Massachusetts, was eligible for $565 in 1996, $618 in 2008, and $618 in 2010 (Schott & Finch, 2010). Even modest increases over time are not universal. In states such as Arizona and Florida, cash grants were frozen between 1996 and 2005 at $347 and $303, respectively, for a single-parent family of three. In 2009, Hawaii and Arizona reduced benefit levels by 20% (Schott & Finch, 2010). In 2011, California cut its TANF benefits by 8%, reducing monthly cash aid for a family of three from $694 to $638 (Schott & Pavetti, 2011).

In 2011, only two states had higher TANF benefits in 2011 than in 1996 (CBPP, 2012b). Recipients in other states were less fortunate. Since 1996, TANF benefits have declined 0–10% in 8 states, 10–20% in 7 states, 20–30% in 28 states, and more than 30% in 6 states (CBPP, 2012b). With many states facing enormous budgetary shortfalls and help from emergency TANF funds set to expire, states may consider further benefit reductions. Already, state TANF offices nationwide have cut back on staffing due to the Great Recession. The US Government Accountability Office (GAO, 2010c), found that of 31 states reporting changes to local offices, 22 had decreased the number of TANF staff, 11 had reduced work hours, and 7 had decreased the number of offices – all changes that likely mean reduced access to services and staff availability, and longer processing and wait times for clients.

Not surprisingly, TANF benefits do not lift a family out of poverty. In 2008, Alaska was the only state that provided cash benefits that were greater than half of the federal poverty level (FPL; $1,467 for a family of three per month in all states except Hawaii and Alaska, which have higher FPLs of $1,833 and $1,686, respectively; Schott & Levinson, 2008), but by 2010, this was no longer the case (Schott & Finch, 2010). In 2010, cash benefits were below 30% of the FPL in 29 states. Even when TANF benefits are considered along with food assistance, only a handful of states have benefit levels that extend above 75% of the poverty line (Schott & Finch, 2010). Keeping benefits low ensures that cash assistance does not compete with the low-wage labor market, thereby maintaining a pool of low-wage workers (Piven & Cloward, 1993).

It is important to note that low benefit levels are not unique to TANF. TANF's precursors – mothers' pensions, Aid to Dependent Children (ADC), and subsequently Aid to Families with Dependent Children (AFDC) – were not generous programs. For example, the maximum monthly ADC grant established by the Social Security Act of 1935 was $18 a month for a first child and $12 for a second child compared with the $30 per month received by elderly Social Security beneficiaries (Blank & Blum, 1997). And, as remains the case today, benefit amounts varied dramatically across states, with states with higher percentages of Black residents providing notoriously limited support. In 1940, the national ADC payment averaged approximately $13.00 per month per child, but in Arkansas, Black families received just $3.52 per month per child and slightly above $4.00 per month in South Carolina (Gilens, 1999). These low benefits were institutionalized by legislators who successfully advocated for the removal of a clause from the Social Security Act of 1935 mandating that ADC provide "a reasonable subsistence compatible with health and decency" (Gilens, 1999, p. 105).

That TANF does not provide the financial support necessary to lift a family out of poverty is indisputable. What is less clear is the extent to which TANF helps keep children living with their parents or relatives, another goal of the legislation. Compared with other dimensions of welfare reform, TANF's impact on child–family arrangements has been the focus of less empirical attention. However, some research suggests that low TANF benefits undermine this goal. For instance, Brandon and Fisher's (2001) analysis of data from the Survey of Income and Program Participation (SIPP) found that in lower benefit states, the risk of children living apart from their parents was greater than in states with higher benefits. Newborns and teenagers were found to be at greatest risk of living apart from their parents, as were children with a parent with a disability (Brandon & Fisher, 2001). Based on these findings, the researchers conclude that poor single parents are more likely to seek alternative living arrangements for their children when cash benefits are low.

Other studies seek to disaggregate such findings by examining similarities and differences across states, ethnic and racial groups, and various regulations (e.g., time limits and sanctions). Bitler, Gelbach, and Hoynes' (2003) analysis of national data on children's living arrangements between 1989–2000 illustrates the complexities of evaluating reform across diverse groups and state policies. Post-reform, they found an increased probability of Black children living with neither parent, but this was not the case among Hispanic and white children. Such findings speak to the heterogeneity of the welfare population and the importance of examining the underlying causes of changes in living arrangements but leave many questions unanswered – most notably, the potential harm and benefits associated with various living arrangements.

Ending "Dependence": At What Cost?

TANF's most fundamental goal and the criteria upon which it is most commonly judged is its ability to "reduce the dependence of needy parents on government benefits by promoting job preparation, work, and marriage" (PRWORA, 1997, SEC 601). From this vantage point, it is reducing caseloads, not poverty, that is of central importance. If declining caseloads alone are the measure of success, welfare reform has succeeded. Between 1996 and 2002, TANF caseloads dropped from 4.6 million to 2.1 million families (Urban Institute, 2006). At end of fiscal year 2006, TANF caseloads stood at approximately 1.9 million families nationally (US Department of Health and Human Services (HHS), 2009). Despite sky-rocketing rates of unemployment rates and deep economic recession, 18 states reduced their TANF caseloads during 2008, and the number of cash aid recipients remains at or near the lowest rates in more than 40 years (DeParle, 2009). In September 2009, 1.8 million families received TANF benefits (HHS, 2012); during an average month in 2011, 1.95 million families received TANF (Loprest, 2012).

Many factors have contributed to declining TANF enrollment. The strong economy of the 1990s undoubtedly played a significant role in boosting the earnings of some low-income families; however, more than half of the drop in caseloads since the mid-1990s is attributed to declines in the share of families that received support from TANF rather than a decline in the number of poor families who were eligible for assistance (Parrott & Sherman, 2006). According to one estimate, 87% of the drop in welfare caseloads can be explained by the decline in eligible families participating in the program (GAO, 2010c).

Declining access is vividly illustrated by comparing program participation rates in AFDC versus TANF. In the early 1990s, more than 80% of eligible low-income families were served by the AFDC program, compared with the 48% of low-income eligible families receiving TANF in 2002 (Parrott & Sherman, 2006). Under TANF, the percentage of poor children receiving welfare has declined, falling from 62% in 1995 to 24% in 2007 (Legal Momentum, 2009). The impact of declining rolls is made "real" by considering that if the same 62% of poor children continued to receive TANF in 2007, then 8 million children would have received TANF benefits instead of the 3.1 who did (Legal Momentum, 2009). A GAO (2010a) report estimates that 800,000 fewer children would live in deep poverty (i.e., below half the federal poverty threshold) if TANF participation rates rose to their pre-PRWORA 1995 level of serving 84% of eligible families. Mandatory work requirements, time limits, state diversion strategies (e.g., the provision of one-time benefits instead of TANF enrollment), and sanctions for not meeting work and other program requirements are all posited to play a role in the declining enrollment of needy families (GAO, 2010a).

When Work Does Not "Pay". TANF's "work first" policies position work outside the home as central to ending welfare "dependency." TANF promotes work-force participation by requiring recipients to take part in designated "work participation" activities, short-term training, and/or educational programs that can lead to immediate work placement, and through time-limited benefits. The value that TANF places on paid "work" is not solely about reaping the rewards of increased earning power, it is also about promoting work, in and of itself, as good and morally righteous regardless of wages per se. The Protestant work

work ethic / = culture

ethic, the belief that hard work is laudable and will ultimately be rewarded, provides ideological justification for requiring paid labor force participation even if tangible monetary benefits are not immediately (or ever) realized (Christopher, Zabel, Jones, & Marek, 2008). Moreover, work requirements deter program enrollment, with strict regulations and unappealing options, preventing some eligible parents from applying for benefits. Work requirements, particularly "workfare" programs in which TANF recipients essentially work for their benefits, may encourage recipients to leave the program even if they do not have other sources of income.

In the years immediately following TANF's implementation, work requirements increased, ultimately reaching a maximum rate of 50% for single-parent families and 90% for two-parent families (GAO, 2010b). As such, at least 50% of all TANF families were expected to participate in one or more of the 12 permitted work activities for an average of 30 hours per week. Under PRWORA, states failing to meet work requirement rates could be subject to federal penalties (e.g., reduced block grant funding). Most states were able to lower their required work participation rates well below 50% – in some cases to zero – through credit granted to states for recent caseload declines (GAO, 2002). As a consequence, mandated work participation rates have varied considerably across states. Moreover, state interpretations of eligible "work" activities have also varied. Nevertheless, nationally approximately 30% of adult TANF recipients met federal work requirements (GAO, 2002), suggesting that states, overall, adhered to TANF's work mandates to a greater degree than was required.

When TANF was reauthorized as part of the DRA of 2005 (2006), a top priority for some policymakers was enforcing higher state work participation rates, and the adoption of stricter work activity definitions and a new formula for calculating work participation credit has helped to advance this objective (GAO, 2010c). However, actual work participation rates did not significantly rise. In fiscal years 2007 and 2008, the 2 years following TANF reauthorization, approximately 29–30% of TANF families met their work requirements (GAO, 2010c). Post-DRA work participation rates have been attributed to the economic downturn as well as tougher federal work activity definitions (GAO, 2010c). Both with TANF and after its reauthorization, the most common work activities have remained the same: unsubsidized employment, job search and job readiness assistance, vocational training, and work experience (GAO, 2010b).

Following PRWORA's adoption, labor force participation among single mothers increased from 44% in 1994 to 66% in 2001 (Blank, 2006). The overall health of the US economy in conjunction with the "push" provided by TANF's "work first" policies are generally credited for higher employment rates among single mothers. Yet despite this growth, poverty did not decline as rapidly as might be expected, and women's participation in the paid labor market outpaced exits from poverty, making it clear that employment in and of itself does not necessarily mean an end to poverty. With the favorable economic conditions of the late 1990s long since cooled, unemployment rates among female-headed households have increased. In 2009, 49.4% of households headed by women were unemployed (US Bureau of Labor Statistics, 2010a). Indeed, it appears that any early labor gains among single mothers during TANF's early years have disappeared (CBPP, 2012b).

In weaker and stronger economic times, primary labor force participation has not necessarily translated into greater financial stability, or relief from poverty, for female-headed households. From the mid-1980s through the mid-1990s, single mothers earned an annual average income of approximately $18,000; this figure rose to approximately $23,000 between 1995 and 2001 (Blank, 2006). In 2011, the median income for female-headed households was $33,637 (US Census Bureau, 2012a). Gender and ethnic disparities contribute to women's low earnings. In 2011, women who worked full-time earned 77 cents for every dollar earned by men (US Census Bureau, 2012a). This gap is even larger for women of color with African American women earning 64 cents and Latinas bringing home 55 cents for every dollar earned by white non-Hispanic men (National Women's Law Center (NWLC), 2012). The wage gap is evident across all educational levels. In 2007, the median income for women who completed high school was $21,219, while their male counterparts earned $34,435; at the associate's degree level, women earned $27,046 to men's $41,035; and women with bachelor's degrees earned just $38,628 compared with $57,397 for men (Mink, 2010). Again, when ethnicity is considered, these gaps grow even wider. In 2006, white men with a high school diploma earned $36,539, almost as much as white women who had graduated from college ($39,006; Mink, 2010). These disparities persist.

Although not a panacea, education is one of the few routes to higher wages and upward mobility. Better job opportunities, higher self-esteem, and an enhanced sense of contributing to society, as well as improved study habits and better grades among children are frequently reported benefits of college attendance (Institute for Women's Policy Research (IWPR), 2006). Yet by emphasizing work over educational attainment and making higher education difficult to pursue, TANF does little to prepare low-income women to successfully compete for higher paying jobs. And, with states required to engage at least 50% of TANF families in approved "work" activities or face financial penalties, there is little incentive to encourage higher education. Vocational training can count toward meeting all of a recipient's work participation hours but only for 12 months – an insufficient amount of time to gain significant skills. After 12 months, states can only count a recipient's hours in higher education toward meeting required participation rates if she *also* participates in a "core" work activity (e.g., subsidized or unsubsidized employment or work experience) for at least 20 hours per week (Hamilton & Scrivener, 2012). The dilemma is obvious – how to balance the demands of school, required work activity, and family responsibilities? Not surprisingly, the number of welfare recipients enrolled in postsecondary degree

focuses on work
→ can't have work w/o
education

programs has significantly decreased since TANF's adoption (IWPR, 2006; Mazzeo, Rab, & Eachus, 2003).

Job readiness programs are not a substitute for formal educational opportunities. Such programs, which typically last between 1 and 6 weeks, are mandatory in some regions. Basic skills, such as preparing resumes, interviewing skills, dressing appropriately, and the importance of getting to work on time are typical curricular units (GAO, 1999a). Perhaps women with extremely limited work experience could benefit from such training; however, it seems unlikely that most program participants would gain much new knowledge from these remedial classes. Low-income women are well aware that many training programs are a dead end. For example, in Latimer's (2008) analysis of 665 West Virginian welfare leavers' responses to open-ended questions about their state's welfare program, access to useful training and better educational opportunities were among the most commonly identified needs. Computer skills were viewed as particularly important because as one respondent explains, "as it is now the only job skills provided is to work 35 hours per week cleaning schools" (Latimer, 2008, p. 82).

Critics contend that limited access to education and work requirements, in conjunction with time limits, leave low-income women with no choice but to take low-paying jobs. Viewed through this lens, a punitive welfare system and weak safety net function to provide employers with a plentiful low-wage labor force rather than serve the needs of poor families. Low paying jobs in retail, food preparation, temporary agencies, and clerical support are common among TANF recipients and leavers (Parrott, 1998). These same jobs are the bedrock of the working poor labor force. In 2008, "service occupations with 2.9 million working poor, accounted for nearly one-third of all those classified as working poor" (US Bureau of Labor Statistics, 2010b, p. 2).

During the 1990s, the ranks of the working poor grew, and in 2008, 8.9 million adults were considered "working poor," meaning that these individuals spent at least 27 weeks in the labor force (working or looking for work) during a given year, but still had incomes below official poverty thresholds (US Bureau of Labor Statistics, 2010b). In 2008, female-headed households and Blacks and Hispanics were twice as likely as their counterparts, male-headed households and whites and Asians, respectively, to be among the ranks of the working poor. With job growth in the low-wage service sector outpacing other areas, the number of working poor is likely to further increase. Between 2008 and 2018, it is estimated that very low (less than $21,590) and low paying ($21,590–$32,380) jobs will account for 55% of the growth among those occupations with the largest anticipated increases (Metzgar, 2010).

These are the labor market realities that greet so-called welfare "leavers." A GAO (1999b) report on the status of former welfare recipients released just several years after PRWORA's passage provided early evidence of the economic hardship confronting welfare leavers. In the GAO's eight-state review, the average quarterly earnings of former recipients ranged from $2,378 to $3,786.

Annual average family earnings, assuming these wages were continuous, would range between $9,512 and $15,144. Only if these wages were coupled with food stamps and other supports would these earnings be sufficient to lift a family above poverty thresholds. Findings from Acs, Loprest, and Roberts' (2001) national study of "welfare leavers" are similarly troubling. Employed "leavers" averaged between $7.00 and $8.00 per hour, earnings above the federal minimum wage at the time but still far below self-sufficiency wages. For most "leavers," employment was unreliable. Following their exit from TANF, approximately three-quarters of all "leavers" were employed at some point during the year, but only a little over one-third were employed during all four quarters (Acs et al., 2001). Few find jobs that provide health insurance, paid vacation, or sick leave (Parrott, 1998). Loss of other benefits also limits economic well-being. In Moore and Arora's (2009) analysis of Wisconsin's highly acclaimed welfare program, earning gains were eroded by losses in benefits and, as a consequence, there was no significant change in the average incomes of poor female-headed households between 1993 and 2006.

In sum, although some modest gains in earnings are found among welfare "leavers," most families continue to experience economic hardship and live in poverty or near-poverty conditions (Cherlin, Frogner, Ribar, & Moffitt, 2009; Parrott, 1998; Parrott & Sherman, 2006; Slack et al., 2007). Among former welfare recipients only one-fourth to one-fifth are likely to qualify for unemployment benefits (Boushey & Wenger, 2006). Not surprisingly, many return to welfare. Since PRWORA's adoption, the probability of returning to TANF within 2 years of exiting the system has increased – a likely outcome of leaving TANF for reasons other than secure employment (e.g., sanctions) and the tough economic climate. About one-quarter to one-third of families return to TANF within a year of leaving the rolls (Acs et al., 2001).

Barriers to Work. A sizeable body of literature has sought to identify the factors that distinguish welfare "leavers" from nonleavers. Much of this research focuses on "barriers to work," with the aim of designing interventions to move recipients into the workforce. Mental health issues, physical health concerns, disabilities, limited educational attainment, and little or no work experience are consistently identified as significant obstacles to finding and keeping a job (Kissane & Krebs, 2007). In Danziger, Kalil, and Anderson's (2000) analysis of survey data from 665 former and current welfare recipients in Michigan, human capital (e.g., not completing high school or an equivalency degree and employment in fewer than 20% of years since the age of 18), physical health (e.g., self-reported poor health and being in the lowest quartile of physical functioning), and mental health and substance dependence (e.g., presence of depression, generalized anxiety disorder, post-traumatic stress disorder, and alcohol or substance dependence) barriers were present among slightly more than half of the sample (52.6%). Among those with barriers, 34.7% met the diagnostic criteria for post-traumatic stress, generalized anxiety, or depression; 18.7% reported having physical health difficulties; 16.2 reported human capital limitations; and 5.6% experienced substance abuse problems (Danziger et al., 2000). Women with co-occurring human capital, physical health, and mental health barriers had significantly longer welfare histories than other groups and also had the lowest employment rates at each of the two assessment points. Such findings underscore the need for supports (e.g., education, mental health services, and sound health care) to help women move into the workforce, as well the reality that paid labor force participation may be unlikely for some recipients. Although states are permitted to exclude a percentage of their caseload from meeting work requirements while receiving TANF, the high prevalence of workforce barriers belies TANF's fundamental premise that *all* recipients can and should work outside the home.

Questions about the ethics of work requirements and time limits are explored in Hildebrandt and Ford's (2009) longitudinal interview study of 41 former TANF recipients in a Midwestern city who had "timed out" of welfare and not successfully transitioned from welfare to work. Respondents described complex, intersecting barriers to economic security ranging from health problems to limited education and skills to domestic violence. Discussing the obstacles that she confronted, one former recipient explained:

> I went through a domestic violence situation from [my children's] dad. He was drinking heavily because he was unemployed and I guess he started trying to take it out on me. . . . So he had to do six months and I didn't have a job. I had been unemployed for about six months at that time myself. He ended up in jail and I ended up in a shelter. He'd had his job for 13 years. (Hildebrandt & Ford, 2009, p. 299)

Such complex life circumstances are not amenable to quick or easy solutions. Commenting on TANF's shortcomings, the researchers' observe,

> 'Fixing' their job skills did not fix a domestic violence issue or their chronic health problems or meet the special needs of their children . . . multiple barriers to work that cannot be adequately addressed within the narrow get-a-job scope of current TANF programming. There is reason for logical and ethical concern here. (Hildebrandt & Ford, 2009, p. 301)

Women with multiple barriers are at heightened risk of becoming "disconnected" – being without "work and welfare income over the entire past year" and not reporting education as a "primary activity" (Blank, 2007a, p. 186). More "generous" definitions also consider women with very limited income or public assistance support as "disconnected." The number of "disconnected" mothers has risen dramatically, with the percentage of low-income single mothers reporting no income rising from 11.6 in 1995 to 19.6 in 2004 (Blank, 2007a).

Loprest's (2011) comprehensive review indicates that 20% to 25% of low-income single mothers are disconnected from both TANF and work. Relatively little is known about how "disconnected" families make ends navigate such extreme hardship, but there is growing concern that in the coming years, more low-income women will lack all income support as they hit welfare time limits and are unable to find work. Ninety-seven percent of "timed out" former TANF recipients in Hildebrandt and Ford's (2009) study lived below official poverty thresholds. Moreover, changes made to federal TANF policy in January 2006 mandate higher work participation rates, and as a consequence, states may find it preferable to drop hard-to-employ families from the rolls rather than provide training and comprehensive support services or grant work requirement exemptions to long-term recipients (Blank, 2007a).

How federal and state welfare policy should address the improbability for many participants of "work first" (as well as "work eventually") is contested. Among those who believe work requirements should be upheld, creating a temporary partial waiver program for women with multiple barriers to work is an appealing solution. Under such an initiative, program participants would receive support services to bolster "work readiness," be granted income supplements for part-time employment, and participate in periodic assessments to gauge potential to fully meet work requirements (Blank, 2007a). Although labor intensive and costly, such a program would have the advantage of allowing states to assist more long-term recipients without hitting their allowed percentage of caseload exemptions (Blank, 2007a).

Feminist and critical scholars contend that work requirements themselves are problematic, and that changing program rules to accommodate "hard-to-employ" recipients may bring immediate relief to families but fail to address the underlying structural roots of inequality and poverty. By equating "work" with labor outside the home, TANF excludes caregiving within the home as a form of labor. One consequence of this devaluation is that caring for one's own children does not count toward meeting TANF work requirements. Ironically, however, caring for other women's children (e.g., providing child care) could meet TANF regulations. This double standard reflects the deep-rooted devaluation of the daily labor that women perform in their homes and in caring for their families, and although women across social classes, most notably mothers, are affected by the failure to recognize and compensate caregiving labor, poor women bear much of the financial and social brunt of these expectations. Middle-class women, especially white middle-class women, are encouraged to stay home and care for their children full-time (and are sometimes chastised for "choosing" to work outside the home and placing their children in daycare); however, TANF recipients do not have this option. This double standard is aptly summarized by a welfare recipient and mother of three in Gemelli's (2008) semi-structured interviews examining single mothers' attitudes toward work and family:

working
expectations —
class
issue

> It's funny that low-income women or women living in poverty can stay at home
> and be a bad role model, but a middle class mother or wealthy mother is not a bad
> role model when they stay home. It's like America has two standards and it's based
> on class. Why can't a mother who lives in poverty have the same things as a middle-
> class mother? (pp. 101–102)

Multiple aspects of this dilemma are expanded upon by Mink (1998a):

> . . . lacking earnings for their economic and social contributions, women who work
> full- or part-time as caregivers for their children are ideologically unequal in a
> political culture that prizes income-producing work as the currency of virtue.
> Further, unwaged mothers do not have marital freedom: lacking the financial means
> to exit marriages, they lack the freedom to choose to stay in them. When they do
> dare to exit or avoid marriage, mothers do not enjoy vocational liberty: unpaid for
> their work in the home, they are forced either by law or by economic circumstance
> to choose wages over children. (p. 58)

Interviews with TANF recipients make clear that low-income women are well
aware of these limitations. This is powerfully communicated in women's belief
that mothers should be able to stay home with their children full-time if they
wish to. A 49-year old TANF recipient and mother of three aptly summarizes
this perspective:

> There are a lot of parents out there – it would drive them crazy to stay home and
> take care of their kids all the time. . . . But if a certain person does not want to
> work, I don't think she should be forced to have to go to work. If your choice is
> to stay home and be a *good mother*, take care of your baby, then that should be
> your choice. And you don't have that choice anymore, it's gone. (Hennessy, 2009,
> p. 164)

This sentiment is echoed throughout Hennessy's study of 39 low-income
respondents residing in a northeastern city. Informants consistently described
TANF policies as unfairly requiring poor women to pursue paid work outside
the home at their children's expense, with one respondent simply summing
up the overriding message from caseworkers as, "Work first, kids second" (Hennessy, 2009, p. 166).

Further insight into the barriers confronting working mothers is revealed in
Dodson's (2007) analysis of data from approximately 300 low-wage mothers
pooled from three qualitative studies. Respondents described jobs that failed to
provide economic security and that placed them in unhealthy working conditions
and their children in substandard, dangerous child care. In response to these
unacceptable conditions, some women asserted their right to parent by blurring
the lines between home and work (e.g., finding surreptitious ways to monitor
their children while working), creating their own "flextime" (e.g., arranging
schedules to accommodate children's needs as much as possible), and prioritizing

personal and family well-being over workplace demands (Dodson, 2007). The high priority placed on family responsibilities is reflected in one respondent's comment, "You have to choose and what mother's choosing this job over her child?" and another informant's observation that, "They think they got you. But I say, I will always get another job but I can't get another son" (Dodson, 2007, p. 266). Dodson (2007) sees these responses as reflecting a shared "moral economy" in which mothers prioritize children over jobs when work fails to provide even the most basic resources needed to care for loved ones (p. 259).

In doing so, low-income women values that position income and the market over family, relationships, and well-being (Dodson, 2007). Poor women's refusal to tolerate risky working conditions is recounted in a story by Dorothy, a participant in Dodson's (2007) study, who quit her job rather than jeopardize her health:

> The thing you have to remember is that they don't care . . . if your child is safe or out in the street alone . . . they don't care if you are pregnant and the job is going to make you sick. . . . Okay, I was five months pregnant last year working at a (fast food restaurant) doing cashier and cooking. So I cleaned bathrooms too but the point is they said I have to use bleach . . . to mop the floor . . . and the (toilet). So I need a brush . . . (but) he's going to tell me to put my hands . . . to get my nigger hands and get a towel and wash out the inside of the commode . . . it was the men's bathroom, it was filthy. I said 'I can catch hepatitis . . . but he's like 'oh yes you are going to do that' and, yeah, I quit. I walked out to his face. (p. 273)

Narratives such as this stand in sharp contrast to stereotypes of welfare recipients as lazy or disinterested in work, or as passive victims. They are also a powerful reminder of why we must delve deeply into work participation and separation statistics to understand the employment trajectories of low-income women and barriers to employment. Moreover, if moral economies or alternative understandings of dominant paradigms are ignored or dismissed, social policy, whether progressive or conservative, cannot succeed (Dodson, 2007). Listening to the concerns of poor women, it is clear that TANF's emphasis on work over family and use of "sticks" (e.g., deterrents such as sanctions) for enforcement is guided by assumptions about the motives, values, and decision making of low-income women that run counter to the reality of women's values and priorities.

Securing Quality Child Care: Another Obstacle to Work Outside the Home. Feminist critiques of work requirements extend beyond disagreement with TANF's philosophical underpinnings to the structural shortcomings of "reform" that make program compliance difficult if not impossible. Support for child care and early education comes from multiple programs (e.g., Head Start, Child Care and Development Fund (CCDF), Social Services Block Grant), and through increased state flexibility to use TANF funds to provide child care for current recipients, recent program leavers, and other low-income families.

Child care is not an entitlement and remains in short supply, particularly for infants and toddlers, children with special needs, and families requiring care during nonstandard hours such as evenings and weekends (GAO, 1999c). Bureaucratic regulations and cumbersome parental requirements also block access to childcare benefits (Holcomb et al., 2006). This is particularly true for parents transitioning off of welfare who may need to reapply for care or schedule in-person visits or follow-up meetings (Holcomb et al., 2006). During any given month of 2008, it is estimated that only one in six children eligible for childcare assistance from the Child Care and Development Fund received it (Children's Defense Fund (CDF), 2011). Limited funding means that only 3% of eligible infants and toddlers are able to participate in Early Head Start (CDF, 2012).

States vary in terms of the accessibility of child care but in at least one-third of states shortages mean that eligible families are put on waiting lists or sent away (CDF, 2005). In California alone, 187,516 children were on the childcare waiting list in April 2011 (CDF, 2012). Many states set cut-off rates so low as to exclude many needy families. For example, in 18 states, eligibility for childcare subsidies is restricted to families with incomes below 175% of the poverty level ($32,043 for a family of three; CDF, 2011). Reflecting the devaluation of caregiving work, childcare providers themselves frequently earn poverty level wages. In 2009, in California, a state known for its high cost of living, Head Start teachers earned a mean salary of $31,794 and childcare workers a median salary of $23,730 (CDF, 2011).

Quality, in addition to access, remains a pressing concern. Many states set low payment rates for providers which, in turn, contributes to inadequate wages, untrained and undertrained staff, and limited incentives for the expansion or improvement of services (Pearlmutter & Bartle, 2003). Less than 1% of family childcare homes and less than 10% of all childcare centers were accredited in 2008 (CDF, 2010).

The strain associated with low quality childcare and poor accessibility is evident in Dodson's (2007) findings from interviews and focus groups with approximately 300 low-income women. Protecting children emerged as a major concern, with almost half of respondents discussing current or previous experiences with substandard care caused by overcrowding, lax caregivers, or lack of control over their children's care needs (Dodson, 2007). In some of the most troubling situations, children's lives were potentially endangered. Discussing her son's allergies and difficulty finding appropriate care, one mother explained,

> He has severe allergies to all milk and dairy and everything, and so that's part of the reason why I work these night shifts, because I don't want anybody else . . . (inaudible). I mean, his throat closes up and everything. And so now when I ask for help (from state children's agencies) finding special needs daycare, they send

[handwritten note: child care not available to all]

me three numbers and two of them is already disconnected. . . . I need to know that my son is going to make it through the day. (Dodson, 2007, p. 264)

Most childcare facilities, particularly those serving low-income families, are ill-prepared to care for with children with special needs and medical conditions, even those as straightforward as allergies, leaving the burden on securing safe appropriate care on already strapped mothers. Although Dodson's (2007) study did not specifically examine the psychological impact of these experiences, she found that "many mothers spontaneously referred to being depressed and angry at their care dilemmas" (p. 265).

These same sentiments are also evident in Pearlmutter and Bartle's (2003) focus group study of mothers' perceptions of childcare subsidy programs in California and Ohio. Difficulties accessing care were common and subsidies often arrived late. Delayed payments have led many caregivers to refuse this form of compensation, further complicating recipients' ability to find child care and putting their employment in jeopardy. Care providers who accept subsidies may risk sinking into poverty themselves. Describing the dilemma facing her child's care provider, a California mother explained,

. . . because they haven't paid her for these three children that she's been keeping for months. She said, 'I'm going to have to stop keeping them because they haven't paid me yet, and no one in the world can keep these kids for free.' She said, [they owe me] . . . nine hundred dollars. She was sitting there crying. . . . I was trying to find a place to get some food from. And, she was asking me where was I going and because she needed some too. . . . (Pearlmutter & Bartle, 2003, p. 167)

Stories such as these underscore the poverty that plagues both mothers and those who care for low-income children, as well as ways in which the subsidy system fails those who rely on it. Although welfare reform has brought increased attention to the need for accessible, quality child care, without further investment, lack of child care will continue to be a major threat to family financial stability and health.

Workplace Discrimination: An Underacknowledged Barrier to Work. Although racism and sexism are well-documented barriers to hiring and workplace advancement (Browne, 1999), employer bias is neglected in evaluation research examining transitions from welfare to the paid labor market and barriers to work. It is also noticeably absent in the political discourse of welfare reform. A field experiment by Pager, Western, and Bonikowski's (2009) dramatically illustrates the extent to which racism skews the employment "playing field." To test for racial discrimination, white, Black, and Latino men posed as job applicants and applied for 340 advertised entry-level jobs in New York City. Fictitious resumes were used to match the educational attainment and work histories of the ethnically diverse "applicants," with each described as steadily employed high school graduates. The magnitude of racial bias was further tested by pitting "clean" Black and Latino applicants against a white applicant who had served 18 months for a drug felony for possession of cocaine with intent to distribute (Pager et al., 2009). Compared with similarly qualified whites, African Americans were only half as likely to receive a follow-up call or job offer, and Black and Latino applicants without criminal records fared no better with employers than a white applicant who had just been released from prison (Pager et al., 2009). These findings provide vivid documentation of "a racial hierarchy" in which young white men are positioned at the "top," followed by Latinos and African Americans at the "bottom" (Pager et al., 2009, p. 793).

The stigma of a criminal record may not tarnish the employment prospects of most welfare recipients; however, intersections of racism, sexism, and classism are equally salient determinants of the employability of welfare recipients. The impact of these intersections on women's employability is illustrated in Kennelly's (1999) study of white employers' stereotypes about Black female workers. Seventy-eight white employers in the Atlanta metropolitan area participated in face-to-face interviews. Supervisors stereotyped Black women workers as single mothers regardless of whether this was accurate, and in turn, associated single parenthood with absenteeism, tardiness, and poor work skills (Kennelly, 1999). Racism, classism, and sexism were also evident in employers' equation of Black single mothers with poor mothering skills.

Welfare receipt itself carries its own negative associations of poor work ethic. In Alfred's (2007) focus group and interview study of 15 employed African American TANF recipients and their employers, both sets of respondents described discrimination against welfare recipients as widespread. As one low-income respondent put it, ". . . I think being on welfare make employers not want to hire you because they think you don't want to work" (Alfred, 2007, p. 302). Jacob's (2005) experimental investigation of hypothetical hiring decisions made by 81 employees of temporary employment agencies brings these sources of bias into sharper focus. Participants reviewed fictitious resumes of job applicants who were described as TANF or non-TANF recipients and as African American or white. Applicants were portrayed as applying for a position as a fast food restaurant cashier or an administrative assistant. Hiring decisions were mediated by job type, with TANF recipients and African Americans less likely to be recommended for an administrative assistant position than as a fast food cashier (Jacob, 2005). These findings suggest that bias against hiring welfare recipients and women of color may be particularly strong in decisions involving higher status positions (Jacob, 2005). Of course, higher status positions also tend to pay higher wages.

Research investigating labor force dynamics and employer demand for different types of workers lends further insight into discrimination and other structural barriers. For example, in a telephone survey of 750 firms in Chicago, Cleveland, Milwaukee, and Los Angeles, Holzer and Stoll (2003) found that demand for Black and Hispanic welfare recipients lagged behind their representation in the population of poor, female-headed households. Hiring decisions, especially those involving African Americans, appeared to be less related to overall demand and desired skill sets and more closely connected with location (e.g., central cities) and discriminatory preferences among employers. Workplace retention rates of employed welfare recipients are also suggestive of discriminatory bias. In Holzer, Stoll, and Wissoker's (2004) multicity study, Black workers had higher discharge rates and more negative employer evaluations than Hispanic workers. It may be the case that anti-Black attitudes contribute to the greater perceived salience of problematic work behaviors (e.g., "bad attitudes" and absenteeism) among employers.

Collectively, these findings underscore the realities of workplace discrimination, a reality that is largely neglected by policymakers who support time limits and work requirements without acknowledging how discrimination restricts opportunities, and researchers who largely situate "barriers to work" within the individual rather than broader societal factors. Failing to conceptualize job discrimination as a "barrier to work" in research evaluating welfare reform, negates poor women's multifaceted and intersecting experiences of discrimination and leaves larger power hierarchies unquestioned and undisturbed.

Sanctions: Penalizing Low-Income Women and their Families. Many TANF exits are involuntarily, with families leaving the welfare system due to sanctions. Financial sanctions were also part of the previous AFDC system, but under PRWORA, states have greater latitude to define the scope of penalties (e.g., sanctioning the entire family versus adults only and the duration of sanctions) and types of punishable behaviors. In 2008, 219,000 cases were closed due to full family sanctions (12.8% of all closed cases), and each month, approximately 85,000 families or 5.2% of the average monthly caseload were subject to partial family sanctions (Legal Momentum, 2010b). These figures likely underestimate true sanction rates (Legal Momentum, 2010b). Although time limits have received more public attention than sanctions, four times as many families may be affected by sanctions than time limits (Bloom & Winstead, 2002).

The most economically vulnerable recipients appear to be the most likely to be sanctioned. Compared with other welfare recipients, sanctioned families have lower levels of educational attainment, lower earnings, and higher rates of physical and mental health issues (Bloom & Winstead, 2002; GAO, 2000; Kalil, Seefeldt, & Wang, 2002; Lens, 2006). They also tend to have greater difficulty accessing reliable transportation and child care and report higher rates of domestic violence (Goldberg & Schott, 2001). These characteristics increase the difficulty of complying with welfare regulations, especially work requirements; they are also associated with longer-term welfare receipt, thereby increasing potential opportunities to be sanctioned.

Reviews of sanctioned cases vividly illustrate how common "barriers" heighten the likelihood of being sanctioned; they also reveal the tough standards to which poor women must adhere to keep their benefits (Lens, 2006, 2008, 2009). Health and transportation difficulties are highlighted in the description of the appeal hearing of a 43-year old African American woman who was sanctioned for missing an appointment. The woman, who lived in an emergency shelter and suffered from both shingles and AIDS, tried to make her appointment despite feeling sick. When the bus was slower than anticipated, she called to report that she would be 20 minutes late and learned she was being sanctioned (Lens cited in Legal Momentum, 2010b). Difficulties securing child care are evident in the case of a Texas woman who was sanctioned for missing an orientation and job search class (Lens, 2006). She was told to bring her children with her but that they would not be allowed into the job search room with the computers (Lens, 2006). Unsure who would care for her children in the waiting room, she was sanctioned for not attending the meeting. Ironically, sanctions may be administered even if "noncompliance" is work related. Salma, a California mother of four, was sanctioned for missing a required orientation because she was attending school and working (Moreno et al., 2006). After obtaining a full-time job in a dental office, she still struggled financially but was unable to come into program compliance because of her busy work schedule, and as a result, continued to receive reduced benefits. These impossible competing demands deny poor women their autonomy, forcing them into "no win" situations.

It is not simply a matter of some groups being more "vulnerable" to sanctions than others; sanctions involve layers of state and local choices and decision making, and race and racism figure prominently into the adoption and implementation of sanctions. Numerous studies find that recipients of color are sanctioned at higher rates than their white counterparts (Legal Momentum, 2010b) and racial bias appears at multiple levels of the system (Gooden, 2003). Soss, Schram, Vartanian, and O'Brien (2001) found that states with higher percentages of people of color have adopted stricter sanction, time limits, and "family cap" policies than states with smaller percentages of people of color. Local context also matters, with larger racial disparities in sanctioning occurring in more conservative regions and in states in which local stakeholders are granted discretion over decision making (Fording, Soss, & Schram, 2011).

Racial bias can also be manifested in frontline treatment of recipients. In Gooden's (1998) post-reform interviews with welfare recipients in Virginia, Black respondents reported receiving less transportation assistance and less caseworker support related to education than white respondents. Such patterns echo racist practices earlier in welfare's history, such as Washington, DC caseworkers' use of a more generous standard budget for white than Black recipients (Gordon, 1994). The discretionary nature of sanction and appeal decisions make these prime areas for bias to influence the decision making process. As Lens (2009) observes,

> Sanctions, an inherently discretionary tool, can be applied in different ways. Because all states permit clients to avoid sanctions if they have 'good cause' for not complying

with work rules, sanctions often require individualized, and hence discretionary, determinations. . . . Workers must scrutinize clients' reasons for not complying for sufficiency and truth. (p. 288)

Further examination of how racism is manifested both through the preferential treatment of white families and subtle and overt discrimination against families of color is crucial. Careful investigation of interpersonal and intergroup dynamics is particularly important.

Sanctions are intended to increase participants' compliance with work and other program requirements; however, there is little evidence that they effectively do so (Wu, 2008). They do succeed in increasing family hardship (for a review, see Lens, 2006). In 2008, partially sanctioned families faced an average monthly reduction of $146 or about 38% of a $383 monthly TANF grant (Legal Momentum, 2010b), and not surprisingly, sanctioned families experience more material hardship than nonsanctioned families (e.g., difficulty paying household and medical bills, not having enough food, housing insecurity, and having a utility turned off) and often remain unemployed (Lens, 2006; Parrott & Sherman, 2006). The duration and timing of sanctions is also related to hardship. Wu (2008) found that recipients who received full family sanctions and those who were sanctioned for longer periods of time were more likely to exit the system without a job than to leave with a low-paying job. Sanctions may be particularly damaging to children. Lohman, Pittman, Coley, and Chase-Lansdale's (2004) analysis of a representative sample of low-income urban preschoolers and adolescents in Boston, Chicago, and San Antonio found that preschoolers of sanctioned mothers experienced rates of serious behavioral problems triple that of national norms. The causality of these relationships are difficult to determine and sanctioned families may be more vulnerable than other low-income families to begin with; however, it is also likely that the stress and material hardship of leaving welfare due to sanctions negatively affects children's development.

Sanctions clearly "succeed" in reducing state caseloads (Legal Momentum, 2010b). Sanctions are a primary contributor to reduced caseloads in many states (GAO, 2000; Goldberg & Schott, 2001), particularly full family sanctions (Legal Momentum, 2010b). Goldberg and Schott (2001) estimate that between 1997 and 1999 approximately 540,000 families lost their TANF benefits following a full family sanction. Advocates worry that DRA changes to work participation rates will encourage reliance on sanctions to lower state caseloads.

Critical scholars identify broader economic and social functions served by sanctions. By narrowing poor women's options, sanctions help ensure the availability of a low wage labor pool. Within the welfare system, women must comply with work participation requirements or lose all or a portion of their benefits. Among those outside of the system, the close behavioral oversight associated with sanctions may deter eligible families from seeking assistance. Sanctions serve corporate interests by weakening the safety net and providing a pool of laborers who must accept a job regardless of the nature or conditions of the work (Piven & Cloward, 1993). Sanctions also serve important hierarchy-enhancing functions. Sanctions both gain their legitimacy from and reinforce stereotypes of welfare recipients as unmotivated workers and irresponsible parents who must be coerced to behave appropriately. In doing so, sanctions provide the nonpoor with yet another opportunity to assert their superiority (e.g., "without these rules, welfare recipients would take advantage of the system"; "poor women must be forced to send their children to school") and distance themselves from poverty and the poor. As Fording et al. (2011) assert, "Negative images of target groups guide policy design and implementation, and policy designs are then implemented in ways that reinforce negative group outcomes and reputations" (p. 1652). Lens' (2009) content analysis of a random sample of 255 sanction hearings in Texas lends insight into how perceived deservingness and judgments of morality are manifested in sanction decisions. Rules were often applied narrowly with little consideration of contextual factors or structural barriers to compliance (e.g., being 15 minutes late to a meeting due to child care or transportation difficulties), clearly showing that poor women are rarely given the benefit of the doubt.

Whose Family Values? TANF and Family Formation

TANF's final two goals, the prevention and reduction of "out-of-wedlock" pregnancies and the promotion of two-parent heterosexual families, are among welfare reform's most controversial provisions. To advance these goals, PRWORA created new rules for teenage mothers (i.e., making TANF eligibility for mothers under the age of 18 contingent on living with a responsible adult, usually a parent, and participation in school or training), permitted states to adopt disincentives to having additional children while receiving TANF (e.g., "family cap"), introduced incentives for reducing "out-of-wedlock" births (i.e., state bonuses for reducing births to single parents without accompanying increases in abortion rates), supported abstinence and marriage promotion education, and required mothers to identify biological fathers and cooperate with child support enforcement (GAO, 2001). TANF reauthorization via the DRA sought to further strengthen marriage and responsible fatherhood efforts through the allocation of $150 million annually from 2006 to 2010 to support these efforts (Handler & Hasenfeld, 2007). States can also use their TANF block grants and their own funds to support marriage and fatherhood activities (Mink, 2010).

High poverty rates among single mothers (US Census Bureau, 2012a) are commonly cited as the rationale for these changes. According to this logic, encouraging marriage and the formation of two-parent families will help to reduce poverty by having two rather than one potential wage earner in the home. However, the cited benefits of two "breadwinners," and two-parent families, more generally, only partially explain the adoption of these initiatives. Classist, racist, and sexist stereotypes about single motherhood, sexuality, and parenting skills are integral to these and other "reform" initiatives.

Welfare scholars are quick to point to a long history of attempts to regulate poor women's sexual behavior and marital status. Mothers' pension or aid programs, the first US "welfare" programs for poor women and their children, limited eligibility to only the most "deserving" women (Katz, 1986). Widowed mothers were eligible for benefits, whereas divorced mothers were not. "Suitable home" rules further whittled down eligibility by making "immoral" behaviors, such as "out-of-wedlock" births, drinking alcohol, housing boarders, or "foreign" forms of childcare or housekeeping, used as grounds for ineligibility (Gordon, 1994). Poor immigrants were often the intended targets of "suitable home" rules (Gordon, 2004).

These practices continued and evolved under Aid to Dependent Children (ADC; later renamed Aid to Families with Dependent Children, AFDC). Although not legally restricted to widows, ADC, particularly in its early years, was primarily viewed as a program for families who had lost an earner, with "suitable home" violations (e.g., "out-of-wedlock" children, the presence of a man in the house) providing cause for termination (Gordon, 1994). During the 1940s and 1950s, "morality" was enforced through the intense surveillance of ADC recipients:

> Across the country three levels of surveillance emerged: 1) a home was watched during the day or night or both; 2) two investigators made a surprise visit with one at the front door, the other at the back door, in the hope of apprehending an errant man; or 3) the investigators demanded entry and searched the premises for a man or evidence that a man might be included in the family unit . . . the 'surprise element' of the actual visit was considered to be one of its chief merits. (Bell cited in Gordon, 1994, p. 298)

This process was intended not only to humiliate targeted families, but also deter potential applicants.

Southern states were particularly brutal in their enforcement of "suitable home" rules, with Black women disproportionately judged as violating these standards (Lindhorst & Leighninger, 2003). In Louisiana, comments by public officials lay bare perceived connections between "illegitimacy," welfare use, and race. For example, during a discussion of single mothers, a member of Louisiana Board of Public Welfare claimed, "Negroes in the South don't look upon illegitimacy as anything wrong," with the Governor, a segregationist, expressing his perception of "charity hospitals as baby hatcheries for unmarried women" (Lindhorst & Leighninger, 2003, p. 569). Strict enforcement of "unsuitable home" rules resulted in the termination of 22,501 Louisiana children or 28% of the state's caseload in July 1960 (Lindhorst & Leighninger, 2003). Ninety-five percent of terminated children were Black, with most families living in urban areas. In most instances, "guilty" mothers were allowed to continue caring for their children, but the loss of cash assistance resulted in considerable hardship (Lindhorst & Leighninger, 2003; Piven & Cloward, 1993).

It was not until the 1960s that a series of rulings undermined "suitable home" policies. The Supreme Court's 1968 ruling in *King v. Smith* sent one of the strongest messages against "immorality" as grounds to terminate benefits. The plaintiff, an African American mother of four who earned $16.00 a week as a waitress, was denied AFDC benefits after the state of Alabama claimed that she had a male partner who could provide parental support (Gooden, 2003). This allegation was based on Alabama's practice of considering an ongoing sexual partner as a "substitute father" regardless of actual financial obligation (Gooden, 2003). The Supreme Court struck down the regulation citing that Alabama lacked the authority to modify "the federal statutory definition of parent to include a 'substitute father'" (Gooden, 2003, p. 262). Claims that the regulation was essential for combating "immorality" were rejected on the basis that such practices were inconsistent with AFDC's goal of child protection (Gooden, 2003).

The legacy of "suitable home" rules and other aspects of earlier welfare programs – discouraging single motherhood, regulating sexual behavior, and excluding women of color – are alive and well in contemporary family formation initiatives. Commenting on how these older practices ground current policy, Gordon (1994) explains:

> Not only did mothers' aid shape the welfare state, but the debate about it introduced the themes and questions that still dominate welfare policy discussions today. These include concerns about how to help single mothers without encouraging single motherhood and the proper role of women, as well as the most fundamental questions about what entitles a person to help. Who is deserving? . . . Does the state have an obligation to police the behavior of those who receive public funds? (p. 37)

The years leading up to PRWORA's adoption were dominated by alarm about rising nonmarital births and single motherhood, particularly among teenagers and low-income women of color. TANF's "family formation" goals were among the most hotly contested, with political and religious conservatives claiming that the welfare system itself was responsible for the dissolution of the traditional nuclear family by serving as a "surrogate husband" that enables poor women to raise children on their own (Harris & Parisi, 2005). This perspective is illustrated in former Senator Kay Bailey Hutchinson's characterization of the welfare system as "a self-perpetuating monster that sustains the most distressing ills of our society – illegitimacy, the disintegration of the family, weakening of the work ethic and crippling dependency" (Hutchinson, cited in Onwuachi-Willig, 2005, pp. 1671–1672). Although conservative support for "reform" policies encouraging the formation of two-parent families was strong, pregnancy prevention goals, unless grounded in abstinence education, were met with ambivalence due to their association with sex education (Orth & Goggin, 2003).

Mainstream news depictions of welfare recipients, particularly African American women, as sexually available and as bad mothers, reinforced dominant stereotypes about single motherhood and irresponsible parenting (Bullock, Wyche, & Williams, 2001; Kelly, 2010; Schram & Soss, 2001) and lent credibility to conservative claims. Kelly's (2010) analysis of television news coverage of US welfare reform from 1992 to 2007 documents the prevalence of these images in mainstream news outlets. Consistent with other analyses (Bullock et al., 2001; Gilens, 1999), African Americans were overrepresented in news stories about "reform," and stereotypical depictions were common, including representations of welfare mothers as childlike (e.g., too unintelligent or naïve to leave welfare), hyperfertile (e.g., having larger families than is typical of nonwelfare families, bearing children "out-of-wedlock," and starting families during adolescence), lazy (e.g., unmotivated to pursue school or job training), and weak role models (e.g., rejecting mainstream "American" values and engaging in unhealthy behaviors). By reflecting and reinforcing classist, racist, and sexist stereotypes, these images set the stage for conservative reform.

Feminists and other critics counter that the conditions of single motherhood – low wages, lack of family supports, discrimination – are the root problems, not single mothers or single motherhood, per se (see Mink, 1998a, 1998b, 2001, 2010). Accordingly, resources should be directed to training and education that prepare TANF recipients for higher paying jobs rather than marriage promotion programs and other family formation initiatives. It is further argued that TANF's emphasis on heterosexual marriage institutionalizes its normative status and negates the legitimacy of gay and lesbian families (Lind, 2004). And, in promoting heterosexual two-parent families over female-headed households, welfare reform simply replaces reliance on cash aid with dependence on male partners (Harris & Parisi, 2005). Initiatives to make welfare receipt contingent on establishing paternity and implementing child support are criticized for their potential to incite hostility and violence from male partners, deepening the risk of abuse (Catlett & Artis, 2004). Family caps are rebuked for overtly seeking to regulate the childbearing decisions of poor women and for endangering family well-being through the reduction of benefits. Collectively, these policies are condemned as overt attempts to regulate the marital and childbearing behaviors of poor women (see Mink, 2010; Onwuachi-Willig, 2005; Roberts, 1995), with some critics calling such policies a modern incarnation of the eugenics movement (Pierson-Balik, 2003). More general reservations about the role of government in matters as personal as marriage and family formation are also central concerns.

Marriage as a Solution to Poverty? Early welfare reform efforts focused more heavily on "welfare to work" efforts than family formation, with state variability in the implementation of policies and/or activities to promote marriage, strengthen two-parent heterosexual families, and discourage divorce (Harris & Parisi, 2005; Ooms, Bouchet, & Parke, 2004; Orth & Goggin, 2003). Many states revised their TANF eligibility rules to treat single and two-parent households similarly, making it easier to provide benefits to married families (Ooms et al., 2004).

Orth and Goggin's (2003) 18-state review identified four main categories of marriage promotion initiatives: (1) campaigns to reduce "out-of-wedlock" births and supportive statements by policymakers or leaders; (2) the formation of coalitions and/or advisory groups to oversee marriage promotion efforts and the prevention of nonmarital births; (3) the launching of educational initiatives centered on relationship skills; and (4) financial incentives (e.g., cash bonuses for married TANF recipients, income disregards for a spouse who marries a TANF recipient, and elimination of financial penalties for two-parent families).

Although married households tend to have higher incomes than single female-headed households (Thomas & Sawhill, 2005), marriage is not a guarantee of upward mobility and two-parent married couples can remain poor (Onwuachi-Willig, 2005). Evaluation studies find little effect of family formation initiatives on marriage rates among recipients (Blank, 2007b; Donley & Wright, 2008; Kissane & Krebs, 2007). In Graefe and Lichter's (2008) comparison of pre- and post-PRWORA data, for example, welfare reform was not strongly associated with changes in marital status among single mothers. Another study found increased rates of cohabitation, an outcome that is ironically at odds with PRWORA's goals, but the likely consequence of an increased need to share resources (Cherlin & Fomby cited in Blank, 2007b).

As with all social behaviors, the decision to marry, live together, or remain single is motivated by complex, multifaceted intentions and circumstances. In welfare reform's wake, researchers have sought to understand the reasons underlying lower marriage rates among poor women and women of color. One line of research examines marital attitudes and expectations among so-called fragile families, and in doing so both debunks stereotypes about the devaluation of marriage in poor communities and offers insight into reasons for delaying marriage (e.g., Edin & Kefalas, 2005; Edin, Kefalas, & Reed, 2004; Edin & Reed, 2005; Gibson-Davis, Edin, & McLanahan, 2005). In Gibson-Davis et al.'s (2005) interviews with 47 unmarried, romantically involved couples with children, financial concerns, relationship quality, and fear of divorce emerged as the most frequently cited reasons for waiting to marry, with many respondents identifying more than one of these factors as influencing their relationship decisions. Although the majority of couples (77%) lived together at the time of the interviews and ostensibly had established households together, perceived financial obstacles still loomed large. Participants saw economic hardship as undermining marriages and wanted to build their assets and achieve greater financial stability before marrying. And, echoing dominant cultural representations of marriage, respondents hoped to have the means to plan a "nice" wedding and reception (Gibson-Davis et al., 2005, p. 1308). The desire to enter marriage on firm economic grounding and in a relationship they trusted as strong is indicative of the high value placed on marriage.

These findings coupled with the results of evaluation studies raise deep questions about the effectiveness of marriage promotion efforts, particularly those geared toward "teaching" respect for marriage as an institution, many of which are geared toward white, middle-class groups (Orth & Goggin, 2003). Critiquing both the practical consequences and philosophical underpinnings of these initiatives, the NOW Legal Defense and Education Fund (n.d.) asserts,

> Federal marriage promotion diverts welfare funds from basic economic supports, lacks public support, coercively intrudes on fundamentally private decisions, places domestic violence victims at increased risk, wastes public funds on ineffective policies, and inappropriately limits state flexibility. It sends the message that the way out of poverty for women is dependence on someone else to act as a breadwinner rather than economic self-sufficiency. (para. 2)

Continued funding for marriage promotion initiatives and demonstration projects in the face of mounting evidence against their effectiveness is indicative of the degree to which poverty is seen as a moral failing.

Whether marriage promotion efforts are deemed "successful" seems largely contingent on the criteria upon which judgments are based. If the "true" goals of marriage promotion are primarily symbolic – to culturally affirm heterosexual marriage and stigmatize single motherhood – than failure to significantly increase marriage rates, while important, particularly to conservatives, may be secondary to ideological gains. For progressives and critical scholars, marriage promotion efforts are yet another diversion from addressing the structural roots of inequality and women's poverty. Findings from Pandey and Kim's (2008) analysis of national survey data offer insight for moving beyond this stalemate. They found that postsecondary education significantly improved the financial security of mothers regardless of their marital status, and that educated mothers were more likely to be married. Increasing opportunities for postsecondary education under TANF rather than investing in unproven marriage promotion programs may be among the surest routes to achieving goals important to both progressives and conservatives. Unfortunately, the Deficit Reduction Act of 2005 (2006) moved in the opposite direction by tightening how work activities are defined and allocating funds for healthy marriage and responsible fatherhood initiatives.

Births to Single Mothers. During PRWORA's first several years, $100 million was awarded annually to states that achieved the largest reductions in "out-of-wedlock" births providing that abortion rates did not rise. Although discontinued, "out-of-wedlock" birth reduction bonuses, or "illegitimacy bonuses," remain one of the starkest initiatives to reduce births to single mothers. Between 1999 and 2003, 23 "illegitimacy bonuses" of approximately $20–$25 million were granted, with Alabama, Michigan, and Washington, DC receiving 13 of the 23 awards and nearly 60% of the funds (Korenman, Joyce, Kaestner, & Walper, 2006). Korenman et al.'s (2006) analysis of these three bonus recipients reveals that "changes in the racial composition of births accounted for between one-third and 100% of the decline in the nonmarital birth ratio" (abstract). In Washington, DC, reductions in nonmarital birth ratios (nonmarital births/total births) can be explained by declining African American birth rates and a decline in the Black population at peak childbearing age; nonmarital birth ratios rose among Hispanics and whites (Korenman et al., 2006). Such findings raise serious questions about the effectiveness or value of such incentives other than to reinforce the symbolic importance of childbirth within marriage.

"Family caps" are perhaps among the most controversial family formation initiatives (Camasso & Jagannathan, 2009). State policies range from "full child exclusion" (i.e., a new child is excluded from benefits) to "partial child exclusion" (i.e., families with a new child receive a reduced increase in benefits) to "flat grant" practices (i.e., regardless of size, all families receive the same benefits; Smith, 2006, p. 152). Bluntly describing the goals of family cap policies, Vobejda and Havemann (1997) explain:

> It seeks to send a message to poor women that having more children will only increase hardship and deprivation – not bring extra cash. That message is intended to be so clear and harsh that it will reach into the most private sexual relationships, persuading women to stop having children they cannot support. (p. A01)

Although poor mothers are the intended targets of family cap policies, the burden of having less money inevitably deepens hardship for the entire family.

The meaning of these policies for families is powerfully illustrated by reviewing "real" dollar reductions in benefits. For example, in New Jersey, if a second child is born while a family is receiving TANF, the family is denied $102 per month, and a third child (or further children) results in a loss of $64 per month per child (Camasso & Jagannathan, 2009). Based on a GAO (2001) analysis of data from 20 states, family caps were estimated to result in a 20% reduction in cash benefits, or an average of $100 less per month, for a two-person family with one "additional" child (GAO, 2001). Equally unsettling are estimates of the number of families affected. In these same 20 states, 108,000 families (9% of their TANF caseload) were subject to family caps during an average month in 2000 (GAO, 2001).

The financial repercussions of family caps on mothers and their children have not been the focus of extensive systematic evaluation, perhaps in part due to difficulty distinguishing the effects of various benefits (e.g., child support, earnings, and TANF; Smith, 2006). The misperception that these reductions are too small to be consequential may also contribute to a lack of research attention. Also untested is the assumption that family caps save states money (Smith, 2006). Although family caps may reduce state expenditures in the short run, the deeper deprivation caused by reduced benefits is likely to result in greater long-term social and financial costs.

Evaluations of family cap policy on rates of nonmarital childbearing fail to show consistent effects. Some studies document declining nonmarital birth rates, while others show no correlation (see Camasso & Jagannathan, 2009; Dyer & Fairlie, 2003; Kissane & Krebs, 2007; Romero & Agénor, 2009; Smith, 2006). A smaller strand of research examines the impact of family cap policies on abortions. Among the most widely cited finding is Camasso's (2004) study, in which New Jersey's family cap policy resulted in fewer births and increased abortions and contraception use among short-term welfare recipients.

These findings fuel claims that welfare "reform" and its advocates are more interested in limiting the growth of poor families than protecting the "family values" so often evoked in public discourse. Noting this hypocrisy, Mink (1998b) observes:

> The welfare debate revealed that except among the purest of abortion foes, the fact of illegitimacy is more morally freighted than the act of abortion; the need to teach 'those people' not to reproduce unless they can afford it is more urgent than the call to protect the unborn; and the demand to reform welfare is more righteous than the struggle to preserve life. (pp. 100–101)

The selectivity with which supposed "violations" of "family values" are decried (e.g., nonmarital births) or conveniently ignored (e.g., the potential of restrictive policies to increase abortion rates) speaks to both the regressive and conflicted beliefs surrounding welfare "reform." Since PRWORA's passage, federal legislation prohibiting family caps has been introduced but not moved forward; however, some states have phased out or eliminated family caps. Family caps were not a focus of TANF reauthorization, and TANF policy remains silent on the issue leaving these policies at the discretion of the states (Smith, 2006).

Mothers and children pay the price for these coercive (and ineffective) policies. Yet a full-scale overhaul of family formation initiatives in their many forms – marriage promotion, family caps, abstinence-only education, paternity establishment, and responsibile fatherhood initiatives – seems unlikely without also challenging the classist, sexist, and racist stereotypes that give them their legitimacy (see McClelland & Fine, 2008). Empirical evidence repeatedly discredits well-worn myths about poor women's sexual and reproductive behavior: poor women value marriage; welfare benefits are not an incentive to have "additional" children; welfare recipients do not have larger families than nonrecipients; and regardless of family caps, the likelihood of having another child declines with length of time on welfare (Smith, 2006). Yet the focus remains on behavior modification and "creating a culture of marriage" (Harris & Parisi, 2005, p. 855), rather than fostering the positive economic conditions associated with personal well-being and healthy long-term relationships. Scott, London, and Gross' (2007) findings from interviews with 38 welfare recipients about their views on "self sufficiency," work, and marriage reinforce the need for a radically different approach to supporting low-income families, one that prioritizes the perspectives and needs of poor women, and puts economic stability and well-being ahead of the advancement of marriage, per se. They summarize:

> If we were to listen to the women, they might tell us that the more likely path to self-sufficiency involves increased education and training and access to higher paying jobs with benefits. They might also tell us that if the men had more options, and were financially stable and well employed, they would consider marriage to the men in their communities. They certainly would say they do not need to attend programs on marriage education and skills training – they are all for marriage, under the right circumstances. (Scott et al., 2007, p. 622)

Fostering the "right" circumstances – self-sufficiency wages that make it possible for low-income women and men to support themselves and their families, healthcare benefits, and access to quality, affordable child care – would turn current "family formation" policies on their head, and yet ironically might be more effective at achieving PRWORA's articulated goals.

Breaking the Cycle of Women and Children Last

A comparative study of pre- and post-reform public opinion by Hetling, McDermott, and Mapps (2008) offers unique insight into popular understandings and perceptions of welfare reform. Respondents who were aware of welfare reform expressed more positive attitudes toward welfare recipients post- than pre-reform. Interestingly, this attitudinal change was unrelated to the perceived effectiveness of welfare reform; instead, this greater positivity appeared to be largely attributable to the simple fact that "reform" had occurred (Hetling et al., 2008). These findings speak to the symbolic nature of welfare reform, and the extent to which the drive for "reform," in and of itself, can trump the real outcomes of "reform" for low-income women and their children, at least in the public mind. If stereotypes of "out of control" welfare recipients in need of discipline were not so widespread, the harmful consequences of welfare reform on low-income families might gain greater traction in shaping public opinion and discourse.

Much of the research literature evaluating welfare reform clings to the same narrow conceptualizations and in doing so fails to ask the truly important questions: "Are families better off with TANF? . . . Are children better off with TANF? . . . To what extent is the over 50% drop in the welfare rolls due to sanctions? . . . Is TANF really a viable path out of poverty for families? . . . Are welfare applicants and recipients being treated fairly?" (Applied Research Center, 2006, pp. 1–3). A justice-focused research agenda requires taking on these and other questions capable of challenging "mainstream understandings of women's 'success' post-welfare" (Gatta & Deprez, 2008, p. 21) and "shift the focus of research, away from the characteristics of failings of poor people and toward those of a mainstream political economy and culture that relegates so many people to economic insecurity and social marginality" (O'Connor, 2000, p. 557).

Our attention must turn to fostering economic security and asset building (e.g., How can policies be structured to help low-income women and families build assets? What does economic security mean to low-income women?), fully interrogating underlying philosophies and assumptions (e.g., What would welfare policy look like if it were guided by a strength rather than deficit approach? How do individualistic beliefs blind us to structural inequality?), and treating race, ethnicity, gender, class, sexuality, and disability as more than demographic characteristics (e.g., How does welfare policy recreate inequality and privilege? How do power inequities pervade the design, implementation, and delivery of public assistance? How can these dynamics be interrupted?). It also requires ending our overreliance on decontextualized analyses of welfare reform and instead examine women's lived experiences and their recommendations for change (Gatta & Deprez, 2008).

TANF's next reauthorization offers a crucial opportunity to revisit current policies and make changes that will strengthen the safety net and promote economic security. Debates about obligation, morality, and deservingness are steeped in a long history of racism, classism, heterosexism, sexism, and ableism and are unlikely to be resolved, but progress is still possible. Fifteen years post-reform, some facts are irrefutable. Poverty remains a significant and growing problem, and TANF serves fewer eligible families than its predecessor did. Work-first policies, by and large, have not increased women's economic security, and marriage promotion efforts have not yielded significant increases in two-parent families. Welfare reform's only consistent success appears to be reducing the caseloads.

Alleviating poverty, not simply reducing welfare caseloads, requires that a "human welfare first" approach replace the current "work first" philosophy (Bullock & Limbert, 2008). Access to higher education, safe jobs with self-sufficiency wages, reliable health care, high-quality child care, affordable housing, benefits that make it possible for recipients to care for themselves, and programs that treat *all* recipients with dignity and respect are key elements of creating a real safety net (see Chapter 6 for a further discussion of policy recommendations). Without comprehensive changes to TANF and significant investment in other support programs, the burden of poverty will continue to fall on women and children.

5

Low-Income Women, Critical Resistance, and Welfare Rights Activism

Co-authored with Wendy M. Limbert and Roberta A. Downing

> *In the final weeks before Clinton signed the act, the prowelfare effort was a beautiful bud of a coalition, which included welfare recipients and professionals, gay activists and straight feminists, white poverty lawyers and Black members of the Rainbow Coalition, liberal Washington insiders and outsider college professors. But it was only a bud, and whether it ever flowers into something more politically significant remains to be seen.* (Kornbluh, 1998, pp. 65–66)

This passage, written by a member of the Committee of 100, a feminist initiative that organized against the adoption of oppressive welfare "reform" policies, reflects the ongoing hope that broadscale collective action will generate sufficient social and political pressure to overhaul Temporary Assistance for Needy Families (TANF). In this chapter, we examine one crucial aspect of building a strong movement for economic justice, the political mobilization of low-income women against restrictive welfare policies. We are guided by welfare rigths activists Baptist & Bricker-Jenkins' (2001) observation that welfare recipients are "only the first and most visible targets" of welfare "reform" (p. 144) and that welfare reform's "ultimate objective . . . is a downsized standard of living for the majority of Americans, justified by a restricted vision of human rights (p. 144). From this perspective, welfare rights are about much more about than just welfare policy, and include the creation and protection of a network of policies and programs that advance the needs and well-being of the poor and working and middle classes.

We draw on findings from focus groups conducted with current and former welfare recipients who attended a retreat organized by an activist organization

Women and Poverty: Psychology, Public Policy, and Social Justice, First Edition. Heather E. Bullock.
© 2013 Heather E. Bullock. Published 2013 by John Wiley and Sons, Ltd.

to illustrate some of the factors that contribute to collective action. Our goals are twofold: (1) to illuminate how low-income women understand and describe their engagement in welfare rights activism; and (2) to contextualize core social psychological dimensions of collective action. Consistent with Wright, Taylor, and Moghaddam (1990), we define collective action as any time a group member acts "as a representative of the group and the action is directed toward improving the conditions of the entire group" (p. 995). This broad definition allows for the inclusion of a range of behaviors including those that are visible (e.g., participating in protest planning and demonstrations) and those that are less visible (e.g., letter-writing and helping others navigate the welfare system). Throughout our analysis, we attend closely to social psychological and structural factors that facilitate or inhibit collective action.

Welfare Rights Activism

Necessary in the 1960s and 1970s, Necessary Now

Although often overshadowed by the civil rights movement, welfare rights actvism during the 1960s and 1970s made significant strides toward economic justice and greater access to welfare benefits. Advocacy by poverty lawyers, progressive caseworkers, and other professionals were crucial to these efforts; however, at its core, welfare recipients and other low-income people powered this movement (Kornbluh, 1998). The National Welfare Rights Organization (NWRO), the public "face" of this movement, worked to coordinate the efforts of 540 local Welfare Rights Organizations (WROs; Kornbluh, 1998). As with other political and social movements, disputes over leadership and goals were common (see Piven & Cloward, 1977).

Women were crucial to these efforts. Nationally, early welfare rights leaders were men, but women, especially African American women, were prominent at the grassroots level (Edmonds-Cady, 2009). The demographic composition of these local organizations is difficult to determine, but archival documents suggest that approximately 85% of members were African American, 10% were white, and 5% were Latina (Kornbluh, 1998; Nadasen, 2002). A small number of Native Americans also participated. Most welfare rights activists were women, typically brought together by shared experiences of poverty and welfare receipt (Kornbluh, 1998). Describing the origins of the welfare rights movement, Nadasen (2002) explains:

> They organized primarily in response to local problems with welfare departments, such as a recipient unjustly removed from the welfare rolls, unable to buy basic necessities, or treated unfairly by caseworkers. Although stringent eligibility criteria and unfair practices were long associated with AFDC, in the late 1950s and early 1960s these policies became even harsher and more repressive . . . using avenues opened up by the relatively liberal political climate, mothers receiving AFDC joined

with friends and neighbors to share grievances, show one another support, and influence the policies and practices of the welfare department. (p. 275)

Membership was not limited to low-income groups, and some middle-class women were also active in the movement. Edmonds-Cady's (2009) oral histories with 12 women who participated in the welfare rights movement between 1964 and 1972 offers insight into the political mobilization of economically and racially diverse women. Although intersections of race, gender, and class cannot be disentangled, welfare recipients tended to emphasize class as their primary motivator (e.g., lived experiences of poverty and classist discrimination). White nonrecipients described gender-based standpoints as powerful motivators (e.g., the importance of being a woman and knowing another woman who needed assistance), whereas African American nonrecipients focused on race as a key factor (e.g., race as point of solidarity and racist discrimination). These findings illustrate the complex lenses through which women view activism, and how social location and intersectionality shape political mobilization.

The goals of the welfare rights movement are as relevant today as they were in the 1960s and 1970s: adequate income, justice (e.g., for institutions to equitably serve both the poor and wealthy, access to fair hearings before benefit termination), dignity (e.g., freedom to make decisions about parenting and sexuality), and democracy (e.g., inclusion in political decision making; Kornbluh, 1998; see also Abramovitz, 2001). Nadasen's (2002) discussion of the welfare rights movement lends insight into interconnections among these goals and how fighting for welfare rights involves taking on racism, sexism, and classism:

They fought for an increase in welfare benefits or a guaranteed annual income which would provide the means to make choices about parenthood, employment, and sexuality otherwise closed to them. They believed that economic assistance was not a form of dependency but a source of liberation. They also constructed a political platform that challenged the racist and sexist stereotypes associated with Black single motherhood. The movement, then, was as much a women's movement as a poor people's movement, as much about feminism as Black liberation. (p. 294)

The extent to which these same goals and struggles continue to define welfare rights activism is striking. Receptive political environments in which poor people's concerns are taken seriously remain elusive (Campbell, Cornish, Gibbs, & Scott, 2010). The fight for self-sufficiency wages and welfare benefits that support families, access to high-quality health and child care, fair treatment within the welfare system and broader community, control over their own lives, and freedom from the image of "welfare queen," and other destructive stereotypes are as relevant today as they were in the 1960s and 1970s. TANF's time limits, sanctions, and work first policies, it could be argued, have intensified the need for welfare rights activism.

Although the NWRO ended in 1975, local and national organizations continue to advocate broadly for welfare justice. One of this chapter's coauthors, Wendy Limbert, was deeply engaged with San Diego's Supportive Parents Information Network (SPIN), a grassroots organization founded by 12 low-income parents and a former ACLU attorney who came together "to find a way to complete their educational training instead of being forced to take low-wage, temporary jobs to satisfy welfare reform demands" (Supportive Parents Information Network (SPIN), n.d., para. 2). SPIN's goals – to provide advocacy training to low-income parents, end the isolation of poverty, and include low-income people in political and community processes and decision making – echoes those of national and local goals currently pursued by countless other organizations across the country.

In the wake of welfare "reform," welfare rights organizations have faced increased need and new challenges. SPIN collaborated with the San Diego Office of the Public Defender to develop a diversion program that would minimize the devastating consequences of fraud prosecution. In doing so, SPIN played a pivotal role in educating the broader community that "welfare fraud" typically involves small sums of money and is more likely the result of errors calculating erratic income than intentional deception (Swan et al., 2008). Across the United States, mobilization efforts against workfare programs and work requirements have also been launched (Cohen, 2006; Reese, 2002). Deepening poverty means that significant attention must be dedicated to ensuring that basic needs, such as heating and other basic utilities, are covered (George Wiley Center, n.d.). It is also the case that TANF policies have resulted in confusion about eligibility and concern about how policies are being implemented at the state and local levels. In response, welfare rights organizations have mounted efforts to educate recipients about TANF regulations, inform low-income group, particularly immigrants, about eligibility for benefits, and ensure fair treatment in light of greater caseworker discretion. Other efforts have focused on fighting welfare privatization (Reese, Geidraitis, & Vega, 2005).

Welfare rights organizations are working to raise awareness of restrictive welfare policies. High visibility protests against marriage promotion, for instance, have sought to capture public attention, and hopefully, public support for directing federal and state funds toward job training and education rather than marriage counseling. By strategically planning antimarriage promotion events on holidays, such as Valentine's Day, and including children in rallies against proposed state budget cuts to CalWORKS, California's cash aid program, LIFETIME has sought to both garner media attention and humanize the plight of poor families (LIFETIME, n.d.). SPIN (2010) launched a major campaign to raise awareness of how difficult it is to access food assistance and how few food-insecure families receive this support. Welfare Warriors (2010) sang their own holiday carol "CPS

(Child Protective Services) is Coming for You" outside the Milwaukee Bureau of Child Welfare to raise awareness of the watchful eye of the state in poor women's lives.

Grassroots organizations have also played an important role in documenting the impact of sanctions and diversion policies on recipients. In Wisconsin, advocates raised concerns about civil rights violations against immigrants and ethnic minorities because recipients were not receiving written materials in their primary languages (Reese, Geidraitis, & Vega, 2006). The case was particularly extreme for Hmong immigrants, many of whom read little or no English and often had limited literacy in Hmong (Moore & Selkowe, 1999). As a consequence, making sense of and adhering to welfare regulations was difficult if not impossible for these families. Complaints helped build the case for welfare agencies' compliance with accessible language requirements.

Other functions of welfare rights organizations, although less tangible, are equally important. In bringing low-income women together, welfare rights organizations create a "safe space" for members to share their experiences, break the silence and stigma that surround poverty and welfare receipt, (re)claim voice in their communities, and work for social and economic justice through direct action. In addition to these crucial community-building functions, personal benefits are also likely. In interviews with participants in feminist consciousness-raising groups, Weitz (1982) identified a number of individual benefits, including a greater sense of control, externalization of attributions of blame, and increased self-esteem. Similar outcomes are likely to occur among members of other activist groups.

In their pursuit of economic justice, welfare rights organizations provide an alternative to deeply entrenched class, race, and gender hierarchies, and in doing so, challenge the very foundation of dominant economic and social institutions. And, through consciousness raising and other activities, welfare rights organizations also foster personal and political development. We have, by necessity, only scratched the surface of the rich, varied activities of these organizations and their impact. Understanding the factors that contribute to collective action proves equally complex.

Barriers and Correlates of Collective Action

Social psychologists have identified a number of individual (e.g., locus of control and political efficacy) and group-level factors (e.g., relative deprivation and social identity) that influence collective action (Kelly & Breinlinger, 1996; Thomas & Louis, 2013). Group-oriented theories of collective action, particularly Taylor and McKirnan's (1984) five-stage model of intergroup relations, with its emphasis on stratification, ideology, and the perceived permeability of group boundaries, is especially relevant to welfare rights activism. According to this model, collective action is contingent on disadvantaged individuals seeing themselves as discriminated against to the same extent as other members of their group (Taylor & McKirnan, 1984). With respect to welfare rights activism, two sets of beliefs are central to this process: a shift from individualistic ideologies that justify differential status in terms of personal shortcomings (e.g., meritocracy and individualistic explanations for poverty) to structural explanations that focus on external factors (e.g., discrimination and structural explanations for poverty) and recognition that group boundaries are not permeable (e.g., an individual cannot easily move from a low- to a higher-status group; Kelly & Breinlinger, 1996; Taylor & McKirnan, 1984). These beliefs are likely to be salient for understanding welfare rights activism in the United States.

Individualism, Belief in Meritocracy, and the American Dream

Individualism is characterized by beliefs emphasizing independence and personal responsibility (Bullock & Limbert, 2009). Recognized as a core facet of US identity and political thought, the strength of individualism as a dominant ideology distinguishes the United States from much of the world, including other western countries (Uhlmann, Poehlman, & Bargh, 2009). Long a defining US value, there is growing concern that the cultural revolution of the 1960s and rise of Wall Street in the 1980s has fueled a radical individualism characterized by extreme distrust in institutions and a misplaced confidence in personal autonomy (Sullivan, 2011). The passage of restrictive welfare reform in 1996, which was spurred on by concerns about systemic corruption and the belief that recipients can and should "pull themselves up by their bootstraps," is illustrative of radical individualism.

Individualism is evident in the US tendency to view both poverty and wealth as resulting from individual effort or lack thereof (Bullock, 2008; Feagin, 1975; Furnham, 2003; Kluegel & Smith, 1986). Individualistic attributions for poverty emphasize personal shortcomings (e.g., lack of thrift, laziness, and antiwork values), whereas dispositional explanations for wealth focus on positive characteristics (e.g., hard work, perseverance, intelligence, and risk-taking). Conversely, structural attributions for poverty (e.g., discrimination, low wages, and poorly funded, inadequate schools) and wealth (e.g., privilege, inheritance, and networks) focus on larger institutions and social structures.

In the United States, individualistic attributions for poverty enjoy greater popularity among European Americans, men, conservatives, and middle-income groups than among African Americans, women, liberals, and the poor (Bullock, 1999; Feagin, 1975; Furnham, 2003; Kluegel & Smith, 1986). Conversely, structural explanations for poverty are endorsed more strongly by less privileged groups (e.g., African Americans, women, and the poor). Similar demographic patterns are found for attributions for wealth (Furnham, 1983, 2003; Kluegel & Smith, 1986; Smith, 1985; Smith, & Stone, 1989). Collectively, these demographic patterns reveal that groups with greater access to resources and those who benefit most from dominant institutions are also more likely to support maintaining the status quo, whereas less powerful groups are more likely to question social structures and perceive current arrangements as unjust.

Beliefs, however, are not always clear-cut, and endorsing one set of beliefs does not necessitate the rejection of another seemingly contradictory set of values. This is true of attributions for poverty. A number of studies with ethnic minorities and low-income groups find support for both structural and individualistic attributions, albeit with lesser support for individualistic explanations (Bullock & Limbert, 2003; Bullock & Waugh, 2005; Hunt, 1996; Seccombe, 2011). This "dual consciousness" or belief in both the importance of individual agency and "the realities of class and caste" (Hunt, 1996, p. 310) acknowledges personal efforts to leave poverty while remaining mindful of powerful structural constraints on individual outcomes. In terms of day-to-day survival, "dual consciousness" may help low-income people remain hopeful that efforts to exit poverty will pay off for themselves and their families while still acknowledging the structural barriers to equality and economic security. Findings from Bullock and Waugh's (2005) study of Mexican American farmworkers illustrate this pattern. Although support was stronger for structural attributions, individualistic explanations were also endorsed. Along these same lines, the majority of respondents saw racism as blocking upward mobility and regarded Mexican immigrants as having fewer opportunities than other ethnic groups, but also believed that they would be financially secure in the future and that their own chances of getting ahead were good if they worked hard. These dual beliefs may be indicative of the individual perseverance needed to endure the harsh conditions of immigration and awareness of structural barriers to accessing resources (Bullock & Waugh, 2005). Unfortunately, individualistic attributions may also neutralize the potentially radicalizing aspects of structural understandings of inequality.

Several lines of research offer insight into the relevance of causal attributions to welfare rights activism. As "legitimizing beliefs," attributions for poverty and wealth "minimize group conflict by creating consensus on ideologies that promote the superiority of one group versus another" (Pratto, Sidanius, Stallworth, & Malle, 2004, p. 741). The legitimizing functions of attributions and their potential consequences for collective action are, perhaps, most directly documented by studies examining predictors of support for welfare and other redistributive policies. Individualistic attributions for poverty and wealth are correlated with restrictive welfare policies and decreased funding for welfare programs, whereas structural explanations are associated with support for progressive welfare policies and increased welfare spending (Bullock, Williams, & Limbert, 2003; Kluegel & Smith, 1986). Although not sufficient, structural attributions for poverty and wealth are likely to be important correlates of welfare rights activism because these beliefs provide an ideological foundation for questioning the distribution of resources and acting on behalf of more generous welfare policies. Why would programs designed to support low-income families and level the playing field be championed if poverty were attributed to characterological flaws and wealth to individual initiative and skill? Likewise, why would strict time limits on welfare receipt be supported if discrimination and privilege were perceived as primary sources of poverty and wealth?

Classic social psychological research on attributional patterns and stigma lend further insight into potential relationships among attributions and welfare rights activism. Consistent with the actor-observer effect (Jones & Nisbett, 1972) by which individuals attribute their own setbacks to situational factors but others' negative outcomes to personal causes, welfare recipients have been found to distinguish their own poverty from the economic hardships of others (Davis & Hagen, 1996; Seccombe, 2011). For example, in Seccombe's (2011) interviews with welfare recipients, women focused on situational causes (e.g., lack of jobs and shortage of child care) or factors beyond their control (e.g., illness) when explaining their own plight, but emphasized individual traits, such as laziness and lack of interest in bettering oneself, when discussing other women's poverty. Put simply, women viewed their own poverty and welfare use as an exception to larger trends (Seccombe, 2011). In echoing dominant myths about others' welfare use, welfare recipients distance themselves from other poor women with whom they may share life circumstances and political interests, and potentially even a group identity.

The stigma and negative stereotypes associated with welfare receipt encourage distancing and disidentification from public assistance (Briar, 1966; Davis & Hagen, 1996; Goodban, 1985; Williams, 2009). These dynamics are documented in Davis and Hagen's (1996) investigation of coping with welfare stigma. During focus groups with welfare recipients, welfare mothers in general were stereotyped, with respondents differentiating themselves from other recipients and focusing on external causes (e.g., the high cost of medical care) of their own welfare receipt:

> I think most people look down on people on welfare who are trying to do something for themselves. It's because they hear the story about people getting on welfare because they have so many kids, and so the more kids they have, the more money they get, and many of them are on drugs. But people like myself, I do not use drugs, nor do I drink. I have pride in myself. (pp. 328–329)

Attributing others' poverty to personal shortcomings may help recipients manage welfare stigma; unfortunately, this distancing may discourage participation in welfare rights activism.

In the United States, individualism is deeply intertwined with belief in meritocracy and the American dream. Meritocracy emphasizes the role of individual effort and talent in advancement (McNamee & Miller, 2009). The belief that status is based on merit is a central facet of the American dream – that anyone regardless of family of origin, class, race, or gender can rise to the "top" of the class hierarchy through hard work and perseverance (Hochschild, 1995).

Meritocracy is evident in all facets of US life, from political discourse to popular culture (Hochschild, 1995). "Horatio Alger" or rags-to-riches stories tell of individuals who overcome significant disadvantage (e.g., poverty, lack of education, and racism) to achieve "success," typically in the form of material or "earthly" rewards (Uhlmann et al., 2009). Barack Obama's (2004) address as a US senatorial candidate at the Democratic National Convention embodies the belief in unbounded opportunity:

> They [my parents] shared an abiding faith in the possibilities of this nation. They would give me an African name, Barack, or 'blessed,' believing that in a tolerant America your name is no barrier to success. They imagined me going to the best schools in the land, even though they weren't rich, because in a generous America you don't have to be rich to achieve your potential. (para. 7)

Such claims go largely uninterrogated, contributing to a cultural backdrop in which wealth, power, and status are seen as reflecting individual merit (e.g., intelligence, effort, skill, and perseverance) and justifying the status quo even when it is personally disadvantageous.

As with support for individualistic attributions, belief in meritocracy and the American dream can provide much-needed hope in the face of hardship but may limit collective action. Foster, Sloto, and Ruby (2006) illustrate these dynamics in their study of women's responses to personal discrimination. Among women who reported experiencing personal discrimination, stronger belief in meritocracy was associated with decreased collective action and lower self-esteem; conversely, for those who reported little personal discrimination, stronger meritocratic beliefs predicted higher self-esteem. Drawing on social identity theory, the researchers posit that the conflict or "shattered assumptions" that result from endorsing meritocracy and personally experienced discrimination contribute to negative social identification (Foster et al., 2006). Consequently, lack of participation in collective action may be motivated by the desire to distance or disassociate from groups and/or situations that heighten the threat of being personally discriminated against or that bring these conflicts to the forefront. It is also the case that belief in meritocracy may contribute to the minimization or dismissal of discrimination (Foster et al., 2006). Experimental research by McCoy and Major (2007) lends further insight into meritocracy's legitimizing function. In two complimentary studies, meritocracy primes led low-status group members to justify personal and group disadvantage by decreasing perceptions of discrimination and increasing endorsement of stereotypes that justified their subordinate status. Collectively, these findings document the role of legitimizing beliefs in deterring collective action, and consistent with Taylor and McKirnan's (1984) framework, they also show how alternative understandings may facilitate collective action.

Beliefs about Social Mobility

tokens = representative

According to Taylor and McKirnan's (1984) model, the perceived permeability of group boundaries has important implications for collective action. Individuals who see movement from a lower to higher status group as blocked may be more likely to engage in collective action because such actions are seen as necessary to challenging structural inequity and barriers to mobility (Wright et al., 1990). On the other hand, individual effort may be seen as sufficient when entry into a higher status groups is viewed as fluid. "Tokens" or exemplars, individuals who have successfully moved up the socioeconomic ladder, communicate that individual initiative is all that is needed to move out of poverty, dampening interest in group mobilization efforts (Wright & Taylor, 1998).

Perceived permeability is especially relevant to welfare rights activism and other economic justice initiatives because social class in the United States, unlike gender and race, is largely perceived as an earned or achieved rather than an ascribed status (Weber, 1998). Upward mobility is also a central premise of the American dream, evident in belief that that through hard work and perseverance, anyone can improve their station in life. In the wake of the Great Recession, Americans have grown more pessimistic about their own financial status and their children's economic chances, yet belief in the American dream and mobility remains strong. In an Economic Mobility Project (2011a) survey of 2,000 respondents, 68% believed that they have or will achieve the American dream, 54% expected they will be better off in 10 years, and 68% anticipated that their children would be at least as well off as they are now. Hard work, ambition, and quality education were rated as the most important factors in getting ahead (Economic Mobility Project, 2011a).

Widespread belief in prospects for upward mobility does not correspond with the probability of upward mobility in the United States. International analyses challenge the belief that the United States affords greater opportunities and mobility than other countries (Isaacs, n.d.; Sawhill & Morton, 2007). The United States ranks below Canada, Denmark, Sweden, Germany, and France in terms of intergenerational mobility. US children are more likely than their counterparts in these countries to end up in the same income distribution as their parents, indicating that low income is more of a barrier in the United States than other countries (Isaacs, n.d.). These findings make clear that although economic mobility in the US is certainly possible, it is not easy, and perhaps, not as likely as is widely believed. Recognizing these complexities – ease, likelihood, and structural obstacles – may be pivotal to collective action.

The Current Study

We drew on Taylor and McKirnan's (1984) model of intergroup relations to ground our analysis of low-income women's engagement in welfare rights activism. Consistent with their model, we were interested in how perceived discrimination, structural attributions for poverty and wealth, and belief in limited upward mobility and/or barriers to class permeability are related to political mobilization. Through focus groups, we hoped to gain a more contextualized understanding in women's own words about the relationship of beliefs about inequality and class permeability to collective action.

However, focusing exclusively on attitudes and beliefs yields a narrow understanding of collective action. A wide range of situational factors, such as the proximity and public visibility of advocacy organizations, are also likely to play an important role in collective action. Moreover, understanding the impact of discrimination or negative experiences in particular settings, not simply perceiving oneself and one's group as discriminated against, can lend deeper insight into contextual dimensions of low-income women's political mobilization. Poor women's interactions with social services and healthcare professionals may be particularly important in terms of radicalization because there is so much at stake (e.g., denial of benefits or access and sanctions). To allow for a multifaceted understanding of low-income women's participation in welfare rights activism, our examination of the correlates of collective action was threefold: *experiential* (e.g., classist, racist, and sexist discrimination; termination of benefits); *ideological* (e.g., attributions for poverty wealth, beliefs about upward mobility/ permeability of class boundaries); and *situational* (e.g., opportunities for mobilization).

Two further aspects of this analysis warrant mention: our focus on collective action and social class. Although we focus on collective action in the broadest sense, we are mindful not to value these behaviors over other forms of critical resistance. The importance of covert, "unorganized" resistance is documented in Gilliom's (2005) analysis of Appalachian welfare recipients' responses to surveillance (e.g., relationship tracking, involvement with the criminal justice system). To circumvent harsh system rules, women engaged in a range of everyday resistance strategies (e.g., working "under the table" jobs and not reporting petty earnings). These less visible but certainly no less risky behaviors that allow women to "fly under the radar," supplement family income, and maintain a sense of autonomy should not be interpreted as secondary to more visible, collective strategies (Gilliom, 2005). Additionally, our analysis "privileges" social class in that we foreground relationships among class identity, poverty-related experiences, and beliefs about economic inequality to understand welfare rights activism (Ostrove & Cole, 2003). In doing so, we aim to enrich psychological understandings of class-based beliefs and experiences. We are cognizant, however, that social identities and inequalities intersect rather than act in isolation, and are careful to attend to the full range of our informants' experiences (Choo & Ferree, 2010; Cole, 2009).

Method

Participants

Twenty-five women ranging in age from 23 to 51 ($M = 33$; $SD = 7$) participated in one of four separate focus groups held on-site at a weekend-long advocacy summit sponsored by a nonprofit organization that helps low-income parents pursue postsecondary education and access public assistance programs. In terms of organizational involvement, 44% were current participants of the program; 20% were program staff; 20% were new to the organization; and 16% were volunteers. Political action ranged from testifying before the state legislature and taking part in organized protests to those whose attendance at the retreat was their first formal action.

All respondents were current or former welfare recipients. Eighty percent of informants were receiving TANF at the time of the study, 76% were receiving food assistance, 60% were participating in a state Medicaid program (Medi-Cal), and 40% were receiving housing assistance. The majority of respondents self-identified as poor or working poor (72%), with 12% identifying as working class, and 16% as lower middle class or middle class.

Twenty-eight percent of respondents self-identified as Black/African American; 24% as white, 16% as bi/multiracial (e.g., African American and Chicano and African American and white), 12% as "other" (e.g., Filipina), 8% as Latina/Chicana, 8% as Asian/Pacific Islander, and 4% as Native American. With one exception, a participant who was pregnant at the time of the study, all respondents were mothers. Consistent with national US norms (US Census Bureau, 2004), the average family included 1.7 children. Children ranged from 4-month-old infants to 22-year-old adults. Most participants were the head of their household, with 80% reporting their marital status as single, separated, or divorced; the remaining 20% were living with a partner or were legally married. Our sample was overwhelmingly liberal, with slightly less than half (48%) identifying as a Democrat, 32% as "other" (i.e., Socialist, Green Party, "no affiliation – all are crooks"), and 12% as independent. Eight percent of respondents did not answer this question.

Given the organization's focus on education, it is not surprising that our sample was more highly educated than welfare recipients nationally (Committee on Ways and Means, US House of Representatives, 2008). Forty percent of respondents had obtained a high school diploma/GED, 32% held an associate's degree/certificate as their highest degree, 24% had earned a bachelor's degree, and 4% held a masters degree.

Context

The mission and work of the nonprofit convener of the summit provides an important context for our focus groups, understanding our respondents, and our findings. Founded by student mothers who earned college degrees while receiving public assistance, the organization focuses on empowering low-income parents to pursue higher education and access support programs. With a strong welfare rights mission, activities include educating recipients about their rights to education under TANF and rights under the welfare system more generally (for a discussion of poverty law and community activism, see Loffredo, 2001), staging high visibility protests against controversial policies and funding cuts to public assistance, and advocating for local, state, and national policy change. The organization has generated interest in its programs by having a strong presence at community colleges, among other venues. Their protests, some of which capitalize on "political spectacle" (Farrar & Warner, 2008), have attracted media attention.

Funding for the summit allowed for participants' transportation, housing, and food expenses for the weekend to be covered. Some women brought their children, and child care was provided while they took part in the sessions. These supportive resources, which made participation in the summit possible, as well as the organization's community presence, are important facilitators of collective action that should not be overlooked.

Procedure

Past and current TANF parents who attended the summit received flyers inviting their attendance at one of four 90-minute focus group discussions of how people become involved with welfare rights organizing and suggestions for strengthening welfare policy. Approximately six women participated in each focus group. As an important feminist tool for "understanding the person within the social world," focus groups were selected as the most appropriate methodology for this study (Wilkinson, 1998, p. 111). A distinguishing advantage of focus groups over individual interviews is that "focus groups involve the interaction of group participants *with each other* as well as with the researcher/moderator" (Wilkinson, 1998, p. 112). This contextualized, relational approach allows for the social co-construction of meaning unlike more individual-focused methods (Wilkinson, 1998). Moreover, the group structure, at least during data collection, shifts the power dynamics away from the researcher to the participants (Wilkinson, 1998). These considerations were crucial in determining the most effective strategy for learning about low-income women's life experiences.

All focus groups were held on two consecutive evenings after formal summit activities had concluded. Respondents were assured that their responses would not be shared with caseworkers, that their participation was voluntary and not connected to the summit, and that their comments would not impact support from the organization. Participants received $50 for their participation.

After providing informed consent, participants completed a brief demographic questionnaire (e.g., race and/or ethnicity, perceived social class, receipt of public assistance, and marital status). Respondents selected a pseudonym to be used during the session, and to add a further layer of identity protection, we subsequently assigned new pseudonyms for reporting. After these materials were completed, all participants and the researchers introduced themselves. Two of the three principal investigators, one of mixed ethnic descent (i.e., Chicana and white) and the other white, facilitated the focus groups. Both were middle class at the time of the study.

The focus groups were structured around 10 open-ended questions related to experiences with the welfare system, how people get involved with welfare rights organizing, beliefs about poverty and wealth, and recommended policy changes. Prior to the study, all questions were reviewed by the organization to ensure their relevance and mutuality of interest. Each meeting was tape recorded and a note taker summarized comments and themes on a flip chart.

Analysis

Prior to analysis, a team of research assistants transcribed each focus group recording. Transcript accuracy was established by having multiple research assistants review transcripts while listening to audio recordings and make necessary corrections. One of the principal researchers also reviewed the transcripts and recordings to ensure accuracy.

Thematic analysis was used to analyze the data (Braun & Clarke, 2006). After repeatedly listening to tape recordings of the focus groups and reading the transcripts, the principal researchers (and authors of this chapter) independently coded the transcripts for key concepts and patterns. To allow for exploration of Taylor and McKirnan's (1984) model in relation to welfare rights activism as well as a potentially broader range of factors identified by respondents, our analysis included both deductive and inductive coding strategies. An initial round of coding was guided by aspects of collective action identified by Taylor and McKirnan (1984) and was followed by open coding to identify other themes. After noting common themes, interrelationships among recurring themes were assessed, and themes were recategorized to reflect increasingly abstract levels of analysis. This process involved moving between inductive and deductive analysis as we revisited and revised our interpretations (Flick, 2002).

Our cross-checking process began during the focus groups. To assess whether we were accurately "hearing" our informants, notes and summaries were written on a large flip chart allowing participants to verify conceptualizations of their responses. The principal investigators worked independently to identify core themes and then collaboratively until consensus regarding "core" themes was reached. "Core" themes characterized the experiences and/or perceptions of the majority of discussants, and experiences that were not widely shared are identified as such.

Findings

We describe three core correlates of collective action among our discussants: (1) experiences of interpersonal and institutional discrimination that threatened family survival and/or emotional well-being; (2) structural beliefs about inequality and the oppressiveness of interclass relations; and (3) collective responsibility for fighting economic justice. Because discriminatory experiences were foundational in many respects, we begin our discussion here. Direct quotes are reported using pseudonyms.

Radicalizing Experiences of Interpersonal and Institutional Classism

Among the low-income women that we spoke with, being discriminated against was a unifying experience. With remarkable consistency, our discussants described experiencing classism in what quickly became a familiar set of contexts: accessing medical care for themselves and their children; applying for social services or communicating with their caseworkers; trying to secure housing; in the classroom; and in public spaces where markers of poverty are visible, such as using food stamps in the grocery store or Medicaid insurance cards to access health care. These commonly cited sites of classist discrimination echo other studies of low-income women's experiences (Adair, 2002; Bartle & Segura, 2003; Downing, LaVeist, & Bullock, 2007; Jarrett, 1996; Lott, 2002; McCormack, 2004; Seccombe, 2011). Sharing their experiences with the group elicited nods of recognition and supportive comments like "I've been there." These stories also brought tears of frustration, pain, and empathy as well as supportive laughter and at times even applause for one another.

Experiences of institutional discrimination, which in many cases threatened individual and family survival, appeared to play a large role in welfare rights mobilization. This was the case for women who described first getting involved because they were sanctioned or were worried about benefit termination due to administrative difficulties, in danger of losing their child care or housing, required to work outside the home, or unable to attend school or access the medical care that their families needed. Inadequate access to health care or substandard medical treatment of children was particularly salient. For example, Eve, a white mother of one, recounted a story of her ill son being summarily dismissed at an emergency room due to her pending Medicaid status until she pushed for further attention. Moving between the overt and covert dynamics of the interaction, she described the power imbalance of the exchange:

'Oh well, you have Medi-Cal that's pending. So we're gonna give you the pink stuff and send you home.' And she says, 'And I'm the doctor. And technically, you're on welfare . . . I'm the doctor here. You're on Medi-Cal, do you understand your role?'. . . . And I wasn't raised poor, so I was . . . stunned.

Medi-Cal insurance cards served as a visible maker or indicator of economic status, making welfare recipients easy targets for classist discrimination and as a consequence, discrimination extended to a broad range of healthcare-related settings including pharmacies. Stephanie's story was a familiar one to the other participants in her focus group.

Stephanie [34-year-old multiracial mother of five]: My son had an earache – it was a Friday. I went to drugstore to get his prescription filled. They had a problem running the Medi-Cal card. They told me, 'You need to go talk to your social worker.' They weren't making a phone call. They weren't gonna accommodate me. And they knew I had a son that had chronic pain with his earache. He went all weekend with a terrible earache.
Dina [28-year-old African American mother of one]: Oh god.
Anita [27-year-old white mother of two]: I have had that happen.
Stephanie: The social worker went home early on Friday. I tried to call her. I couldn't get through. So I had a kid in pain all weekend. Monday morning, I'm hot. I call my social worker. 'Well I don't understand. Everything's okay. It should go through. Just tell them it's okay.' I said, 'But it's not working.' So I'm having to fight with the drugstore to get my son's prescription. I go in there, it's a whole rig-a-ma-roll. And the people in the drugstore think I'm some crazy welfare mom.
Eve [white mother of one]: Yeah.
Stephanie: And I get treated differently. And it's really hard to maintain your composure when you're upset.

These situations illustrate the potentially grave consequences of discrimination for low-income mothers and their children. They also underscore the stress of being evaluated and treated as a "welfare recipient" and the pressure not to behave in ways that confirm classist stereotypes. Power dynamics, however, heighten the stakes for poor women far beyond concerns about stereotyping alone. Overt anger or frustration could result in termination of service or care, a considerable risk when conveniently located pharmacies may be difficult to find and a declining number of California physicians accept welfare recipients as patients, in part due to low Medi-Cal reimbursement rates (Russell, 1995).

Difficulties with cash benefits were equally threatening to well-being, putting women and their families at risk of falling into deeper poverty or possible eviction from their homes. Welfare regulations were overwhelmingly viewed as punitive and interactions with caseworkers were frequently identified as problematic. After being repeatedly assured that her recertification application was moving forward, Dina, a 28-year-old African American mother of one, grew increasingly apprehensive when her benefits card failed to arrive. Describing a complex web of paperwork, requirements, and frustration, Dina recounted:

> I filled out the big packet of papers and nothing happened, I still didn't get my check. And so therefore, I had to pay 50 dollars late fee for it . . . and I'm late for my rent. And rent is important . . . I called the lady [caseworker] and she said, 'Oh, you had a recertification on this date.' And I said, 'Okay, I went to that recertification.' And they said, 'Well, we already cut your benefits.'

Due to administrative error, Dina was required to recomplete her application materials and unnecessarily participate in a TANF orientation program. She explained:

> And for a whole month and a half I didn't have anything. And they just, they still didn't do anything until I had to finally write an appeal about 'em and . . . I talked to everybody and I had everything clear. And so they really made me mad about that and I'm not gonna never forget that. They made me go up there every day . . . and I was missin' school and work and everything was going crazy.

Eventually her benefits were reinstated but for struggling families such as Dina's, the consequences of lost time at school, work, and lag in cash assistance can be catastrophic. These experiences also communicate to recipients that the "the system" is not on their side or trustworthy, and that following rules does not ensure positive outcomes. As Isabel, a 24-year-old Chicana and mother of two put it, "The whole system is so penalty driven, it's not like a support system." Advancing this point, Eve, a white mother of one, explained, "The one word in welfare is: compliant. Hundred percent compliant! Because that's not good enough. What is good enough? . . . I find it very intimidating. . ."

The onerousness of welfare regulations was compounded by the lack of privacy and surveillance that have long been central to feminist critiques of the welfare system (Hays, 2003; Mink, 2001). Anita, a white 27-year-old mother of two, recounted being intimidated when caseworkers conducted a home visit after the birth of her first child. After being questioned about the quality of lighting in her apartment and her parenting skills, she subsequently left the state, afraid that that her child would be taken from her. She had more recently been investigated for welfare fraud because her status as a student intern on a research project raised suspicion about her financial need. Another respondent described undergoing unwanted disability testing and being erroneously labeled as schizophrenic, while another respondent was sanctioned because she continued attending school rather than accept a job that paid barely above the minimum wage. Ultimately, an exemption was granted so that she could continue her studies but only after telling her caseworker her "personal business."

There was a shared understanding among respondents that the welfare system is structured to limit recipients' freedom. Regulations that restrict postsecondary education to programs directly related to employment are but one example. Commenting on these barriers, Stephanie, a 34-year-old multiracial mother of five, reported:

coercion

I had a caseworker tell me that as long as I'm on welfare I am married to them. So I better change my coursework. I was told that I need to stick to my educational plan. I chose to change my educational plan. I took authority over that. But that's a form of discrimination.

welfare controls your whole path life

Since welfare reform's passage, college attendance by welfare recipients has dropped considerably, and despite successful efforts in some states (Price, 2005) and at some colleges and universities (Adair, 2008) to expand access, significant barriers remain especially for participation in baccalaureate granting programs.

Other aspects of TANF regulations were viewed as facilitating broader discriminatory treatment: ʻ

Stephanie [34-year-old multiracial mother of five]: Welfare families have to take what's called a verification of enrollment to our children's school, I believe like once every six months to make sure that they're in school and so that you can continue getting your benefits. And this is a problem because that makes your children discriminated against at school by the staff, the faculty, and you as a parent. It's really difficult taking those forms into the school saying, 'I need this . . .' They know those are from the welfare parents and our children get treated differently. And, we're discriminated against as parents, like if our children have an issue at school with behavior . . .
Anita [27-year-old white mother of two]: Oh yeah.
Stephanie: . . . or grades or something, it all goes back, 'Oh well, that they're welfare families.'
Anita: 'What do your parents do?'
Eve [white mother of one]: Yeah, yeah, 'What do you expect?' They are expected to be 'high-risk' kids.
Stephanie: This to me is a form of discrimination against . . . our children and us as parents, and our kids know what those green envelopes represent 'Oh, that's for welfare . . .' they know that they're treated differently on account of that.
Eve: Yeah, they criminalize us.

Some schools have sought to reduce classist discrimination by minimizing the presence of visible makers of poverty such as "free lunch" cards; however, other practices, such as frequent verifications of need mean that TANF recipients must repeatedly disclose low-income status to school systems. Feminist and critical scholars view such practices as intentionally designed to humiliate recipients, and the legitimacy of women's concerns about the impact of poverty and welfare receipt on teachers' judgments of children and their families is amply documented in the research literature. In an experiment by Darley and Gross

(1983), participants viewed a videotape of a hypothetical fourth grade girl taking a test in which she was portrayed as coming from a high or a low socioeconomic (SES) background. Although the child's academic performance was identical in both conditions, participants rated the abilities of the high SES target as above grade level but as below grade level when they thought she was poor. Further research documents the disrespectful treatment low-income parents frequently experience when interacting with their children's teachers (Lott, 2001).

Interpersonal discrimination was as pervasive as institutional discrimination with respondents describing being treated as "less than" – "looked down on," ignored, scrutinized, insulted, and treated as "lazy and stupid." Jasmine, a 28-year mother of one who identified as African and European American, aptly summarized the insidiousness of interpersonal classism, "I think there's always this . . . stereotype where . . . people I don't know, they kinda smirk." For our respondents, the pervasiveness of classist stereotypes – that welfare recipients are neglectful mothers, unmotivated to work, and sexually available – meant that interpersonal discrimination was an omnipresent possibility and with caseworkers, family members, classmates, landlords, and strangers (e.g., people in grocery stores making "casual" antiwelfare comments) among the most commonly cited perpetrators this appeared to be the case. Consequently, "everyday" classism was in many respects as threatening to women's survival and well-being as institutional classism. We found that classist stereotyping and stigma not only deterred women from applying for much needed assistance (Stuber & Kronebusch, 2004), it also threatened self-efficacy and self-esteem (Major & O'Brien, 2005).

In the welfare system, stereotypes were frequently described as underlying dehumanizing treatment (Hays, 2003; Soss, 2005). Describing an interaction with her caseworker, Jasmine stated, "You're already making assumptions and stereotypes and you're not even helping me with what the issue is . . . You're looking at me as if I'm some . . . number instead of looking at me as a human being." Judgments of "undeservingness" were also common. When attempting to continue her coursework, Michelle (23-year-old Filipina and Italian mother of two) recalled her employment counselor saying, "People like you, immigrants, coming to this country and getting all this education." Initially, Michelle believed that she was "supposed to take all this shit" because she was a "welfare mom," but she eventually reported her TANF employment counselor to the state Civil Rights Bureau. Although the locus of responsibility was often placed on individual caseworkers and perhaps, rightly so, we see the working conditions of frontline social work – high caseloads, low salaries, limited time to get to know clients, and caseworkers' role as enforcers but not creators of restrictive welfare policies – as creating fertile conditions for mistreatment and discrimination.

Families were not "safe havens." For example, Alena, a 35-year-old Native American mother of one, was so fearful of the stigma associated with welfare receipt that she applied only after her mother urged her to do so. Ironically, her mother subsequently made Alena's life miserable by "complaining about how

don't want to be sponges → feel indebted

we're living and sucking and sponging [off the system]." Reutter et al.'s (2009) study of class-based stigma and discrimination in Canada reveals similar distancing by family members and claims of "sponging:"

> [My brother-in-law said] I'm tired of supporting welfare people like you. Tired of supporting your kids. You had your kids, you raise your kids. Why should I go out to work to pay for welfare to look after you and your kids? I have to work for a living. Why can't you work? (p. 301)

Regardless of the setting, or whether a family member or stranger was involved, interpersonal classism was a source of humiliation. An experience shared by Jocelyn (43-year-old Chicana mother of one) resonated with other participants in her group:

> I've been treated crappy at the grocery store because of my food stamps . . . I used to tear them all out and put them in my wallet so I wouldn't lose them. . . . Apparently you're supposed have them in the book when you use them and so they made me go all the way home and get all my book covers . . . I came back with the books and she stood there with all these people in line watching and compared the serial numbers on each food stamp to the serial numbers on the front of the book. . . . It took like ten or fifteen minutes and I was completely humiliated . . . and I'm like you guys just made me feel more freakin' demeaned than any other grocery trip I've ever made in my entire life.

Although paper food stamps have been replaced with electronic benefit cards, stigma remains with program participants reporting continued scrutiny about their purchases.

Collectively, institutional and interpersonal discrimination threatened every aspect of our respondents' lives – their health, economic viability, and emotional well-being. These experiences were painful but also mobilizing (Stewart & Gold-Steinberg, 1996). Institutional classism, whether related to welfare benefits or health care, delivered a blunt mandate: learn one's rights and how to navigate the system. Getting involved with a welfare rights organization was essentially a matter of survival and staying involved, by becoming a staff person or a parent leader or volunteer, was a way to "give back" and help others "make it." Even women who felt they had advocated fairly well on their own believed that a deeper understanding of welfare regulations would be helpful. As Ara, a 28-year-old mother of three, explained,

> I knew there was some problems with my case and I've been advocating for myself pretty well but I knew there was some laws I didn't know about so I really wanted to find out . . . some of the policies so that I could get the most out of CalWORKS while I'm on it.

The complexity of welfare regulations coupled with perceived caseworker negligence required having someone on "your side." Lena, a 26-year-old Black mother of one, summed it up this way:

> I got involved . . . because I was trying to educate myself so that I can . . . have power in trying to take care of the things that I needed to take care of with the county. I didn't like being told 'no' and I knew that it was wrong so . . . I did a lot of research to find out . . . how I . . . can use those facts to tell them what they were telling me was wrong.

Similarly, Rosa, a 27-year-old Chicana and mother of one, explained:

> You're not informed, they don't tell you . . . sometimes even sanction you without even informing you, or cuttin' you off without informing you. So you don't know when . . . the clock starts, when the clock end . . . and you're kind of afraid to go and ask because what if your clock didn't really start . . . so you don't want them to go well 'Hey, you forgot, you didn't sign something, so let's, you know, get this thing signed.'

The financial hardship caused by sanctions coupled with limited understanding of the policy, troubling error rates and bias in their application, and challenges to successfully reversing sanction decisions make this a crucial area of mobilization for recipients and antipoverty advocates (Legal Momentum, 2010b; Lens, 2006, 2008, 2009).

Interpersonal classism also fueled political mobilization. Discussing how she became a welfare rights activist, Jocelyn, a 43-year-old Chicana and mother of one, explained:

> [Former] Governor Pete Wilson made me an activist [laughter from the group]. When he went on the news and said the typical welfare mother lives in a world of prostitutes and pushers. . . . It made me so mad to hear him talk about moms like me the way he did as if we were worthless . . . the worst in society. . . . That's really when I starting getting politically active.

Jocelyn's story illustrates how the degradation and anger associated with being the target of classism can spur political mobilization, and although her comments and other stories told by respondents frequently emphasized a specific event, "put downs" and their impact may well be cumulative in nature.

It should be noted that although our focus is on classism and its relationship to welfare rights activism, our respondents were quick to identify intersections of classism, sexism, and racism, to view welfare recipients as situated at the nexus of these forces, and to regard fighting classism as inexorably intertwined with alleviating sexism and racism (Neubeck & Cazenave, 2001). Intersections of classism and sexism are revealed in Stephanie's (a 34-year-old multiracial mother of five) description of being turned away by a potential landlord:

If you put down welfare [as a source of income], well, automatically they don't want you. I had a situation where a landlord said to me, 'I turned [over] a new leaf. I only rent to complete families.' That was his way of saying, he won't rent to me, I'm a welfare mom.

In this case, "complete family" is code for both financial security and an intact heterosexual two-parent family. Comments such as this reveal the long-standing convergence of morality and sexuality in judgments about poor single mothers (Neubeck & Cazenave, 2001; Onwuachi-Willig, 2005).

The ease with which respondents perceived racism, particularly within the welfare system, as an important dimension of their experiences is illustrated by two respondents who recounted differential treatment by the same employment counselor. Jackie, a 30-year-old African American mother of one, described experiencing so much difficulty being reimbursed for her transportation expenses that she eventually complained to her counselor's supervisor about his lack of responsiveness. Despite working with the same counselor, Janet, a white 35-year-old mother of one, encountered no such difficulties. Racism was immediately introduced and supported as a possible explanation with Michelle, a 23-year-old Filipina and Italian mother of two, stating, "Only thing I can think of is because Janet is white and Jackie is Black." Ara, a 28-year-old Asian mother of three, advanced this explanation by pointing out that discrimination could occur in the absence of face-to-face meetings because caseworkers can also infer client race or ethnicity from name, voice, or accent, and due to priming that positions welfare recipients as "the lowest of the low." For welfare recipients of color, who are at risk of class and race bias, proving their "deservingness" to caseworkers may be fraught with difficulties. Lens and Cary (2010), for instance, found that in their interactions with caseworkers, women of color sought to deflect racial stereotypes by monitoring their behavior for emotions (e.g., anger and "attitude") and behaviors (e.g., aggressiveness) that could be interpreted as "street."

Welfare racism, "the organization of racialized public assistance attitudes, policymaking, and administrative practices" (Neubeck & Cazenave, 2001, p. 36), is well documented in social science literature (Gooden, 1998; Neubeck & Cazenave, 2001; Soss, Schram, Vartanian, & O'Brien, 2001) and was deeply understood by our respondents; however, we suspect that the isolation of welfare receipt provides relatively few opportunities for most low-income women to compare their experiences with a specific caseworker or discuss their treatment more generally. Moreover, a distinguishing aspect of this exchange and others that occurred regarding race is the extent to which respondents were unified rather than polarized by race and perceived racism. Although white respondents could have chosen to minimize the significance of racism, subtly distancing themselves from women of colors' narratives, or responding defensively or competitively in terms of severity of hardship, this was not the case (for an illustration of white welfare recipients distancing from recipients of color, see Cleaveland, 2008). Nor were the prevalence of sexism or classism minimized by respondents. This shared perspective is likely to be an essential dimension of working collectively to alleviate systemic racism, classism, sexism, and heterosexism in the welfare system.

In sum, personally experienced institutional and interpersonal classism (as well as racism and sexism) was understood as pervasive, systemic, and based on group membership. This open acknowledgment of personal and societal discrimination contrasts with the oft-reported tendency in the social psychological literature to deny or minimize the prevalence of bias, even among those who are the target of it (Crosby, 1984). It may be that two of the underlying reasons for denial of discrimination – the need to maintain a sense of control over outcomes and self presentation concerns – were less salient than other concerns for the women in this study (Sechrist, Swim, & Stangor, 2004). Denying personal discrimination is believed to play a self-protective function by shielding targets from negative emotions and a sense of helplessness, but acknowledging and sharing these experiences can also be a unifying source of empowerment (Foster, 2000). Indeed, these experiences played a crucial role in the political mobilization of our respondents, and survival literally depended on "getting involved" because it provided a direct route to learning one's rights and how to navigate the system. However, welfare rights activism also provided less overtly tangible benefits, such as support and solidarity. We now turn to these and other dimensions of collective action.

Structural Beliefs about Inequality and the Oppressiveness of Interclass Relations

Consistent with previous research investigating attributions for poverty and wealth made by low-income groups (Bullock & Limbert, 2003; Feagin, 1975; Furnham, 2003; Kluegel & Smith, 1986), our respondents articulated highly politicized, structural understandings of poverty, wealth, and inequality. Both wealth and poverty were primarily understood as structural rather than individual problems. Tax cuts, being born wealthy, inheritance, and family connections, particularly being able to attend elite schools, were commonly cited causes of wealth, whereas underfunded public schools and lack of access to higher education, discrimination, limited opportunity, low-paying jobs, and capitalism were perceived as leading causes of poverty. Opportunity was not seen as equally distributed. As Rosa (27-year-old Chicana and mother of one) put it:

> I think a lot of it, um, comes down to opportunity . . . that goes for education, um, access to resources, um, just basic information . . . I was reading an article . . . about President Bush and how . . . he got his MBA from like Harvard or Yale . . . he was a very mediocre student . . . and he got into that school because . . . his family knows someone, or pays or . . . whatever, and . . . that's why he is where he

is . . . because of his family. He had the opportunities to move up faster [than] if he was just . . . a poor boy from Texas then . . . I don't think he would have rose as far.

Extending this analysis, Isabel, a 24-year-old Chicana and mother of two, explained wealth and inequality more broadly as integral to capitalism:

nobody @ top started from 0

The wealthiest people in this country, they're not wealthy 'cause they worked so hard all their lives, and they start at the bottom and work their way up, they're wealthy 'cause of inheritance and real-estate. I mean that's where the wealth is. . . . As far as poverty and wealth goes, that's how this economy strives. It . . . is the way our capitalistic system is set up. It would never survive if there was more equality among people so . . . I believe it's done intentionally.

The extent to which our respondents perceived inequality as built into the structure of the US economic system was striking, standing in sharp contrast to widespread belief in meritocracy and the openness of US society (Bostrom, 2002; Hanson & Zogby, 2010). The wealthy were consistently viewed as deliberately blocking access to valued resources to protect and advance their own power and advantage. Drawing parallels between our current system and the feudal arrangements of serfs and nobility, one of our respondents (Alena, 35-year-old Native American mother of one), described the maintenance of inequality this way:

People who are in poverty usually stay in poverty because the ones who have the wealth have been maintaining it by force of arms and they don't share what is rightfully belonging to all of us, like say the planet. [Laughter of group]. You know, the water, the air, the land which belongs to every person on it . . . They are actually keeping it from us. . . . That is the real problem of poverty versus wealth, and why. . . . I'd say the 'have-nots' can't end up having an equal and fair share is because the 'haves' prevent it intentionally and specifically and really forcefully.

These inequalities were seen as being maintained and recreated through a network of institutions, social policies, and classist beliefs that privilege some groups over others. Tax policies that favor elites were frequently mentioned:

When you hear about tax cuts too for these people . . . it's awful . . . I see a professional baseball player or movie star, and then I hear about the tax cuts because it's supposed to help the economy. . . . It's like a realization . . . it's ridiculous . . . where we're gonna spend money on more and we have all these people that are hungry that are homeless that are being hurt every day, but somehow they're poor, stupid, and lazy; you know and they're not worth helping [Lisa, 26-year-old white mother of one].

Nevertheless, structural inequality was seen as worth challenging. Discussing policymakers' resistance to progressive welfare policies, Eve stated:

They wanna keep us vulnerable, that way their life doesn't get threatened – their lifestyle, their nice cars, their paycheck, they don't have to share at the top. And the thing is, we're not gonna let them get away with it; we really aren't. We're gonna keep showing them we have the wits, we have the ability.

Given the strength of respondents' structural critique, it isn't surprising that they also doubted the permeability of class boundaries and expressed skepticism about their own potential for upward mobility. Among respondents, there was a sense that the possibility of upward mobility was declining or perhaps never as possible as meritocratic ideals promise. As Eve stated, "I think that's [upward mobility] a thing of the past. And I think they're sort of closing the door to that." Classist attitudes and beliefs, characterized as a "pull-yourself-up-by-your bootstraps" bias, were regarded as detrimental to mobility as structural obstacles. Describing these barriers, Isabel (24-year-old Chicana and mother of two) noted:

Fifty years ago I'd believe that you could be . . . working poor and buy a house, and support a family, but now-a-days . . . especially with children you just cannot start from the bottom and work your way up, go out and get that minimum wage job, and ten years later there is no guarantee that you'll be much better off than where you already started. . .. So many myths that are part of what the American people think really need to be dispelled 'cause it's harming . . . society's most vulnerable population . . . children. . . . The myth, again, is poor people are lazy. What about a child that's born into poverty? And, then you just get thrown out there and told, 'Hey go get a job, any job, it don't matter if it's . . . enough for you to barely survive' . . . . People can definitely change but there needs to be strong support systems in place . . . because you know people from day one, from when they're born, are not as advantaged as others, and you can't just compare everybody, and say that, 'Well if these people did it, everyone should be able to do it.'

Low wages were identified as a major obstacle to upward mobility. This was an especially distressing topic, in part because several informants held baccalaureate degrees, a level of education that was expected to significantly ease if not end economic hardship; however, this was not necessarily the case. With many respondents pursuing social service careers, low earnings were illustrative of both the devaluation of human sector labor and the wide gap between earnings and self-sufficiency wages – the income needed to meet basic (i.e., housing, food, child care, health care, and transportation) and other essential expenses (Insight, 2008). In 2008, a family in California consisting of one adult with one preschooler and one school age child was estimated to need an annual income of $44,768 to cover basic expenses (Insight, 2008). Given that many respondents were currently receiving some form of assistance, we assume that few if any respondents were earning close to this salary.

An emotionally charged exchange between two 34-year-old informants, Stephanie, a multiracial mother of five and Olana, an Asian/Pacific Islander and mother of three, both of whom had earned college degrees, vividly reveals the persistence of economic hardship and the accompanying frustration of feeling that economic progress is blocked:

> Stephanie: I'm looking for work and it's scarce. I've got classified ads saying they'll pay me $8.00 an hour, B.A. required . . . the hiring freeze . . . the county won't take me . . . I can't get into universities [jobs], they are laying off people . . . I've worked so hard. Raising my kids on my own, going to school for six years. And now, I want a . . . good paying job, to get out of poverty. I want it so bad and I can't achieve it to save my life [Stephanie begins crying]. . . . It's like a huge brick wall that I can't break down. . . . There's things around me I can't change . . . and I'm almost thinking it's a lie, ya know? . . . It's a miracle if people escape poverty, and I'd like to meet some people that have done it. I want to see some legitimate people who have walked in similar circumstances cause I don't know where they are. I do not. Maybe in the movies but not in my life.
>
> Olana: I agree with you . . . I'm similar, I just don't have as many kids. I have three which is still hard as a single mother . . . I have my BA also, in social work but I can't find a job that's paying enough for me to become self-sufficient . . . you're making me cry.
>
> Stephanie: This is our life, it's emotional.
>
> Olana: Let me just say it, the bullshit, is not fair. You go through six years of college to get your family to place where you feel like you're doing something and then, the wall shoots up. It's like okay, 'I broke down the wall for welfare, I broke down the wall for education, and now you're putting another fucking wall up on me?' And it's ten times bigger . . . I'm supposed to be in a better position because I did this and I succeeded and everybody keeps telling me 'I succeeded' but why can't I see the success? . . . I'm still living in poverty, I'm still struggling, and you don't know when that day's going to come, but you know it's soon, that you're gonna to be out on the street because you don't have anything.
>
> Stephanie: I'm four months behind my rent.
>
> Olana: I know, believe me I know. . . . I had nothing to show for that B.A. saying that I have a job and I have a career and I have something that I am going to be fine at . . . that me and my kids . . . we're gonna make it to that middle class.

The perceived improbability of moving into the middle class was a source of great frustration and hardship, but also a potential source of mobilization.

Despite deep skepticism about class mobility, even for those with postsecondary education, education was viewed as one of the few possible routes to upward mobility (Haskins, Holzer, & Lerman, 2009). Respondents we spoke with regarded education as a possible "door" out of poverty, if not for themselves then for their children, the next generation. Education was perceived as a source of power if not financial gain. Commenting on her hopes for her children and what community college meant to her, Michelle, a 24-year-old mother of two who identified as Filipina and Italian, stated:

> It takes . . . more than a generation to . . . upgrade your class. If we just go by the. . . working poor, middle class, and upper middle. . . . I will never make . . . middle class. So I realize . . . there is another way to go about this . . . that's why I'm getting education . . . because . . . as far as money goes, I'll be always working poor. So, in order to move out of that kind of . . . stigma, I chose education so . . . money couldn't really . . . define me.

With education perceived as the only viable pathway out of poverty, TANF policies that restrict access to education were seen as a yet another attack on the poor. As Jocelyn, a 43-year-old Chicana mother of one stated,

> They don't want to invest in education and training for women on welfare because they think we're too stupid to benefit from it because . . . we're poor. . . . They shut the doors to these opportunities for you, little by little by little. If you're on welfare the door is shut.

As a "work first" policy, TANF emphasizes paid employment over human capital development. Under TANF, adult single-parent recipients engaged in job training or education must work at least 20 hours per week (30 hours per week for two-parent families) in subsidized or unsubsidized employment or community service to count toward meeting a state's required work rates (Lower-Basch, 2008). Additionally, states have a built-in disincentive to discourage education in that they risk penalty if more than 30% of their caseloads meet work participation requirements via educational activities. These and other TANF regulations have introduced new demands to the already complex equation of balancing family and school, effectively discouraging TANF recipients from starting or completing degree programs. Since PRWORA's passage postsecondary enrollment of welfare recipients has dropped considerably (Price, 2005) and respondents, many of whom had personally experienced difficulty accessing education programs, were quick to see TANF as intentionally blocking access to education and advancement more generally.

Being advised to lower expectations, particularly by academic advisors and counselors, was described as further diminishing opportunities for upward mobility. Respondents recounted having their professional goals downgraded by those from whom they sought support and guidance. This undoubtedly compounded the sting of this advice. Describing this dynamic, Lena, a 26-year-old Black mother of one, explained, "Try to tell somebody that you want to be a lawyer and then hear 'I think you should just . . . be a cook . . . maybe a cosmetologist?' They do that all the time." Describing the systematic nature of this bias, Jocelyn, a 43-year-old Chicana mother of one, asserted:

> You're the third young Black mom I've met who wanted to be a lawyer, and all they [guidance counselors] did was tell each one of you, 'no' . . . It's remarkable . . . that anybody from . . . our kind of background can still have that kind of dream and then not have . . . the gatekeepers to those opportunities telling you from whatever their place lower your standards or. . . . 'Why don't you be a cheerleader?'

The negative impact of these messages, typically communicated by authority figures and often times by those with discretion to approve activities (e.g., caseworkers), should not to be underestimated.

Outrage concerning the deliberate barring of upward mobility was particularly strong when it came to their children's educational opportunities. In all four of the groups, discussion invariably turned to the lack of resources in their children's schools and the effects that underfunding in poor communities would have on their children's educational achievement. Expressing frustration with difficulties pursuing her own educational goals and with her child's school, Lena (26-year-old Black mother of one) said:

> So you're telling me now that I can't get educated you know, because I'm a single parent and I'm lazy and I just can't do anything right . . . . But now you're telling me since I'm here in the ghetto you're gonna give my son a bad school too so he can also fail in his future.

The shortcomings of public schools in low-income areas were consistently perceived as a systemic problem, an intentional attempt to train poor children to be poor, "docile" adults. Grace, a 30-year-old Filipina and mother of two, powerfully communicates this perspective:

> Our children are being taught to memorize answers instead of becoming critical thinkers and being leaders . . . they're being taught and trained to become followers . . . it's kinda like some of these schools are pre-prisons. And in certain states they have schools set up and in certain proportion, they say, 'Okay, well these are your test scores. We're going to have to invest more money in prisons' . . . If you score . . . low then the only future you have is to be a criminal. They're setting up prison cells for our children.

Respondents were quick to connect their children's inferior schools with reduced life chances and ultimately, the school-to-prison pipeline (Children's Defense Fund (CDF), 2007; Kim, Losen, & Hewitt, 2010). Neighborhood men with limited employment prospects other than participation in the secondary labor market embodied this dead-end route. Selling drugs, although certainly not condoned by the women we spoke with, was regarded as one of the few ways for poor men to put their skills to use and earn money. As Lena, a 26-year-old Black mother of one, described,

> Dealing drugs . . . it takes a lot of wits. . . . They're entrepreneurs, they're businessmen but they're sitting there in the ghetto and there's no other there's no way out, there's no resources, and you know that the intelligence level is there but that's as far as it's gonna go.

As with economic inequality, the prison industrial complex was seen not just as ensnaring poor people and people of color, but as benefiting the nonpoor.

These dynamics were aptly described by Jocelyn, a 43-year-old Chicana and mother of one:

> I know a lot of young fathers who are out there slingin' drugs every November . . . They'll all be hustling even more cause they wanna have Christmas money for their babies and I'm like, there is something wrong with the picture when young men have to go hustle drugs and face the possibility of life in prison, cause there's a multi-billion dollar industry designed to put them away for life. And there is no equivalent industry to help them realize their potential and get a real opportunity. Something's wrong with the damn picture.

The conviction and pervasiveness with which structural inequalities were invoked to explain "what is wrong with the picture" are consistent with research that identifies external attributions, the rejection of meritocracy, and the perceived impermeability of group boundaries as important to collective action (Kelly & Breinlinger, 1996; Taylor & McKirnan, 1984). Our informants' structural critique, although particularly pointed, is also largely consistent with previous research examining attributions for poverty and beliefs about inequality among less privileged groups (Bullock & Limbert, 2003; Feagin, 1975; Furnham, 2003; Kluegel & Smith, 1986). These beliefs provided an ideological foundation for collective action, and when coupled with institutional and interpersonal classism, an impetus for action.

Collective Responsibility for Fighting for Economic Injustice

The women we spoke with expressed a strong sense of collective responsibility for social change and obligation to other low-income women and their families. Although being personally "wronged" by the welfare system frequently precipitated action, individual mistreatment was seen as connected with the plight of other low-income people. The transition from advocating for oneself to advocating on behalf of others is revealed in Lisa's comments (26-year-old white mother of one):

> The ultimate . . . factor . . . that inspired my work. . .was being told that information I had researched and had in writing . . . was wrong . . . being told that I . . . couldn't get supportive benefits and . . . in addition . . . they were trying to make . . . me work . . . I couldn't believe that I had it in writing . . . their laws . . . and they [caseworkers] had no idea what it was . . . I think that ignorance is what's kept me going, and . . . now it's the people that I meet everyday . . . that are gonna get cut off next week and I don't know how they're gonna live . . . There's no programs to help them. I meet these people and their kids, they are moms that quit work so that they could watch their children because they've got to . . . They're trying so hard to do what is right and the county is not giving them child care . . . It's just things like this that, over and over again and now it's not even me, it's the people that I meet and I just can't believe the awful things that they're going through . . . I just want to help them.

Isabel, a 24-year-old Chicana and mother of two, recounted a similar story:

> I see my best friend sleeping in a car with a one month old baby . . . I know people that's prostituting and selling drugs just to make it, but they get blamed, and the whole thing about the blaming the victim, that's what made me say . . . I found a way to get ahead, but I'm not going to be satisfied until I can help others that want to do the same thing, have that opportunity, cause right now you know it's just not available. . . . Sometimes, I want to cry when I think about my people stuck where they are in the struggle . . . so I feel like it's my duty . . . it's my community, my children, other generations.

[handwritten margin note: power in Community]

This level of connection required that respondents realize that they weren't alone and that their situation was not unique. These were not, however, easy or immediate realizations. The stigma associated with poverty and welfare receipt not only contributes to social distancing by the nonpoor (Lott, 2002; Williams, 2009), it also functions to isolate recipients from each other, contributing to self-blame and devaluing of other recipients (Davis & Hagen, 1996; Goodban, 1985; Seccombe, 2011). As one respondent put it, "We're all so isolated. Because we have kids and we're stuck at home all the time. But everybody has such an amazing story of like how . . . they were treated like animals." Similarly, Isabel, a 24-year-old Chicana and mother of two, explained:

> A long time I suffered, I was like internally oppressed and you know I never thought I could do any better for myself and I just wanted to be isolated and deal with the people in my little community who understood what I was going through . . . I couldn't really face society with it, but now with [organization's name] they've empowered me to not be ashamed of, you know, my economic situation, where I come from.

Or, as Lena (26-year-old, Black mother of one) described:

> Being a student and being a welfare mother, for me, it has a lot of feelings of isolation . . . You just go through the motions but you're never really going to accomplish anything. And to be sitting in a room full of women that are talking about isolation and the feeling that they are not supported by society made *me* feel supported . . . I don't . . . get a lot of problems or anything with my worker but when I do, I can come here.

These comments underscore the importance of both practical and emotional support, suggesting that the communality and self-worth gained from sharing common experiences were as integral to political mobilization as learning to navigate welfare regulations. The transformative potential of these types of interactions are amply documented in analyses of the feminist movement and women's empowerment through consciousness raising groups (Keating, 2005).

The same core principles of feminist organizing – seeing the personal as political, realizing commonalities in women's lives, and deconstructing dominant power relations – are evident in welfare rights organizing and are illustrated in East's (2000) focus group study of active members of an antipoverty grassroots coalition. Her informants reported an increased sense of voice, greater control over their lives, commonality with other women, and a shared sense of responsibility. In echoing these same sentiments, our respondents provide further evidence of the importance of viewing individual experiences as connected to one's group and the relationship of group consciousness to collective action (Duncan, 1999).

Joining in solidarity with other TANF recipients involved more than learning about shared experiences. It also meant refusing to believe that "if you're receiving a handout, then you have to put up and shut up" (Eve, white mother of one). Luna (2009) and McCormack (2004, 2005) identify the rejection of pervasive classist beliefs as a form of critical resistance, and informants' flat rejection of the "welfare mother" stereotype is a conscious turning away from these beliefs and the formation of an identity that stands in opposition to them. Eve, a white mother of one, described the process this way:

> I started to internalize it [classist stereotypes] and then I got pissed off. That's when I decided to become, I guess, an activist, for myself. And then when I realized that it wasn't just me being affected and hiding it, it was . . . a whole lot of other people that I didn't even know. But I knew that if they knew that they were gonna be affected by . . . the welfare reform, they would get pissed off too. So in terms of the activism . . . I just kinda got this fire in me and ran with it and I've been running ever since.

Decrying classist beliefs allowed women to break from welfare stigma, identify with other recipients and their experiences, and mobilize on behalf of economic justice.

Ultimately, coming together fostered the development of a positive group identity or what Apfelbaum (1999) refers to as regrouping, a process of "positive revaluing" and rediscovery of "cultural roots and historical background" (p. 271). Stephanie, a 34-year-old multiracial mother of five, explains:

> Since I met the people at [organization's name] I have stayed involved with them because they have the same values as myself. And I didn't even think there was other people like me that even existed that had, you know, the same values and went through the same . . . crap. Pardon my language, but . . . it's really, really hard [sigh] to keep your spirits up, get an education, and escape poverty and raise your kids, do *everything*, and feel good about yourself . . . I spent many years feeling poorly about myself because I buy groceries with food stamps, and because I don't have . . . money to get nice things for my kids. And it's not because I'm lazy . . . and so I was really pleased with [this organization] because I got to meet a lot of people who . . . want to better themselves and we want to break those stereotypes. And

we want to . . . have good jobs and be educated, and there's a lot of bright people here. We're not stupid. We don't fit into the mold of the stereotype.

In turning away from pervasive stereotypes, respondents challenged dominant constructions of welfare recipients and in doing so not only embraced an alternative, positive understanding of their group, but also a platform for social change. Identified areas for action were far reaching, and included safe, affordable housing and child care, access to quality public education at all levels, tax reform, opening up the political system so that "regular" candidates can run for election not only millionaires, neighborhood investment, and the expansion of grassroots activism and "real" welfare reform (e.g., elimination of time limits and ending poverty instead of reducing welfare caseloads). Public education campaigns to reduce stereotyping of welfare recipients, and training caseworkers to be sensitive to racism were also discussed. Karen, an African American 36-year-old mother of two, offered a concise summary of her focus group's recommendations:

> [We] want equality whether it's in housing, which is my issue, education, jobs, money, all of those things and you know we want into that privileged class where all those things are available . . . we want to work and we want to stand before the people who do have that stuff and say, 'Hey, you know, we want that same thing too.' And, we may not get to the upper classes but we want enough to say this is what America was founded for . . . and we're gonna demand that from you.

In positioning a push for equality as contested and oppositional, Karen's statement reinforces the extent to which class relations were perceived as oppressive and connected with respondents' belief that access to resources are deliberately blocked. It also positions the positive, shared identity forged by respondents as an act of critical resistance intended to challenge interclass relations.

By no means did informants think the social change they sought would come quickly or easily but connecting current battles to other major social and political movements, most notably, the civil rights and feminist movements, brought strength and insight. As with other movements, massive uprising was viewed as essential:

Ignoring the issue ≠ solution

> People that are in power seem to think that if they pull all the resources away from people like us then we'll just disappear and shrivel off the face of the earth. . . . We're not going nowhere. We're still here. . . . They haven't gotten that concept yet, at all. . . . It's getting worse . . . and that's why I was saying earlier today about the civil rights thing. We're right back in the sixties . . . if there is not a movement across this nation, we are all gonna be screwed. [Olana, 34-year-old Asian/Pacific Islander and mother of three]

Janet, a white 35-year-old mother of one, also referenced the civil rights movement, pointing to the potential sacrifice and violence that accompanies upheaval, as well the power of large-scale mobilization:

The last time a big change happened was in the civil rights movement . . . and people suffered, people were killed, but . . . it took something that drastic to make a change. . . . We need to try and organize something big. . . . People that have been organizing for 50 years, people like me for three or four years . . . it all boils down to the same thing, it's gonna take something that strong like the civil rights movement to really make change . . . because it's that top five percent up there with all the money and the power . . . and, they don't give a shit.

Frequent calls for "revolution" were made in reference to the scope of needed structural change and the overturning of class hierarchies. Large-scale participation was seen as necessary for success, but also as offering protection against retribution by caseworkers and other authorities who might punish individual recipients for their involvement. Not surprisingly, fear of being "cut off" or "reported" was seen as a major deterrent to the political mobilization of many low-income women.

Associating welfare rights activism to other movements also provided an anchor for identification as an "activist" and collective responsibility for economic justice. This point is underscored by Jocelyn's (43-year-old Chicana and mother of one) remarks about being inspired by learning about other social change movements and her desire to learn from civil rights activists:

I sought out people that were activists and I sought to learn from them and then I started learning more, and learning more about more that was going on, and more kinds of oppressions . . . the more you learn about what's going on the truth – all over the world – the more I became resolved. I was like 'Gosh, you know, this whole world has so many ways . . . that we can make it better. If, we, just every one of us take a role, whatever role we feel moved to take at any time and, and work in that area to make things a little better, you know, a lot better'. . . . So, I'm doing everything I can . . . I spend every breath I have on all that.

With an extensive history of welfare rights activism, Jocelyn's identity was tied to being an activist. Activist identity is an important correlate of collective action (Kelly & Breinlinger, 1995) and our informants varied considerably in this respect, with respondents such as Jocelyn strongly identifying as an activist, and others only beginning to consider or embrace this identity. With ongoing political engagement, activist identity may form through the continued interaction of beliefs and actions via the fusion of "being" and "doing" (Kelly & Breinlinger, 1995, p. 54). A strong activist identification may be particularly important to sustaining engagement when prospects for meaningful change are limited (Kelly & Breinlinger, 1995). Given the depth of resistance to progressive welfare policies in the United States and the scope of necessary structural reform (Piven, 2001), the development of a strong activist identity may prove to be a crucial aspect of building a strong political movement.

Respondents were highly cognizant of the oppositional dynamics of social movements and the strategies used to discourage political mobilization. Describing these practices, Anita, a white 27-year-old mother of two, explained:

> This always happens along the way with every feminist movement. There's a backlash that's created and . . . all to try to push women back into the roles as unpaid labor, a class of unpaid labor who are raising the next generation of workers. . . . We're made to feel inadequate and . . . self-insufficient while we are trying to gain self-sufficiency. . . . As long as we are made to feel this way then we'll remain docile and we won't either have the time or energy or the self-esteem or the resources or the knowledge to be able to fight against what's happening . . . I think that what we need in order . . . to really change things is a real upheaval of the . . . institutional racism, the institutional discrimination against poor, against women, against people with disabilities. All of these things would have to change. . . . I think that . . . the feminist agenda from the seventies is still really valid!

Low benefit levels that enable little more than survival were also identified as dampening mobilization. In their seminal analysis of welfare policy as a means of social control, Piven and Cloward (1993) argue that welfare benefits are expanded to quiet protest and contracted to ensure the availability of a low-wage labor force. Karen, a 36-year-old African American mother of two, makes a related argument, and in doing so identifies a silver lining in the current attack on welfare recipients:

> Part of me wants them to cut all this stuff because people don't react until their survival is challenged. So, part of me is happy when they start cutting things [welfare benefits] even though it's my check they cuttin' too because I think that people will finally decide that it's worth reacting to, it's worth protesting. As long as they're a little bit comfortable and a little bit complacent, and they can actually survive somewhat on what they're doing, then they're gonna go ahead and . . . think, 'Oh, well, I got mine, so you get yours.' But, sometimes I, I hope for the worst so that we can, um, fight for the best.

Reese et al.'s (2005) four city analysis of mobilization against welfare privatization highlights the complex dynamics of threat-based mobilization. Greater threat was associated with wider participation, with more disruptive mobilization taking place when opportunities for political impact were perceived favorably (Reese et al., 2005). For organizers, the lessons from these findings are twofold – the potential of current attacks on the welfare system and other safety net programs to mobilize a strong base and the importance of developing strategies that build on political openings. In this respect, local and regional mobilization efforts that can build a record of "small wins" may be especially powerful agents of change (Lott & Webster, 2006).

With their sights set on meaningful social change, even "revolution," our respondents were united by a shared sense of responsibility for each other and for economic justice. By rejecting classist stereotypes and seeing commonalities among their experiences, women moved from isolation and individual action to a commitment to working on behalf of the hardships facing other poor women. Shared responsibility in many respects appeared to serve as the much needed "glue" to move from individual to collective action.

Economic Justice for Poor Women

One of our discussants noted that any economic revolution must begin with the poor and working classes, and our findings provide valuable insight into some of the beliefs and experiences that contribute to welfare rights activism. Class-based discrimination was radicalizing and pivotal to respondents' initial decisions to seek assistance from a welfare rights organization; however, a network of structural beliefs about inequality and class relations were also central. It is difficult if not impossible to disentangle or sequentially organize correlates of collective action in our respondents' lives, and we see all of the factors discussed in this chapter, individually and in concert with each other, as facilitating welfare rights activism. Consistent with Taylor and McKirnan's (1984) framework, respondents perceived personal discrimination as consistent with the extent to which their group is discriminated against, rejected individualistic beliefs and meritocratic ideology, endorsed structural attributions for poverty and wealth, and perceived class boundaries as impermeable.

A truly formidable economic justice movement – one that can win the battle for self-sufficiency wages, safe workplaces, universal health care, a humane welfare system, and quality education and child care for all – will ultimately require the participation of people across the economic spectrum, including middle-class professionals who are employees and supervisors in institutions that reinforce class-based hierarchies, elites with the power and resources to shape social policy, and working-class groups who compete with the poor for scarce resources. Completing this chapter in the midst of the occupy movement (Occupy Together, n.d.), we grew increasingly hopeful in the possibility of large-scale, cross-class mobilization on behalf of economic justice. With the income and wealth gap rising to levels not seen since the 1920s (Sherman & Stone, 2010), this national movement seeks to unify the bottom 99% of the population around rising inequality and policies that benefit elites at the expense of all other groups. While the top 1% of the population has prospered exponentially, the poor and working and middle classes have suffered declining wages, cuts to public schools, reduced access to higher education and ballooning student loan debt, skyrocketing health-care costs, rising poverty and economic insecurity, and chronic underemployment and unemployment. It seems we have reached a "tipping" point in terms of what we as a society are willing to tolerate in terms of inequality, with meritocracy and the fate of the American dream being questioned deeply, broadly, and publicly. Whether the occupy movement is able to generate meaningful change remains an open question but we regard these protests as indicative of a powerful and growing concern in policies, institutions, and governments that are skewed toward economic elites and a desire for structural change. As we learned from our discussants, nothing less than their survival is at stake.

Acknowledgments

We wish to thank the courageous and insightful women who shared their experiences with us. They are working to create a better world for all women. We are grateful to Shakila Flentroy, Carolina Garcia, Laura Phillips, Harmony Reppond, Isela Reza, and Tania Texidor for their assistance with transcription.

6

Women and Economic Justice: Pitfalls, Possibilities, and Promise

The devastating consequences of poverty on women's life chances are amply documented throughout this book and in a vast body of social science literature (Arangua, Andersen, & Gelberg, 2005; Belle & Doucet, 2003; Goldberg, 2010). Class disadvantage cumulates and grows over time, magnifying inequalities in health, income, wealth, cognitive development, and career opportunities (DiPrete & Eirich, 2006). The hardships associated with poverty are not invisible to the nonpoor. In Reutter and her colleagues (2005) study of Canadians' lay understandings of poverty, poor health, difficulty securing housing and obtaining healthy food, and reduced community participation were perceived as likely outcomes of poverty. That such avoidable suffering is not acted on swiftly, comprehensively, and definitively speaks to the insidiousness of classism and its intersections with other "isms" in legitimizing inequality and promoting economic injustice.

Our lack of action is not caused by a shortage of viable solutions. For instance, the Center for American Progress Task Force on Poverty (2007) called for the establishment of a national goal for cutting US poverty in half over a 10-year period and outlined a concrete plan for doing so. Their 12-step strategy includes imminently doable policy initiatives proven to effectively combat poverty: raising and indexing the minimum wage to half the average hourly wage ($8.40 an hour in 2006); expanding the Earned Income Tax Credit (EITC) and Child Tax Credit; encouraging unionization; guaranteeing childcare assistance to low-income families and encouraging early education; increasing the number of available housing vouchers and supporting equitable development; connecting disadvantaged youth with school and employment; simplifying and expanding Pell grants and making public higher education accessible to all low-income students; updating safety net programs to provide a decent standard of living; helping formerly incarcerated people reintegrate and secure stable employment; ensuring equity for low-wage workers in the unemployment insurance system; and expanding opportunities for saving for education, homeownership, and retirement

Women and Poverty: Psychology, Public Policy, and Social Justice, First Edition. Heather E. Bullock.
© 2013 Heather E. Bullock. Published 2013 by John Wiley and Sons, Ltd.

(Center for American Progress Task Force on Poverty, 2007). Estimated to cost $90 billion annually, just 0.8% of the gross national product, this amount would be easily paid for by recouping the revenue lost from the Bush administration's tax cuts for the wealthy (Center for American Progress Task Force on Poverty, 2007). Unfortunately, austerity rather than these human capital investments have guided recent policy decisions. However, it would be a mistake to see this stinginess as a new trend. Spending on social programs as a percentage of the gross domestic product (GDP) has long been far lower in the United States than in other OECD countries, including those in Scandinavia, Northern Continental Europe, Central and Southern Europe, and so-called "Anglo" countries such as Canada and the United Kingdom (Martin & Caminada, 2011). Meanwhile, the "cost" paid daily by poor women and their families for not adopting such policies is incalculable, and the price of inequality is one we all pay in terms of reduced cohesiveness, trust, and well-being (Wilkinson & Pickett, 2009).

Social science research holds a pivotal role in advancing an economic justice agenda, whether via documenting the causes, correlates, and consequences of poverty and economic disparities, illuminating the factors that contribute to class disadvantage and privilege among diverse social groups, deconstructing the attitudes and beliefs that fuel understandings of class status, economic inequality, and policy support, revealing the impact of political and popular discourse, designing and testing the effectiveness of interventions, programs, and social policies intended to reduce poverty, and ultimately, informing policymakers, advocates, and other key players who can bring sound solutions to the fore.

In this final chapter, I draw on insights from policy studies, feminist and critical theory, and social psychological research to explore why we as a society continue to put women and their children last and how these patterns can be reversed. Attitudinal and institutional barriers to the formation of a more economically just society are considered along with areas of possibility and promise. Special emphasis is placed on strategies for reframing poverty discourse, challenging classist beliefs, practices, and policies, and potential roles for social psychologists and justice-oriented researchers in these efforts. In doing so, I build on the ideas presented throughout this book to focus broadly on areas in which macro- and micro-level social and cultural transformation is needed, attending closely to institutional, intergroup, and individual change.

Reordering Our Values: Re-Visioning Democracy and Social Policy

Economic Justice and Feminist Values

Economic justice in its broadest sense demands an end to poverty and calls for the just distribution of resources (e.g., income, wealth, power, and access to valued resources such as education, health care, and housing). Economic justice can be conceptualized as incorporating three central principles: participation (e.g., engagement in economic systems via work and other activities that are characterized by equal opportunity and freedom from discrimination), distribution (e.g., just wages, prices, and profits), and restraint (e.g., restrictions to prevent individuals or groups from gaining an unfair advantage over others; Center for Economic and Social Justice, cited in Mason, 2012).

Economic justice figures prominently in progressive feminists' call for a new US democracy that:

> embodies consideration for humanity and cooperative models of public life. This new democracy . . . will more energetically seek to include all voices in public life by promoting innovative, promising strategies for building power together. . . . It will connect people with political leaders by creating more responsive, ongoing channels for communication and by seriously addressing the power of money in political processes. . . . It will value the dignity of all human beings, regardless of race, ethnicity, class, culture, religion, sexuality, or age. And it will more actively support families of all types by helping individuals build healthy relationships in conditions of physical and economic security. (Caiazza, Hess, Clevenger, & Carlberg, 2008, p. 3)

These recommendations are not only guided by recognition of the need for a new more participatory government, but also new understandings of community and relational power (Collins, 2010). The shared responsibility for economic justice articulated by politically mobilized former and current welfare recipients (see Chapter 5) offers insight into the embodiment of these goals.

It is difficult, if not impossible, to envision significant institutional or interpersonal change without a reordering of dominant US ideology to emphasize shared over personal responsibility, and community over individual "success." Deeply entrenched beliefs in meritocracy, individualism, and the Protestant work legitimize class position, fueling the perception that social class is earned rather than ascribed, and that individuals are responsible for their place in the class hierarchy (Hochschild, 1995; Weber, 1998; see also Chapter 3). The problematic nature of these belief are implicated in research documenting their role in classist scapegoating of the poor, dominant attributions for poverty and wealth, and support for policies that heap further rewards on the rich and punish the poor (e.g., restrictive welfare policies such as sanctions and work requirements, limited funding and accessibility of safety net programs; Bensonsmith, 2005; Bullock & Fernald, 2005; Bullock, Williams, & Limbert, 2003; Henry, Renya, & Weiner, 2004; Kluegel & Smith, 1986; Smith, Allen, & Bowen, 2010).

Activists have much to offer in terms of identifying values necessary to guide such a major transformation. In interviews with 120 women activists working with national or grassroots organizations, seven interrelated values or principles emerged as pivotal to democracy and social change (Caiazza et al., 2008). These same values are central to overturning dominant beliefs and discourse that associate poverty with individual failure and dependence, and building support for progressive antipoverty policies:

- Community (e.g., gathering places in which people can come together to define and pursue a common good)
- Family (e.g., connection, care, and support)
- Equality (e.g., recognition of class, gender, race, and all forms of injustice in public and private life; the space to exercise authority over one's life)
- Power that is shared and responsive to diverse voices
- Compassion for others that motivates the elimination of injustice
- Balance (e.g., negotiation of complex demands, need, and spheres)
- Practice (i.e., acting on values); (Caizza et al., 2008).

Unifying these values is a sense of a common good and shared responsibility that has long been central to feminist critiques of the US welfare system and the ideology of individualism more generally. Hartmann, Hegewisch, and Lovell (2007, p. 6) articulate this perspective in their observation that:

Societies not only *can* produce the quality of life people want, but they have a *responsibility* to do so. A progressive vision of our future must be one that places caring at its center. . . . These values come primarily but not exclusively from women because it is women who have done the majority of care giving and relationship building in our communities.

In concrete terms, building an economy that prioritizes women and their families would mandate a wide range of policy changes, including increasing workplace flexibility to increase alignment between family and work responsibilities (e.g., requiring paid sick days, expanding the Family and Medical Leave Act; reducing the standard 40-hour work week; eliminating wage and benefit penalties associated with reduced-hour jobs; and reducing discrimination in the workplace against caregivers); paid leave for caregiving to ensure income continuity (e.g., providing income through social insurance programs and establishing state-based paid family care leave); and subsidized child and elder care (e.g., establishing universal early care and education programs and long- and short-term elder care). Family policy is antipoverty policy (Hartmann et al., 2007).

Of course, reducing women's poverty requires many other social and economic policies, including the promotion of full employment in jobs that pay self-sufficiency wages, a strong welfare system that provides and allows families to get back on their feet rather than punishing women and their children, attention to race, gender, and class discrimination, universal access to high-quality health care and education, and progressive tax policies that protect low-wage workers and require the wealthy to pay their fair share (Eamon, Wu, & Zhang, 2009; Edelman, 2012; Gans, 2011; Romich, Simmelink, & Holt, 2007; Yoshikawa, Aber, & Beardslee, 2012). Advancing these policies and garnering widespread support is unlikely without national scrutiny of individualism, a conscious rejection of strictly merit-based interpretations of class status and need, and a willingness to adopt a poverty measure that accurately assesses the prevalence of poverty and economic hardship (see Chapter 1 for a comprehensive discussion of poverty measurement).

The bottom line is a justice-focused approach to women's poverty, and economic inequality requires more than viewing poverty as a structural issue, it also means implementing structural solutions. Rank, Yoon, and Hirschl's (2003) musical chair analogy in which there are more players than seats vividly illustrates this point. Even with improved skill, some players must inevitably "lose" unless more seats are added. If "infrastructure" is unmodified, the "game" will remain unchanged.

Fighting for Economic Justice in a "Winner-Take-All-Society"

The values and policy initiatives by feminist and progressive scholars and advocates diverge dramatically from the individualism and the "winner-take-all-economy" that dominates the United States both in practice and ideology (Tropman, 1998; Twill & Buckheister, 2009). Poverty is a central, and many would say necessary, facet of capitalism and a "money maker" for economic elites. Predatory lending practices ensure that the poor pay more for basic goods such as cars, and also that they pay enormous fees on services such as home rental furniture, in some instances with annual interest rates equaling 520% (Duke-Lucio, Peck, & Segal, 2010; Karger, 2003). Major retailers like Walmart could raise wages without making a dent in their enormous profits. If Walmart paid a minimum hourly wage of $12.00, 41.4% of the pay increase would go to workers in families with incomes below 200% of the poverty line, with these workers earning an additional $1,670 to $6,500 annually (Jacobs, Graham-Squire, & Luce, 2011). Even if the full cost were passed on to consumers, the average impact on Walmart shoppers would be an additional annual expense of $12.49 (Jacobs et al., 2011). These figures reveal how easily wages could be increased if there was the will to do so. The lack of sustained political pressure to address corporate greed and stagnant wages among all but the very top of the economic spectrum is indicative of our ambivalence toward equality and government interference with the "market" (Hochschild, 2006; McCall & Kenworthy, 2009).

The destitution and stigma of welfare receipt ensure that businesses and corporations have a pool of expendable laborers who will work for low wages rather than seek assistance (Piven & Cloward, 1993). As Schram, Soss, Houser, and Fording (2010, p. 739) aptly observe:

> the degrading conditions and stigma associated with welfare have never been incidental to the purposes of public aid; they have an object lesson, instructing low-income populations that even the meanest wages and work conditions are better than the shameful status of the 'welfare poor.'

And, "welfare reform" has brought new opportunities for profiteering. The privatization of welfare has meant lucrative contracts for corporate "service providers" in spite of complaints of racial and gender discrimination against the poor women they are charged with serving (Berkowitz, 2001; Brophy-Baermann & Bloeser, 2006). Davis and Craven (2011, p. 192) see privatization and other aspects of welfare reform as the inevitable shifting of neoliberal governments, such as the United States, away from "assuring social, political, and economic rights" and an overreliance on "market-based patterns of consumption to resolve social inequities and principles that perpetuate fictions of equitable citizenry."

The full impact of market values on welfare policy is laid bare in Schram and his colleagues (2010) analysis of welfare reform and the "new paternalism." They argue that over the past two decades, welfare programs have become more aggressive in their use of surveillance and penalties and more overtly aligned with the interests and needs of business. They explain, "Under neoliberalism, market roles have been elevated as the most essential civic roles. . . . Welfare programs have been restructured to operate according to market logistics, to cultivate market rationalities in service providers and aid recipients, and to serve . . . local markets" (Schram et al., 2010, p. 740–741). The "real-world" application of this perspective is evident in the design of Florida's welfare-to-work program to ensure that "businesses can hire the well-trained workers they need" (Schram et al., 2010, p. 740). Such descriptions make clear that poverty alleviation and family well being take a back seat to business needs. This conclusion is bolstered by evaluations of welfare "reform" that tell a story of biased and capricious application of regulations, and increased hardship for women and their families (Chapter 4; Lens, 2006, 2008, 2009).

These same priorities undergird the failure of the United States to ratify the International Covenant on Economic, Social and Cultural Rights (ICESCR), which includes basic economic rights, such as the right to housing, food, education, health care, and a job offering a living wage (Twill & Buckheister, 2009). Consequently, there is no national requirement in the United States to assist the poor and although not formally recognized as such, economic human rights violations are widespread. In Twill and Buckheister's (2009) study of 57 low-income women and men living in Ohio, participants reported experiencing 301 economic human rights violations in the 30 days prior to being interviewed and 635 violations over their lifetimes. The most common violations were related to food insecurity (e.g., missed meals), housing insecurity (e.g., being homeless), and access to social services (e.g., denied assistance). Such violations occur daily, largely undocumented or unrecognized by broader society as problematic. Groups such as the Kensington Welfare Rights Union, the Women's Economic Agenda Project, and the Poor People's Economic Human Rights Campaign have organized bus tours, rallies, major convenings, and educational initiatives to raise awareness of poverty as a human rights violation and build a movement to end poverty, but the goals of these efforts have yet to be fully realized.

How far we are from accepting economic human rights in the United States is revealed in Republican presidential candidate Mitt Romney's remarks at a private $50,000 a plate fundraiser in which he told a small group of wealthy contributors that many voters would support President Barack Obama because:

> There are 47 percent of the people who will vote for the president no matter what . . . there are 47 percent who are with him, who are dependent upon government, who believe that they are victims, who believe the government has a responsibility to care for them, who believe that they are entitled to health care, to food, to housing, to you-name-it . . . that's an entitlement. And the government should give it to them. And they will vote for this president no matter what. . . . These are people who pay no income tax . . . [M]y job is not to worry about those people. I'll never convince them they should take personal responsibility and care for their lives. (Romney cited in Corn, 2012, para. 2, 3)

This characterization of "nontaxpayers" as dependent "takers" is likely intended to activate classist, racist, and sexist stereotypes of "welfare cheats," African Americans, and other groups perceived as falsifying their needs or claiming "discrimination," "victimhood," or "entitlement" to evade economic responsibility (Bensonsmith, 2005; Gilens, 1999; Seccombe, 2011). However, these images of "nontaxpayers" do not coincide with reality. In 2011, most households that did not pay federal income taxes, paid payroll taxes and of the 18.1% of households that paid neither type of tax, more than half were elderly and those who were not elderly had very low incomes – under $20,000 (Shear & Barbaro, 2012).

Elite discourse, even if overtly biased and grossly inaccurate, may still powerfully impact public opinion. This is certainly the case with welfare policy. Schneider and Jacoby (2005) analyzed National Election Studies data spanning from 1992 to 1996, a time period during which welfare reform initiatives were hotly contested by policymakers and received extensive mainstream media coverage. They found that among highly informed respondents changes in attitudes toward welfare policy and spending corresponded with liberal-conservative ideology, meaning movement that occurred was consistent with elite political discourse, whereas among uninformed respondents opinions were driven by political identification and evaluations of people on welfare. Schneider and Jacoby (2005) see these findings as indicative of the sway that political elites have on public opinion, particularly among well-informed media users. For antipoverty advocates, such findings further confirm why a new progressive discourse surrounding women's poverty must be forged among elites and the dangers inherent in failing to do so (Limbert & Bullock, 2009). In the years immediately preceeding PWRORA's passage, the height of news coverage of surrounding welfare reform, liberals allowed conservatives to define the terms of the debate. In Lens's (2003) content analysis of expert discourse in *The New York Times*, one-third of comments made by liberal experts emphasized structural obstacles to economic security, but only 16% included strategies for improving financial security, and even these suggestions were within the parameters established by conservatives (e.g., recommending education and training opportunities within the context of mandatory work requirements).

Changing the Focus: Reframing Poverty Discourse

A major critique of progressive poverty advocates and scholars is the failure to develop and promote a counter-narrative that can seize the stronghold of conservative constructions of poverty as an individual failing or aberration of mainstream values and goals. Classist, sexist, and racist narratives of poverty, welfare, and inequality are our dominant narratives, and their potency is derived, at least in part, by tapping into meritocracy and individualism (see Chapters 3 and 4). Racial codewords such as "welfare" activate deep biases against poor women, especially women of color, and their perceived violation of "family values" and the fundamental US tenet that hard work pays off (Gilens, 1999; Henry et al., 2004; Neubeck & Cazenave, 2001). Putting feminist values at the forefront of public discourse on women's poverty is crucial to developing strong counter-narratives of poverty, wealth, and inequality. Effective counter-narratives must also support structural understandings of poverty that situate both cause and responsibility within institutions. The liberatory potential of these counter-narratives is evident in the focus groups findings reported in Chapter 5 of this book.

As one possible strategy for reframing poverty, Cassiman (2007) proposes countering mainstream constructions of the "welfare queen" and welfare dependency with a trauma model that conceptualizes poverty as a form of economic/ structural violence. However, as Cassiman (2007) observes such an approach is not without its limitations. If trauma and its connection to poverty are not thoroughly politicized, a "medicalized" view of poverty may inadvertently take hold, reinforcing well-worn beliefs that poor people rather than our society are damaged and need to be "cured."

A more dramatic reframing calls for moving from a poverty-focused paradigm to an asset-based focus. Assets refer to "resources used to promote family mobility and well-being," including "savings, education, good health, home ownership, and the connections people have to each other as pathways or networks to other resources and mutual support" (Institute on Assets and Social Policy (IASP), n.d., para. 2). This broader approach reveals high rates of economic insecurity that should be difficult to dismiss as personal failing. Shapiro, Oliver, and Meschede (2009) estimate that 42% of all working age households in the United States are asset insecure, meaning that they would be unable to pay for 75% of essential household expenses for 3 months if unemployed, even if one family member collected unemployment benefits; 54% of households are estimated to lack sufficient financial assets to invest in opportunities for mobility (e.g., buying a home, starting a new business, and supporting children's education), with only one in five families of color able to do so.

Shifting from what it takes for a family to "thrive" rather than barely "survive," an asset-based approach moves from narrowly focusing on safety net programs to considering a wide range of supportive, interconnected policies, programs, and institutions that foster individual and community well-being and financial stability across the lifespan. The IASP's (2006) "asset opportunity ladder" organizes asset-building policies into a comprehensive matrix spanning the life course. In early childhood, high-quality childcare and the Women, Infants, and Children (WIC) program, which provides supplemental food and healthcare referrals to low-income mothers and children up to age 5, establish a foundation upon which to build assets; programs such as Head Start and the State Children's Health Insurance Program (SCHIP), which provides health insurance coverage to low-income children, strengthen human capacities; and matched savings accounts from birth onward promote financial wealth (IASP, 2006). Of course, these programs not only benefit low-income children, they benefit families too, and ultimately communities by ensuring a solid start in life. In young adulthood, asset development can be fostered by indexing the minimum wage to inflation and eliminating state income tax for low-income earners; human capacities can be strengthened via GED and certificate programs, English as a second language classes, and on-the-job training; and financial security can be encouraged by Youth Individual Development Accounts (IDA), savings accounts that match deposits made by low- and moderate-income savers for specific purposes, such as postsecondary education or homeownership (IASP, 2006). For parents, transportation and childcare subsidies, paid family leave, and dependent care tax credits help provide essential support that makes it possible to work outside the home and raise a family (IASP, 2006).

Viewed through this lens, supporting families is not just about the need for strong cash aid and nutritional programs to protect against crisis but also programs that build human capital and real financial security. Doing so expands the scope of needed policies beyond expanded access to safe affordable housing through Section 8 and other housing programs to also supporting homeownership through refundable mortgage interest tax deduction, refundable first-time homeowner's tax credit, mortgage assistance programs, and matched savings and other incentive programs (IASP, 2006). Shifting from poverty alleviation to an asset-building framework introduces new questions: How can women's long-term economic security be fostered? What programs and policies promote low-income women's upward mobility? What kinds of synergies exist among individual and community asset building initiatives?

Social science research on framing focuses less on macro-level transformations of dominant attitudes and values and more on micro-level strategies for challenging dominant perceptions and understandings of poverty and welfare policy. Not surprisingly, perceived responsibility for creating and responding to poverty is influenced by how poverty is framed or described. In Iyengar's (1991) seminal work on media framing, viewers who watched episodic stories about poverty (i.e., programming focused on a poor individual or family) were more likely than viewers of thematic stories (i.e., programming focused on societal trends) to attribute poverty to individual characteristics and to perceive the poor as responsible for improving their economic status. Conversely, thematic viewers made more structural attributions for poverty and tended to perceive the government as responsible for the plight of the poor.

Frames have a powerful effect on attitudes and beliefs, in and of themselves, but also through their interactions with pre-existing beliefs. This point is illustrated by Shen and Edwards' (2005) study of the impact of values (i.e., economic individualism and humanitarianism) and framing on support for welfare reform. Respondents read a newspaper article that portrayed welfare reform in terms of recipient need and hardship with the headline "Tougher Welfare Restrictions Said to Hurt the Poor and Children" or strict work requirements and personal responsibility with the headline "Welfare Reform Must Require Strict Work Requirements." Significant effects were found for both participants' values and the frames. Strongly individualistic respondents exposed to the strict work requirement frame generated more frame-relevant thoughts and expressed stronger support for restrictive welfare requirements than respondents low in economic individualism (Shen & Edwards, 2005). The same general pattern held true for respondents who scored high in humanitarianism and were exposed to the public aid frame. These respondents expressed greater support for increasing public aid than those with low humanitarianism scores; however, they did not generate a significantly greater number of frame-relevant thoughts leading the researchers to conclude that individualism had a greater impact on responses than humanitarianism (Shen & Edwards, 2005). They posit that as a fundamental dimension of US ideology, individualism may be a more potent, salient device in the framing of welfare reform (Shen & Edwards, 2005).

Indeed, media analyses encourage individualistic conceptualizations by over-representing individualistic constructions of poverty and wealth. An extensive body of research confirms that mainstream media in the United States, whether entertainment, reality, or news programming, portrays poverty and wealth in predominantly individualistic rather than structural terms (see Bullock, Wyche, & Williams, 2001; Kendall, 2011; Limbert & Bullock, 2009). Similar findings are documented in other industrialized nations with high rates of poverty and inequality. In Redden's (2011) analysis of news coverage in Canada and the United Kingdom, rationalizing and individualizing frames dominated news coverage of poverty and immigration. Rationalizing frames were frequently used in news stories in which "the poor" were portrayed as "deserving" and in coverage of immigrants centered on economic costs and benefits. Individualizing frames dominated coverage in which blame or responsibility was ascribed, or when the focus was on politics (Redden, 2011). Social justice frames, on the other hand, were largely absent from mainstream coverage, as were analyses of the role of capitalism and current economic systems in creating poverty. Discussing the system justifying functions of dominant frames, Redden (2011, p. 838) explains,

> news articles bit by bit reinforce market values by reinforcing market-based processes of evaluation and schema of thought by privileging individualizing and rationalizing frames in the representations of poverty and i mmigration. In this way, neoliberal rationality becomes a part of culture and gets embedded in daily life . . . market-based approaches to issues become 'normal' and 'rational'.

In this way, mainstream media plays a central role in reinforcing and perpetuating individual responsibility for poverty.

The media is not a "level" playing field, and the fight to reframe poverty and wealth as structural problems that require structural solutions is a difficult battle. The concentration of media ownership in the hands of just a few giant corporations ensures that "news" serves the interests of economic and political elites, not democracy (Baker, 2007). One consequence is low salience and lack of public knowledge of social and economic policy, particularly of policies benefitting the wealthy. Campbell (2010), for instance, notes that US residents tend not to see the connection between taxes and economic redistribution – a linkage that contributes to the rising fortunes of the top 1%. Campbell (2010) identifies the "informational advantage of the rich" (p. 230) as a key factor, observing that the top 1% are not only well organized with strong lobbies working on their behalf, but also that tax and regulatory policies are governed by complex rules that are difficult to understand (see also Hacker & Pierson, 2010). Welfare and safety net policies are not well understood by the public either. This is evident in claims that "welfare recipients should be required to work for their benefits" when work requirements have been the norm since PRWORA's adoption. These "gaps" in knowledge are not benign; they are crucial to legitimizing the status quo and ensuring that the rich prosper and the poor stay poor.

It is important that research findings on effective framing strategies are shared with policymakers and community leaders, and that these techniques are used to develop persuasive antipoverty campaigns, increase support for progressive policies, and a nurture a politically mobilized public. Building effective counternarratives will require committed efforts on multiple levels (e.g., nationally, state-wide, and regionally) and across spheres of influence (e.g., via mainstream and alternative communication outlets; across policy, programs, and public education initiatives). Organizations such as the FrameWorks Institute, which seeks to "advance the nonprofit sector's communications capacity by identifying, translating and modeling relevant scholarly research for framing the public discourse about social problems" (FrameWorks Institute, n.d., para. 1), offer tremendous insight into "best practices" for framing issues of relevance to low income women and their families.

Promoting Economic Justice: The Need for a Class-Conscious Psychology

Psychology has much to contribute to developing effective strategies for reframing dominant discourse, challenging classist stereotypes, understanding and reducing women's poverty, and ultimately, promoting an economic justice agenda. These activities are aligned with the mission of the American Psychological Association (APA) "to advance the creation, communication and application of psychological knowledge to benefit society and *improve people's lives*" [italics added] (APA, n.d., para. 2). Yet with respect to poverty, psychologists have yet to fully embrace or act on these objectives. As the first two chapters of this book make clear, it is not for lack of evidence regarding the prevalence or impact of economic hardship.

Although progress is being made, most notably APA's (2000) adoption of a Resolution on Poverty and Socioeconomic Status (SES; APA Task Force on Socioeconomic Status, 2007) and the creation of a permanent office and committee on SES housed within APA's Public Interest Directorate (APA Task Force on Socioeconomic Status, 2007), Reid's (1993) claim 20 years ago that poor women are "shut out" of mainstream psychological research remains true (Eagly, Eaton, Rose, Riger, & McHugh, 2012; Lott & Bullock, 2007; Reid, 2011; Reimers, 2007; Saris & Johnston-Robledo, 2000). Poverty has been a core focus of the Society for the Psychological Study of Social Issues (SPSSI) since its establishment during the Great Depression, but attention has waned when other social and economic issues have moved to the foreground (Bullock, Lott, & Truong, 2011).

The general neglect of poverty in psychological literature has been attributed to a wide range of factors, including the misperception that poverty is more closely aligned with the field of sociology than psychology, an overreliance on middle-class undergraduate participants in psychological research, a lack of attention to social context, and classist bias (see Lott, 2002; Lott & Bullock, 2007; Reid, 1993; Smith, 2005, 2010). Psychologists' own privileged socioeconomic status (e.g., highly educated and financially secure) may contribute to distancing from the poor (Lott, 2002). Moreover, the individualism and belief in meritocracy that biases broader thinking about the poor is similarly embedded in the discipline itself and manifested in psychological research (e.g., questions asked, methodologies employed, and interpretations made), teaching, practice, and advocacy (APA Task Force on Socioeconomic Status, 2007; Lott & Bullock, 2007; Smith, 2010). Moreover, we are not immune to the individualism and belief in meritocracy that pervades US society (see Chapter 3). We cannot criticize broader societal values and beliefs without seeing our profession and ourselves as embedded within these same social and cultural frameworks, and perhaps also benefitting from them.

To promote the major transformations that true poverty reduction will require, psychology must undergo the same type of "reordering" and "reframing" that feminist and critical scholars have called for in broader society. As feminist psychologists have long noted, putting women and their needs first means asking different questions and critically analyzing dominant paradigms. For instance, the normative approach in much of the welfare reform literature is to evaluate whether recipients meet program goals but doing so tacitly accepts the tenets of work-first policies and leaves the primacy of work, regardless of its quality, or effects on families and economic security, largely unquestioned (see Chapter 3; Limbert & Bullock, 2005; Steinitz & Mishler, 2001).

 This point is further illustrated by considering the implicit assumption that adolescent or "early" parenting is inherently bad. Breheny and Stephens' (2010) analysis of articles published in healthcare journals documents the prevalence of this perspective. Early motherhood was portrayed as a disease requiring surveillance ("a public health discourse"), as a financial drain on society and to mothers themselves ("an economic discourse"), as resulting from resistance to contraceptives by girls of color ("an ethnicity discourse"), and as a biological problem of the least fit and desirable women reproducing ("a eugenics discourse"). These same frames guide research and advocacy:

> Traditional debates surrounding adolescent pregnancy prevention have focused on the means to the end: Do we promote abstinence-based strategies or teach contraceptive use? What role should parents play and what role should schools play? How can we make messaging more salient to different racial and ethnic groups? Each of these dilemmas examines *how* teen pregnancy is best prevented, without questioning the *why*. In policy and advocacy discourses, why is somehow understood. (Sisson, 2012, p. 57)

This constricted perspective neglects the role of structural inequities in shaping women's lives and consideration of how services and programs could be expanded and strengthened to improve life chances (Sisson, 2012). Also, shortchanged is the reality that regardless of age, childbearing may bring more rewards than challenges, that early parenting may be a rational, fulfilling choice, and that young parents may be far more capable of meeting these challenges than dominant middle-class constructions allow for (Sisson, 2012).

In shifting our focus to encompass these possibilities, we act on "the power of social scientists to interrupt dominant conceptions of social policy, to reframe social problems, and to introduce data typically withheld from popular view" (Fine & Barreras, 2001, p. 177). This redirected focus calls for a vision of reproductive health that not only challenges inequities that contribute to disparate class and race-based outcomes related to motherhood, but also opens educational and employment pathways to allow *all* low-income girls and women to pursue a full range of options (Alzate, 2009). It also brings to the forefront a range of much-needed policy initiatives, including major investments in all levels of public education, job training, and safe, affordable child care.

Classist assumptions and biases blind us to alternative narratives and frames, and it is not simply a matter of the research questions we ask (or do not ask), but also the conclusions we reach. A recent example comes from Kraus' (2012) discussion of differences between the rich and poor. Noting that more affluent, educated groups tend to have more choices across the lifespan than low income, less educated groups, Kraus (2012, para. 5) surmises:

> For these individuals, fewer resources means that there are fewer choices in life (fewer choices at meals, fewer toys to choose from, fewer future job opportunities, fewer choices of neighborhoods to live in, etc.). This early environment increases the likelihood that choices are less valued and important to relatively lower-class individuals. Instead, these individuals would rather blend in than make unique choices to set them apart from others.

Kraus makes the leap from structured inequality and material deprivation to imputing a personal devaluation of choice (a put down in individualistic societies) based on a series of experiments by Stephens, Fryberg, and Markus (2011) and Stephens, Markus, and Townsend (2007) in which respondents from different social classes made choices in the lab. In one study, high school-educated participants selected a pen that looked similar to other pens while their college-educated counterparts chose a pen that stood out from others; in another study, working-class participants reported being pleased by making the same choices as a friend (e.g., buying the same car), while masters' students were irritated by this; and in yet another examination, participants with a high school education were glad to be given a pen as a gift, while college-educated participants wanted to choose their own pen (Stephens et al., 2007, 2011). In focusing on the seeming working-class preference for fitting in, a response that may be a more a matter of politeness, an expression of gratitude, and/or a desire to present oneself positively in an unfamiliar situation, larger issues related to class entitlement and privilege demonstrated by middle-class respondents are overlooked. This same bias leads to the problematizing of poverty, while wealth and inequality remain unscrutinized.

A significant reframing of dominant discourse around poverty is unlikely to succeed if we do not also reject the classist language that pervades psychological research and practice. As Vojak (2009, pp. 936–937) observes,

> Language is seldom neutral; it is infused with meaning, power and status. Language can be a powerful ideological tool that embodies assumptions about how our world is ordered, and how it may be changed. . . . It frames worldviews, sets the parameters of acceptable discourse and preserves existing power differentials in ways that 'may go undetected by those with less power.'

"Ward," "dependent," and even "recipient," a term used in this book to describe women who are granted TANF benefits, can stigmatize and exclude. Phelan, Link, Moore, and Stueve (1997) found that the label "homeless," a term that might seem benign, elicited distancing and negative associations. The frequent use of "lower class" stands out as one of the more blatant uses of classist language in psychological research (cf. Kraus, Piff, Mendoza-Denton, Rheinschmidt, & Keltner, 2012). In everyday interactions, calling someone "low class" is an overt put-down, and similarly, "lower class" carries with it, whether intentional or not, a constellation of classist stereotypes (e.g., ill mannered and uneducated). Low income, in most cases, is likely a more appropriate characterization. Just as we have worked to eliminate other forms of biased language from our professional journals and textbooks, we must commit to eliminating classist language. We cannot expand the scope of justice to include poor women and their families if our language reinforces classist stereotypes.

Ultimately, our efforts to bring values of community and shared responsibility to the forefront of debates about welfare policy and antipoverty programs are contingent on our own willingness to enter the political fray and fully commit ourselves, personally and professionally, to fighting for economic justice for poor women. Smith's (1990, p. 530) pointed critique of APA's limited efficacy advancing social justice initiatives offers insight into the dynamics we must overcome:

> APA has taken an effective leadership role on issues involving justice to the disadvantaged categories of its own membership. On other issues, which have been more controversial APA has been less effective, partly because APA participates in our culture of self-interest and individualism, and partly because identifying the public interest is inherently political.

Of course, these tendencies may not only characterize our professional organizations; they also filter down to our own efforts. Indeed, the desire to remain "objective" and position science as somehow "above" or neatly walled off from the "chaos" of politics remains an underlying principle of psychological research and training. Although such conceptualizations of objectivity have been eloquently and convincingly debunked by feminist and critical scholars (Unger, 1982), the possibility or desirability of an "honest broker" model of science in which "just the facts" are reported to policymakers without any "personal interference" is still largely upheld in much of the social sciences as the default ideal. These tensions vividly play out in debates about psychologists' involvement in the evaluation of welfare reform and the "proper" roles of advocacy, science, and political engagement (Kalil, 2001; Steinitz & Mishler, 2001; Wilmoth, 2001). Meanwhile, poor women and their families continue to be hurt by punitive welfare policies and a turning away of investment in a public good. Findings from welfare "reform" evaluation studies vividly show the consequences – deeper poverty, material deprivation, and reduced access to basic resources such as secure housing and nutritious food (Legal Momentum, 2009, 2010a).

"To be of use" or to "create a legitimate, generative, and messy space in which progressive social scientists might frame and reframe crucial debates about social justice and the future of democracy and inquiry in America" will require recognizing that social science claims of "neutrality often inadvertently (or consciously) ends up supporting the status quo" (Fine & Barreras, 2001, p. 180, 176). This is certainly the case with women's poverty and rising inequality, in which the synergy between deep-rooted beliefs in individualism and meritocracy and social and economic policies that skew the distribution of income and wealth upward, ensure that the rich get richer and the poor get poorer.

Interrupting these processes requires deliberate action, and there are numerous entry points for psychology to move beyond a dichotomous view of science versus advocacy. These traditional boundaries are broken down, for instance, in thoughtful analyses of collaborative partnerships between researchers, practitioners, and community-based antipoverty programs (Brodsky, 2001; Shpungin & Lyubansky, 2006; Smith, Chambers, & Bratini, 2009). These works not only provide insight into the development and nurturance of cross-class alliances, and potential difficulties in building these relationships, but also the power of participatory research methods to challenge class-based status hierarchies in research, practice, and community building. A defining strength of participatory action research (PAR), one strand of action-oriented scholarship, is that the distinction between "researcher" and "researched," is blurred, creating opportunities for participants to identify, define, and address issues facing their communities (Smith et al., 2009). Participatory methods can bring poor women's experiences and perspectives to the forefront in ways that may be less likely in traditional models of research.

The potential of participatory approaches to shatter classist stereotypes and dominant frames of reference is illustrated by Downing, Sonenstein, and Davis' (2006) photovoice project with low-income youth in Baltimore, Maryland. Photovoice is a community-based participatory methodology in which informants use photographs to document important issues in their lives. As with other participatory methods, photos (or data) are used to spur critical analysis and consciousness not only among participants, but also the broader community; photovoice projects often culminate in public showings. When Downing and her colleagues (2006) asked poor youth to select a topic for a photovoice project related to public health, they chose to document "love" in their lives and community – a topic that runs counter to dominant representations that associate poor urban youth with violence, pregnancy, dropout rates, and substance abuse. Their photographs of siblings, parents, friends, and romantic partners with accompanying commentaries relayed the joys of love and the pain of loss (e.g., absent fathers and death) in ways that contextualized rather than pathologized poverty's impact. The desire to refute classist assumptions is evident in the caption that accompanied a photo of a young African American boy playing basketball:

> This is where I live, play, and get stereotyped. People think that we sell drugs, we are in a gang, and we are dumb. We do not sell drugs, we aren't in a gang and we are not dumb. Not by a long shot.

Exhibited widely, including in Baltimore's city hall, the "reach" of this research is evident in a physician's request that the images be shared with local medical residents to counter the dismissal of poor community members to emergency room "cases." Such studies, with their grounding in lived experience and visual presentation, may be particularly apt to garner attention from the media, the general public, and policymakers.

Participatory research is just one example of so-called "reality referencing" or the foregrounding of lived experiences in the struggle for social justice (Triece, 2011). This foregrounding positions members of marginalized groups as expert "insiders" via their direct experience with oppression. Welfare rights activists employ "reality referencing" to discredit punitive policies by contrasting testimony from low-income women about their experiences with poverty and the welfare system with policymakers' typically limited direct experience but considerable discretionary power (Triece, 2011). As one welfare mother asserted during a confrontation with political leaders, "We are tired of being taught to live on air and peanut butter by people who've never had to do that. Let me refute the myth that the poor are miraculously happy. If you see us smiling, it's because we're organizing" (Triece, 2011, p. 437). These comments aim to generate a "reality gap" between real women's experiences and the "welfare queen" stereotype, and to spark questions about whose claims should hold greater weight in public policy (Triece, 2011).

Ultimately, however, the burden of overturning stereotypes, dominant discourse, and restrictive policies cannot fall exclusively, or even primarily, to poor women. Building a large-scale, successful antipoverty movement will require middle class support and strong cross-class alliances. Extensive knowledge of stereotyping and attitude change, discrimination, intergroup relations, framing, the social psychology of social justice, collective action, and the detrimental consequences of poverty make psychologists well positioned to contribute to such a movement. Findings from focus groups with politically mobilized low-income women point to the importance of adopting structural critiques of economic inequality, perceiving class boundaries as impermeable, and embracing a shared sense of responsibility for social change (see Chapter 5).

However, accruing knowledge itself is not enough. Just as it is claimed that poverty reduction will remain out of reach if policymakers lack the political will to champion structural change, our efforts as a discipline will be thwarted if we lack the will to use our "expert" status to critically interrogate the reproduction of class privilege and inequality and mobilize against the preventable everyday injustices endured by poor women and their families. Accepting this challenge will require extending beyond our "comfort zone" to develop communication skills to reach policymakers and other audiences (see Sommer & Maycroft, 2008), the adoption of feminist and critical paradigms that blur the lines between advocacy and science, and that foster self-reflexivity regarding class status, power, and belief systems.

Moving Forward

It is no secret that power begets power, or that power is not easily conceded. As Peter Edelman (2012, para. 16), a Georgetown University law professor and former Clinton appointee who resigned in protest of the signing of the Personal Responsibility and Work Opportunity Reconciliation Act states, "The wealth and income of the top 1 percent grows at the expense of everyone else. Money breeds power and power breeds more money. It is a truly vicious circle." This cycle cannot be interrupted without the creation of a safety net that ends poverty and promotes the accrual of a wide range of human capital and economic assets, without sweeping changes to US tax policies that privilege the very wealthiest among us, and the implementation of a full complement of policies that support women and families (e.g., paid family leave, universal child care, and the adoption of self-sufficiency wages). These are neither risky nor unfounded proposals – ample research and evidence supports their effectiveness. We know how to end poverty if we want to.

Rejecting system justifying ideology that obscures structural (dis)advantage is equally crucial and as formidable a challenge. Since the mid-1980s, the proportion of Americans who perceive a widening gap in living standards between the poor and middle classes has grown, but this has not necessarily translated into greater class resentment or cynicism regarding personal control over life circumstances or the prospect of hard work paying off (Pew Research Center, 2012). Political polarization has hardened dramatically over the same period, with party differences surpassing gender, age, race, and class differences. The greatest divergences are in attitudes toward the safety net. Gaps of 35 points or more were found in a Pew Research Center (2012) poll that assessed beliefs about whether the government is responsible for caring for the poor, whether people in need should be helped even if it means going further into debt, and whether the government should guarantee all citizens food and a place to sleep. Over the past 25 years, support for the safety net among Democrats has remained relatively stable and robust, while the percentage of Republicans endorsing government responsibility for the poor has dropped to a quarter century low, with majorities now rejecting a central role for government (Pew Research Center, 2012). These trends, which are neither surprising nor entirely new, speak to the tough road ahead for antipoverty policy and attitude change.

There is, however, room for optimism. Whether the energy of the occupy movement can be sustained, it has succeeded in making "the 99%" a household word, and record gaps between the wealthy and everyone else may grow wide enough to mobilize antipoverty efforts in earnest. As Edelman (2012, para. 18, 19) points out,

History shows that people power wins sometimes. That's what happened in the Progressive Era a century ago and in the Great Depression as well. The gross inequality of those times produced an amalgam of popular unrest, organization, muckraking journalism and political leadership that attacked the big – and worsening – structural problem of economic inequality. . . . We have the ingredients. . . . The people have the power if they will use it, but they have to see that it is in their interest to do so.

except people don't believe science

Social science research, particularly social psychology, provides a roadmap for confronting these challenges head on. We must deploy our understanding of attitude change, stereotyping, and framing to challenge classist bias; we must use our knowledge of power, stigma, and discrimination to improve class, race, and gender relations, and we must draw on all we know about the antecedents, correlates, and consequences of women's poverty to develop and advance just social policies. For poor women, recognition of our interconnectedness and shared responsibility for each other cannot come too soon.

References

Abramovitz, M. (2001). Learning from the history of poor and working-class women's activism. *Annals of the American Academy of Political and Social Science, 577*, 118–130.

Abravanel, M. D. (2002). Public knowledge of fair housing law: Does it protect against housing discrimination. *Housing Policy Debate, 13*, 469–504.

Acker, J. (2009). From glass ceiling to inequality regime. *Sociologie du Travail, 51*, 199–217.

Acs, G., Loprest, P., & Roberts, T. (2001, November 27). *Final synthesis report of findings for ASPE "leavers" grants*. Retrieved from Urban Institute website: http://aspe.hhs.gov/hsp/leavers99/synthesis02/index.htm

Adair, V. C. (2002). Branded with infamy: Inscriptions of poverty and class in the United States. *Signs, 27*, 451–471.

Adair, V. C. (2008). The missing story of ourselves: Poor women, power, and the politics of feminist representation. *NWSA Journal, 20*, 1–25.

Albelda, R. P., & Tilly, C. (1997). *Glass ceilings and bottomless pits: Women's work, women's poverty*. Boston, MA: South End Press.

Alfred, M. V. (2007). Welfare reform and Black women's economic development. *Adult Education Quarterly, 57*, 293–311.

Alkire, S. (2007). The missing dimensions of poverty data (OPHI Working Paper No. 00). Retrieved from Oxford Poverty & Human Development Initiative website: http://www.ophi.org.uk/wp-content/uploads/OPHI-wp00.pdf

Alkire, S., Roche, J. M., Santos, M. E., & Seth, S. (2011, November). *Multidimensional poverty index*. Retrieved from Oxford Poverty and Human Development Initiative website: http://www.ophi.org.uk/policy/multidimensional-poverty-index/

Alksnis, C., Desmarais, S., & Curtis, J. (2008). Workforce segregation and the gender wage gap: Is "women's" work valued as highly as "men's?" *Journal of Applied Social Psychology, 38*, 1416–1441.

Alzate, M. M. (2009). The role of sexual and reproductive rights in social work practice. *Affilia, 24*, 108–119.

American Association of Retired Persons Public Policy Institute. (2007, June). *Valuing the invaluable: A new look at the economic value of family caregiving*. Retrieved from http://assets.aarp.org/rgcenter/il/ib82_caregiving.pdf

American Psychological Association. (APA). (2000). *Resolution on poverty and socioeconomic status.* Retrieved from http://www.apa.org/about/policy/poverty-resolution.aspx

American Psychological Association. (APA). (n.d.). *About APA.* Retrieved from http://www.apa.org/about/

American Psychological Association Presidential Task Force on Psychology's Contribution to End Homelessness. (2010). *Helping people without homes: The role of psychologists and recommendations to advance research, training, practice, and policy.* Retrieved from American Psychological Association website: http://www.apa.org/pubs/info/reports/end-homelessness.pdf

American Psychological Association Task Force on Socioeconomic Status. (2007). *Report of the APA task force on socioeconomic status.* Retrieved from http://www.apa.org/pi/ses/resources/publications/task-force-2006.pdf

Amnesty International. (2009, October). *The gender trap: Women, violence and poverty.* Retrieved from http://www.amnesty.org/en/library/info/ACT77/009/2009/en

Anderson, T. L., Shannon, C., Schyb, I., & Goldstein, P. (2002). Welfare reform and housing: Assessing the impact to substance abusers. *Journal of Drug Issues, 32,* 265–296.

Apfelbaum, E. (1999). Relations of domination and movements for liberation: An analysis of power between groups (abridged). *Feminism & Psychology, 9,* 267–272.

Appelbaum, B., & Gebeloff, R. (2012, February 11). Even critics of safety net increasingly depend on it. *New York Times.* Retrieved from http://www.nytimes.com/2012/02/12/us/even-critics-of-safety-net-increasingly-depend-on-it.html?pagewanted=all

Appelbaum, L. D. (2001). The influence of perceived deservingness on policy decisions regarding aid to the poor. *Political Psychology, 22,* 419–442.

Appelbaum, L. D., Lennon, M. C., & Aber, J. L. (2006). When effort is threatening: The influence of the belief in a just world on Americans' attitudes toward antipoverty policy. *Political Psychology, 27,* 387–402.

Applied Research Center. (2006). *How existing welfare reform research distorts welfare reality.* Retrieved from http://www.arc.org/content/view/266/135/

Arangua, L., Andersen, R., & Gelberg, L. (2005). The health circumstances of homeless women in the United States. *International Journal of Mental Health, 34,* 62–92.

Associated Press. (2011, August 10). Nebraska: Candidate says he regrets welfare analogy. *New York Times.* Retrieved from http://www.nytimes.com/2011/08/11/us/11brfs-Raccoon.html

Averitt, S. (2003). "Homelessness is not a choice!" The plight of homeless women with preschool children living in temporary shelters. *Journal of Family Nursing, 9,* 79–100.

Baker, C. E. (2007). *Media concentration and democracy: Why ownership matters.* New York, NY: Cambridge University Press.

Baptist, W., & Bricker-Jenkins, M. (2001). A view from the bottom: Poor people and their allies respond to welfare reform. *Annals of the American Academy of Political and Social Science, 577,* 144–156.

Barata, P. C., & Stewart, D. E. (2010). Searching for housing as a battered woman: Does discrimination affect reported availability of a rental unit? *Psychology of Women Quarterly, 34,* 43–55.

Bartle, E., & Segura, G. (2003). Welfare policy, welfare participants, and CalWORKS caseworkers: How participants are informed of supportive services. *Journal of Poverty, 7,* 141–161.

Bartle, E. E. (1998). Exposing and reframing welfare dependency. *Journal of Sociology and Social Welfare, XXV*, 23–41.

Bassuk, E. L. (1993). Social and economic hardships of homeless and other poor women. *American Journal of Orthopsychiatry, 63*, 340–347.

Becker, D., & Marecek, J. (2008). Dreaming the American dream: Individualism and positive psychology. *Social and Personality Psychology Compass, 2*, 1767–1780.

Beit-Hallahmi, B. (1979). Personal and social components of the Protestant ethic. *Journal of Social Psychology, 109*, 263–267.

Belle, D. (2006). Contested interpretations of economic inequality following hurricane Katrina. *Analyses of Social Issues and Public Policy, 6*, 143–158.

Belle, D., & Doucet, J. (2003). Poverty, inequality, and discrimination as sources of depression among U.S. women. *Psychology of Women Quarterly, 27*, 101–113.

Bensonsmith, D. (2005). Jezebels, matriarchs, and welfare queens: The Moynihan report of 1965 and the social construction of African-American women in welfare policy. In A. L. Schneider & H. M. Ingram (Eds.), *Deserving and entitled: Social constructions and public policy* (pp. 243–259). Albany, NY: State University of New York.

Berkowitz, B. (2001). *Prospecting among the poor: Welfare privatization*. Retrieved from Applied Research Center website: http://www.arc.org/pdf/296bpdf.pdf

Bianchi, S. M. (2011). Family change and time allocation in American families. *Annals of the American Academy of Political and Social Science, 638*, 21–44.

Bishop, R. (2008). From a distance: Marginalization of the poor in television ads for Goodwill industries. *Journal of Poverty, 12*, 411–431.

Bitler, M. P., Gelbach, J. B., & Hoynes, H. W. (2003, October). *Welfare reform and children's living arrangements* (Rand Working Paper: WR-111-NICHD/NIA). Retrieved from RAND Corporation website: http://www.rand.org/content/dam/rand/pubs/working_papers/2004/RAND_WR111.pdf

Blank, R. M. (2006). Was welfare reform successful? *The Economists' Voice, 3*, 1–5.

Blank, R. M. (2007a). Improving the safety net for single mothers who face serious barriers to work. *Future of Children, 17*, 183–197.

Blank, R. M. (2007b, June). *What we know, what we don't know, and what we need to know about welfare reform* (National Poverty Center Working Paper 07-19). Retrieved from National Poverty Center website: http://www.npc.umich.edu/publications/u/working_paper07-19.pdf

Blank, R. M. (2008). Presidential address: How to improve poverty measurement in the United States. *Journal of Policy Analysis and Management, 27*, 233–254.

Blank, S. W., & Blum, B. B. (1997). A brief history of work expectations for welfare mothers. *Future of Children, 7*, 28–38.

Blau, F. D., & DeVaro, J. (2006, June). *New evidence on gender differences in promotion rates: An empirical analysis of a sample of new hires* (NBER Working Paper No. 12321). Retrieved from The National Bureau of Economic Research website: http://www.nber.org/papers/w12321

Bloom, D., & Winstead, D. (2002, January). *Sanctions and welfare reform*. Retrieved from Brookings Institution website: http://www.brookings.edu/research/papers/2002/01/01welfare-bloom

Blow, C. M. (2011, December 2). Newt's war on poor children. *New York Times*. Retrieved from http://www.nytimes.com/2011/12/03/opinion/blow-newts-war-on-poor-children.html

Bobbio, A., Canova, L., & Manganelli, A. M. (2010). Conservative ideology, economic conservatism, and causal attributions for poverty and wealth. *Current Psychology: A Journal for Perspectives on Diverse Psychological Issues, 29,* 222–234.

Bornstein, S. (2011). *Poor, pregnant, and fired: Caregiver discrimination against low-wage workers.* Retrieved from Center for WorkLife Law website: http://www.worklifelaw. org/pubs/PoorPregnantAndFired.pdf

Bostrom, M. (2002). *Achieving the American dream: A meta-analysis of public opinion concerning poverty, upward mobility, and related issues.* Retrieved from For an Economy that Works for All website: http://www.economythatworks.com/reports/ AchievingTheAmericanDream.pdf

Boushey, H., & Wenger, J. B. (2006). Unemployment insurance eligibility before and after welfare reform. *Journal of Poverty, 10,* 1–23.

Bradley, C., & Cole, D. J. (2002). Causal attributions and the significance of self-efficacy in predicting solutions to poverty. *Sociological Focus, 35,* 381–396.

Brady, D., & Kall, D. (2008). Nearly universal, but somewhat distinct: The feminizaton of poverty in affluent Western democracies, 1969–2000. *Social Science Research, 37,* 976–1007.

Brandon, P. D., & Fisher, G. A. (2001). The dissolution of joint living arrangements among single parents and children: Does welfare make a difference? *Social Science Quarterly, 82,* 1–19.

Braun, V., & Clarke, V. (2006). Using thematic analysis in psychology. *Qualitative Research in Psychology, 3,* 77–101.

Bravve, E., Bolton, M., Couch, L., & Crowley, S. (2012). *Out of reach 2012.* Retrieved from National Low Income Housing Coalition website: http://nlihc.org/oor/ 2012

Breheny, M., & Stephens, C. (2010). Youth or disadvantage? The construction of teenage mothers in medical journals. *Culture, Health & Sexuality, 12,* 307–322.

Briar, S. (1966). Welfare from below. Recipients' views of the public welfare system. *California Law Review, 54,* 370–385.

British Columbia Law Institute & The Canadian Center for Elder Law. (2010, April 14). *Care/work: Law reform to support family caregivers to balance paid work and unpaid caregiving.* Retrieved from http://www.bcli.org/ccel/publications/study-paper-family-caregiving

Brodsky, A. E. (2001). More than epistemology: Relationships in applied research with underserved communities. *Journal of Social Issues, 57,* 323–335.

Brophy-Baermann, M., & Bloeser, A. J. (2006). Stealthy wealth: The untold story of welfare privatization. *Harvard International Journal of Press/Politics, 11,* 89–112.

Browne, I. (Ed.). (1999). *Latinas and African American women at work: Race, gender, and economic inequality.* New York, NY: Russell Sage.

Brush, M. (2012, January 5). *In Congress, nearly half the members are millionaires.* Retrieved from MSN Money website: http://money.msn.com/investing/latest. aspx?post=70cc8f98-07b4-4e4e-923e-5569bd82627d

Bullock, H. E. (1995). Class acts: Middle class responses to the poor. In B. Lott & D. Maluso (Eds.), *The social psychology of interpersonal discrimination* (pp. 118–159). New York, NY: Guilford Press.

Bullock, H. E. (1999). Attributions for poverty: A comparison of middle class and welfare recipient attitudes. *Journal of Applied Social Psychology, 29,* 2059–2082.

Bullock, H. E. (2004). From the frontlines of welfare reform: An analysis of social worker and welfare recipient attitudes. *Journal of Social Psychology, 144,* 571–588.

Bullock, H. E. (2008). Justifying inequality: A social psychological analysis of beliefs about poverty and the poor. In A. C. Lin & D. R. Harris (Eds.), *The colors of poverty: Why racial and ethnic disparities persist* (pp. 72–95). New York, NY: Springer.

Bullock, H. E., & Fernald, J. L. (2005). Predicting support for the elimination of the dividend tax: The role of framing and attributions for wealth. *Analyses of Social Issues and Public Policy, 5,* 49–66.

Bullock, H. E., & Limbert, W. M. (2003). Scaling the socioeconomic ladder: Low-income women's perceptions of class status and opportunity. *Journal of Social Issues, 59,* 693–709.

Bullock, H. E., & Limbert, W. M. (2008). Moving from "work-first" to "human welfare first:" New frameworks for theorizing about poverty and U.S. welfare policy. In C. Raghavan, A. E. Edwards, & K. M. Vaz (Eds.), *Benefiting by design: Women of color in feminist psychological research* (pp. 44–53). Newcastle upon Tyne: Cambridge Scholars Publishing.

Bullock, H. E., & Limbert, W. M. (2009). Class. In D. Fox, I. Prilleltensky, & S. Austin (Eds.), *Critical psychology: An introduction* (2nd ed., pp. 215–231). London: Sage Publications.

Bullock, H. E., & Waugh, I. M. (2005). Beliefs about poverty and opportunity among Mexican immigrant farm workers. *Journal of Applied Social Psychology, 35,* 1132–1149.

Bullock, H. E., Lott, B., & Truong, S. V. (2011). SPSSI and poverty: Reflections at seventy-five. *Journal of Social Issues, 67,* 150–164.

Bullock, H. E., Williams, W. R., & Limbert, W. M. (2003). Predicting support for welfare policies: The impact of attributions and beliefs about inequality. *Journal of Poverty, 7,* 35–56.

Bullock, H. E., Wyche, K. F., & Williams, W. R. (2001). Media images of the poor. *Journal of Social Issues, 57,* 229–246.

Burnette, D. (2010, May 10). Public housing waiting list to reopen after 10 years: CHA to add 40,000 new names. *Chicago Tribune.* Retrieved from http://articles.chicago tribune.com/2010-05-10/news/ct-met-cha-waiting-list-20100510_1_chicago-housing-authority-public-housing-cha-housing

Caiazza, A., Hess, C., Clevenger, C., & Carlberg, A. (2008). *The challenge to act: How progressive women activists reframe American democracy.* Retrieved from Institute for Women's Policy Research website: http://articles.chicagotribune.com/2010-05-10/news/ct-met-cha-waiting-list-20100510_1_chicago-housing-authority-public-housing-cha-housing

Camasso, M. J. (2004). Isolating family cap effect on fertility behavior: Evidence from New Jersey's family development program experiment. *Contemporary Economic Policy, 22,* 453–467.

Camasso, M. J., & Jagannathan, R. (2009). How family caps work: Evidence from a national study. *Social Service Review, 83,* 389–428.

Campbell, A. L. (2010). The public's role in winner-take-all politics. *Politics & Society, 38,* 227–232.

Campbell, C., Cornish, F., Gibbs, A., & Scott, K. (2010). Heeding the push from below: How do social movements persuade the rich to listen to the poor? *Journal of Health Psychology, 15,* 962–971.

Carter, N. M., & Silva, C. (2011). *The myth of the ideal worker: Does doing all of the right things really get women ahead?* Retrieved from Catalyst http://www.catalyst.org/knowledge/myth-ideal-worker-does-doing-all-right-things-really-get-women-ahead.

Casper, L. M., McLanahan, S. S., & Garfinkel, I. (1994). The gender-poverty gap: What we can learn from other countries. *American Sociological Review, 59*, 594–605.

Cassiman, S. A. (2007). Of witches, welfare queens, and the disaster named poverty: The search for a counter-narrative. *Journal of Poverty, 10*, 51–66.

Catlett, B. S., & Artis, J. E. (2004). Critiquing the case for marriage promotion: How the promarriage movement misrepresents violence research. *Violence Against Women, 10*, 1226–1244.

Center for American Progress Task Force on Poverty. (2007, April 25). *From poverty to prosperity: A national strategy to cut poverty in half.* Retrieved from http://www.americanprogress.org/issues/poverty/report/2007/04/25/2912/from-poverty-to-prosperity-a-national-strategy-to-cut-poverty-in-half/

Center on Budget and Policy Priorities (CBPP). (2009, May 15). *Policy basics: The housing choice voucher program.* Retrieved from http://www.cbpp.org/cms/index.cfm?fa=view&id=279

Center on Budget and Policy Priorities (CBPP). (2012a, December 4). *An introduction to TANF.* Retrieved from http://www.cbpp.org/cms/?fa=view&id=936

Center on Budget and Policy Priorities (CBPP). (2012b, August 22). *Chart book: TANF at 16.* Retrieved from http://www.cbpp.org/cms/index.cfm?fa=view&id=3566

Chafel, J. A. (1997). Societal images of poverty: Child and adult beliefs. *Youth & Society, 28*, 432–463.

Chafel, J. A., & Neitzel, C. (2005). Young children's ideas about the nature, causes, justification, and alleviation of poverty. *Early Childhood Research Quarterly, 20*, 433–450.

Chant, S. (2007). Re-thinking the "feminization of poverty" in relation to aggregate gender indices. *Journal of Human Development, 7*, 201–220.

Cherlin, A., Frogner, B., Ribar, D., & Moffitt, R. (2009). Welfare reform in the mid-2000s: How African American and Hispanic families in three cities are faring. *Annals of the American Academy of Political and Social Science, 621*, 178–201.

Children's Defense Fund. (CDF). (2005, April). *Child care basics.* Retrieved from http://cdf.convio.net/site/DocServer/child_care_basics_2005.pdf?docID

Children's Defense Fund. (CDF). (2007, October 10). *America's cradle to prison pipeline.* Retrieved from http://www.childrensdefense.org/child-research-data-publications/data/cradle-prison-pipeline-report-2007-full-highres.html

Children's Defense Fund. (CDF). (2010, June). *The state of America's children 2010 report – Early childhood development.* Retrieved from http://www.childrensdefense.org/child-research-data-publications/data/the-state-of-americas-early-childhood-development-2010.html

Children's Defense Fund. (CDF). (2011). *The state of America's children 2011 report.* Retrieved from http://www.childrensdefense.org/child-research-data-publications/state-of-americas-children-2011/

Children's Defense Fund. (CDF). (2012, July). *The state of America's children 2012 handbook.* Retrieved from http://www.childrensdefense.org/child-research-data-publications/data/soac-2012-handbook.html

Choi, I., Nisbett, R. E., & Norenzayan, A. (1999). Causal attribution across cultures: Variation and universality. *Psychology Bulletin, 125*, 47–63.

Choo, H. Y., & Ferree, M. M. (2010). Practicing intersectionality in sociological research: A critical analysis of inclusions, interactions, and institutions in the study of inequalities. *Sociological Theory, 28,* 129–149.

Christopher, A. N., & Jones, J. R. (2004). Affluence cues and first impressions: The moderating impact of the Protestant work ethic. *Journal Of Economic Psychology, 25,* 279–292.

Christopher, A. N., Morgan, R. D., Marek, P., Troisi, J. D., Jones, J. R., & Reinhart, D. F. (2005). Affluence cues and first impressions: Does it matter how the affluence was acquired? *Journal Of Economic Psychology, 26,* 187–200.

Christopher, A. N., Zabel, K. L., Jones, J. R., & Marek, P. (2008). Protestant ethic ideology: Its multifaceted relationships with just world beliefs, social dominance orientation, and right-wing authoritarianism. *Personality and Individual Differences, 45,* 473–477.

Christopher, K. (2002). Single motherhood, employment, or social assistance: Why are U.S. women poorer than women in other affluent nations. *Journal of Poverty, 6,* 61–80.

Christopher, K., England, P., Smeeding, T. M., & Phillips, K. R. (2002). The gender gap in poverty in modern nations: Single motherhood, the market, and the state. *Sociological Perspectives, 45,* 219–242.

Clampet-Lundquist, S. (2003). Finding and keeping affordable housing: Analyzing the experiences of single-mother families in north Philadelphia. *Journal of Sociology and Social Welfare, XXX,* 123–140.

Class Action. (n.d.). *What is classism?* Retrieved from http://www.classism.org/about-class/what-is-classism

Cleaveland, C. (2008). "A Black benefit": Racial prejudice among white welfare recipients in a low-income neighborhood. *Journal of Progressive Human Services, 19,* 71–91.

Clinton, B. (2006, August, 22). How we ended welfare, together. *New York Times.* Retrieved from http://www.nytimes.com/2006/08/22/opinion/22clinton.html?_r=1&scp=1&sq=welfare%20reform&st=cse

Cohen, L. (2006). Winning a welfare battle and building bridges. *New Politics, 11,* 60–69.

Cohen, P. N., Huffman, M. L., & Knauer, S. (2009). Stalled progress? Gender segregation and wage inequality among managers, 1980–2000. *Work and Occupations, 36,* 318–342.

Cohen, R. (2012, September 11). Why Mitt and Ann Romney don't understand the poor – Or middle class. *San Jose Mercury.* Retrieved from http://www.mercurynews.com/opinion/ci_21517942/richard-cohen-why-mitt-and-ann-romney-dont

Cohn, J. (2012, February 1). Romney's "let them eat cake" moment. *The New Republic.* Retrieved from http://www.tnr.com/blog/jonathan-cohn/100306/romney-not-concerned-very-poor-safety-net-middle-class

Colbert, S. (2010, December 16). *Jesus is a liberal democrat.* Retrieved from The Colbert Report [video] website: http://www.colbertnation.com/the-colbert-report-videos/368914/december-16-2010/jesus-is-a-liberal-democrat

Cole, E. R. (2009). Intersectionality and research in psychology. *American Psychologist, 64,* 170–180.

Collins, P. H. (2010). The new politics of community. *American Sociological Review, 75,* 7–30.

Committee on Ways and Means, US House of Representatives. (2008, May). *Green book: Background material and data on the programs within the jurisdiction of the committee on ways and means.* Retrieved from http://democrats.waysandmeans.house.gov/2008-green-book

Condon, S. (2011, June 29). *Poll: Most think government should help homeowners in trouble.* Retrieved from CBS News website: http://www.cbsnews.com/8301-503544_162-20075544-503544.html

Conger, R. D., Elder, G., Lorenz, R., Conger, K., Simmons, R., Whitbeck, L., . . . Melby, J. N. (1990). Linking economic hardship to marital quality and instability. *Journal of Marriage and Family, 52,* 643–656.

Corn, D. (2012, September 17). *Secret video: Romney tells millionaire donors what he REALLY thinks of Obama voters.* Retrieved from Mother Jones website: http://www.motherjones.com/politics/2012/09/secret-video-romney-private-fundraiser

Correll, S. J., Benard, S., & Paik, I. (2007). Getting a job: Is there a motherhood penalty? *American Journal of Sociology, 112,* 1297–1338.

Cosgrove, L., & Flynn, C. (2005). Marginalized mothers: Parenting without a home. *Analyses of Social Issues and Public Policy, 5,* 127–143.

Cowal, K., Shinn, M., Weitzman, B. C., Stojanovic, D., & Labay, L. (2002). Mother-child separations among homeless and housed families receiving public assistance in New York City. *American Journal of Community Psychology, 30,* 711–730.

Cozzarelli, C., Tagler, M. J., & Wilkinson, A. V. (2002). Do middle-class students perceive poor women and poor men differently? *Sex Roles, 47,* 519–529.

Cozzarelli, C., Wilkinson, A. V., & Tagler, M. J. (2001). Attitudes toward the poor and attributions for poverty. *Journal of Social Issues, 57,* 207–227.

Crosby, F. J. (1984). The denial of personal discrimination. *American Behavioral Scientist, 27,* 371–386.

Daniels, M. (2012, January 24). Text of the republican response to the state of the union. *New York Times.* Retrieved from http://www.nytimes.com/2012/01/24/us/politics/gov-mitch-daniels-republican-address-to-the-nation.html?pagewanted=all

Danziger, S. K. (2010). The decline of cash welfare and implications for social policy and poverty. *Annual Review of Sociology, 36,* 523–545.

Danziger, S. K., Kalil, A., & Anderson, N. J. (2000). Human capital, physical health, and mental health of welfare recipients: Co-occurrence and correlates. *Journal of Social Issues, 56,* 635–654.

Darley, J. M., & Gross, P. H. (1983). A hypothesis-confirming bias in labeling effects. *Journal of Personality and Social Psychology, 44,* 20–33.

Davis, D. A., & Craven, C. (2011). Revisiting feminist ethnography: Methods and activism at the intersection of neoliberal policy. *Feminist Formations, 23,* 190–208.

Davis, L., & Hagen, J. (1996). Stereotypes and stigma: What's changed for welfare mothers. *Affilia, 11,* 319–337.

Day, J. C., & Rosenthal, J. (2009). *Detailed occupations and median earnings: 2008.* Retrieved from US Census Bureau website: http://www.census.gov/people/io/files/acs08_detailedoccupations.pdf

Deficit Reduction Act of 2005. Pub. L. No. 109-171, 120 Stat 4 (2006).

Delgado, R., & Stefancic, J. (2012). *Critical race theory: An introduction* (2nd ed.). New York, NY: New York University Press.

DeLeire, T., & Lopoo, L. M. (2010, April). *Family structure and the economic mobility of children.* Retrieved from Pew Charitable Trusts Economic Mobility Project website: http://www.economicmobility.org/assets/pdfs/Family_Structure.pdf

DeParle, J. (2009, February 1). Welfare aid isn't growing as economy drops off. *New York Times.* Retrieved from http://www.nytimes.com/2009/02/02/us/02welfare.html

DeWard, S. L., & Moe, A. M. (2010). "Like a prison!": Homeless women's narratives of surviving shelter. *Journal of Sociology and Social Welfare, XXXVII,* 115–135.

D'Ercole, A., & Struening, E. (1990). Victimization among homeless women: Implications for service delivery. *Journal of Community Psychology, 18,* 141–152.

DiPrete, T. A., & Eirich, G. M. (2006). Cumulative advantage as a mechanism for inequality: A review of theoretical and empirical developments. *Annual Review of Sociology, 32,* 271–297.

Dodson, L. (2007). Wage-poor mothers and moral economy. *Social Politics, 14,* 258–280.

Donley, A. M., & Wright, J. D. (2008). For richer or for poorer: The impact of state-level legislation on marriage, divorce, and other outcomes. *Sociological Spectrum, 28,* 133–159.

Downing, R. A., Sonenstein, F., & Davis, N. (2006). *Love through the eyes of Baltimore youth: Photovoice as a youth empowerment tool.* Retrieved from Johns Hopkins University, Bloomberg School of Public Health [recorded presentation] website: https://apha.confex.com/apha/134am/techprogram/paper_136310.htm

Downing, R. A., LaVeist, T. A., & Bullock, H. E. (2007). Intersections of ethnicity and social class in provider advice regarding reproductive health. *American Journal of Public Health, 97,* 1803–1807.

Duke, J. (2010). Exploring homeowner opposition to public housing developments. *Journal of Sociology and Social Welfare, XXXVII,* 49–74.

Duke-Lucio, J., Peck, L. R., & Segal, E. A. (2010). The latent and sequential costs of being poor: An exploration of housing. *Poverty and Public Policy, 2,* 83–102.

Duncan, L. E. (1999). Motivation for collective action: Group consciousness as mediator of personality, life experiences, and women's rights activism. *Political Psychology* [Special issue: Political socialization], *20,* 611–635.

Dyck, J. J., & Hussey, L. S. (2008). The end of welfare as we know it? Durable attitudes in a changing information environment. *Public Opinion Quarterly, 72,* 589–618.

Dyer, W. T., & Fairlie, R. W. (2003). Do family caps reduce out-of-wedlock births? Evidence from Arkansas, Georgia, Indiana, New Jersey, and Virginia. *Population Research and Policy Review, 23,* 441–473.

Eagly, A. H., Eaton, A., Rose, S. M., Riger, S., & McHugh, M. C. (2012). Feminism and psychology: Analysis of a half-century of research on women and gender. *American Psychologist, 67,* 211–230.

Eamon, M. K., Wu, C., & Zhang, S. (2009). Effectiveness and limitations of the Earned Income Tax Credit for reducing child poverty in the United States. *Children and Youth Services Review, 31,* 919–926.

East, J. F. (2000). Empowerment through welfare-rights organizing: A feminist perspective. *Affilia, 15,* 311–328.

Economic Mobility Project. (2009, March 12). *Findings from a national survey & focus groups on economic mobility.* Retrieved from http://www.pewtrusts.org/uploadedFiles/wwwpewtrustsorg/Reports/Economic_Mobility/EMP%202009%20Survey%20on%20Economic%20Mobility%20FOR%20PRINT%203.12.09.pdf

Economic Mobility Project. (2011a, May 19). *Economic mobility and the American dream: Where do we stand in the wake of the great recession?* Retrieved from http://www.pewstates.org/research/analysis/economic-mobility-and-the-american-dream-where-do-we-stand-in-the-wake-of-the-great-recession-85899378421

Economic Mobility Project. (2011b, November). *Does America promote mobility as well as other nations?* Retrieved from http://www.pewstates.org/research/reports/does-america-promote-mobility-as-well-as-other-nations-85899380321

Edelman, P. (2012, July 28). Poverty in America: Why can't we end it? *New York Times.* Retrieved from http://www.nytimes.com/2012/07/29/opinion/sunday/why-cant-we-end-poverty-in-america.html?pagewanted=all

Edin, K., & Kefalas, M. T. (2005). *Promises I can keep: Why poor women put motherhood before marriage.* Berkeley: University of California Press.

Edin, K., Kefalas, M. T., & Reed, J. M. (2004). A peek inside the black box: What marriage means for poor unmarried parents. *Journal of Marriage and Family, 66,* 1007–1014.

Edin, K., & Reed, J. M. (2005). Why don't they just get married? Barriers to marriage among the disadvantaged. *Future of Children, 15,* 117–137.

Edmonds-Cady, C. (2009). Getting to the grassroots: Feminist standpoints within the welfare rights movement. *Journal of Sociology and Social Welfare, XXXVI,* 11–33.

Edsall, T. B. (2012, July 15). The "merit-based society". *New York Times.* Retrieved from http://campaignstops.blogs.nytimes.com/2012/07/15/the-merit-based-society/

Evangelical Social Action Forum & Health Bridge. (2009). *Women's economic contribution through their unpaid work: The case of India.* Retrieved from http://www.healthbridge.ca/HB-%20ESAF%20ER.pdf

Farrar, M. E., & Warner, J. L. (2008). Spectacular resistance: The billionaires for Bush and the art political culture jamming. *Polity, 40,* 273–296.

Feagin, J. R. (1975). *Subordinating the poor: Welfare and American beliefs.* Englewood Cliffs, NJ: Prentice-Hall

Federal Reserve Bank of Boston. (n.d.). *How do we measure "standard of living"?* Retrieved from http://www.bos.frb.org/education/ledger/ledger03/winter/measure.pdf

Ferguson, A., & Hennessy, R. (2010). Feminist perspectives on class and work. In E. N. Zalta (Ed.), *The Stanford encyclopedia of philosophy.* Retrieved from http://plato.stanford.edu/archives/win2010/entries/feminism-class/

Finch, I., & Schott, L. (2011, November 21). *TANF benefits fell further in 2011 and are worth much less than in 1996 in most states.* Retrieved from Center on Budget and Policy Priorities website: http://www.cbpp.org/cms/?fa=view&id=3625

Fine, M. (1982). When nonvictims derogate: Powerlessness in the helping professions. *Personality and Social Psychology Bulletin, 8,* 637–643.

Fine, M., & Barreras, R. (2001). To be of use. *Analyses of Social Issues and Public Policy, 1,* 175–182.

Fine, M., & Weis, L. (1998). *The unknown city: Lives of poor and working-class young adults.* Boston, MA: Beacon Press.

Fisher, G. M. (2008). Remembering Mollie Orshansky – The developer of the policy thresholds. *Social Security Bulletin, 68*(3). Retrieved from Social Security Administration http://www.ssa.gov/policy/docs/ssb/v68n3/v68n3p79.html

Fisher, T., & Reese, E. (2011). The punitive turn in social policies: Critical race feminist reflections on the USA, Great Britain, and beyond. *Critical Sociology, 37,* 225–236.

Fiske, S. T. (2012). Managing ambivalent prejudices: Smart-but-cold and warm-but-dumb stereotypes. *Annals of the American Academy of Political and Social Science*, *639*, 33–48.

Fiske, S. T., Xu, J., Cuddy, A. C., & Glick, P. (1999). (Dis)respecting versus (dis)liking: Status and interdependence predict ambivalent stereotypes of competence and warmth. *Journal of Social Issues*, *55*, 473–489.

Flick, U. (2002). *An introduction to qualitative research*. Thousand Oaks, CA: Sage Publications.

Fording, R., Soss, J., & Schram, S. F. (2011). Race and the local politics of punishment in the new world of welfare. *American Journal of Sociology*, *116*, 1610–1657.

Foster, M. D. (2000). Positive and negative responses to personal discrimination: Does coping make a difference? *Journal of Social Psychology*, *140*, 93–106.

Foster, M. D., Sloto, L., & Ruby, R. (2006). Responding to discrimination as a function of meritocracy beliefs and personal experiences: Testing the model of shattered assumptions. *Group Processes and Intergroup Relations*, *9*, 401–411.

Fox, C. (2005). The changing color of welfare? How whites' attitudes toward Latinos influence support for welfare. *American Journal of Sociology*, *110*, 580–625.

FrameWorks Institute. (n.d.). *Mission of the FrameWorks Institute*. Retrieved from http://www.frameworksinstitute.org/mission.html

Frank, R. H. (2010, October 16). Income inequality: Too big to ignore. *New York Times*. Retrieved from http://www.nytimes.com/2010/10/17/business/17view.html

Fraser, N., & Gordon, L. (1994). A genealogy of "*dependency.*" Tracing a keyword of the U.S. welfare state. *Signs*, *19*, 309–336.

Furnham, A. (2003). Poverty and wealth. In S. C. Carr & T. S. Sloan (Eds.), *Poverty and psychology: From global perspective to local practice* (pp. 163–183). New York, NY: Kluwer Academic.

Furnham, A. F. (1983). Attributions for affluence. *Personality and Individual Differences*, *4*, 31–40.

Gans, H. (1995). *The war against the poor: The underclass and antipoverty policy*. New York, NY: BasicBooks.

Gans, H. J. (2011). Long-range policies for the U.S. economy. *Challenge*, *54*, 80–94.

Garcia, S. M., Hallahan, M., & Rosenthal, R. (2007). Poor expression: Concealing social class stigma. *Basic and Applied Social Psychology*, *29*, 99–107.

Gatta, M., & Deprez, L. S. (2008). Women's lives and poverty: Developing a framework of real reform for welfare. *Journal of Sociology and Social Welfare*, *XXXV*, 21–48.

Gemelli, M. (2008). Understanding the complexity of attitudes of low-income single mothers toward work and family the age of welfare reform. *Gender Issues*, *25*, 101–113.

George Wiley Center. (n.d.). *Utility issues*. Retrieved from http://www.georgewileycenter.org/utility.html

Gibson-Davis, C. M., Edin, K., & McLanahan, S. (2005). High hopes but even higher expectations: The retreat from marriage among low-income couples. *Journal of Marriage and Family*, *67*, 1301–1312.

Gilens, M. (1999). *Why Americans hate welfare: Race, media, and the politics of antipoverty policy*. Chicago, IL: University of Chicago Press.

Gilens, M. (2005). Inequality and democratic responsiveness. *Public Opinion Quarterly*, *69*, 778–796.

Gilliam, F. D. (1999). The "welfare queen" experiment: How viewers react to images of African-American women on welfare. *Nieman Reports, 53*, 49–52.

Gilliom, J. (2005). Resisting surveillance. *Social Text, 23*, 71–83.

Goldberg, G. S. (Ed.). (2010). *Poor women in rich countries: The feminization of poverty over the life course.* New York, NY: Oxford University Press.

Goldberg, H., & Schott, L. (2001, October 1). *A compliance-oriented approach to sanctions in state and county TANF programs.* Retrieved from Center for Budget and Policy Priorities website: http://www.cbpp.org/archiveSite/10-1-00sliip.pdf

Goldberg, M. (2012, April 7). *Wisconsin's repeal of equal pay rights adds to battles for women.* Retrieved from The Daily Beast website: http://www.thedailybeast.com/articles/2012/04/07/wisconsin-s-repeal-of-equal-pay-rights-adds-to-battles-for-women.html

Goodban, N. (1985). The psychological impact of being on welfare. *Social Service Review, 59*, 403–422.

Gooden, S. T. (1998). All things not being equal: Differences in caseworker support toward Black and white welfare clients. *Harvard Journal of African American Public Policy, IV*, 23–33.

Gooden, S. T. (2003). Contemporary approaches to enduring challenges: Using performance measures to promote racial equality under TANF. In S. F. Schram, J. Soss, & R. C. Fording (Eds.), *Race and the politics of welfare reform* (pp. 254–275). Ann Arbor, MI: The University of Michigan Press.

Gordon, L. (1994). *Pitied but not entitled: Single mothers and the history of welfare, 1890–1935.* Cambridge, MA: Harvard University Press.

Graefe, D. R., & Lichter, D. T. (2008). Marriage patterns among unwed mothers: Before and after PRWORA. *Journal of Policy Analysis and Management, 27*, 479–497.

Graetz, M. J., & Shapiro, I. (2005). *Death by a thousand cuts: The fight over taxing inherited wealth.* Princeton, NJ: Princeton University Press.

Grossman, I., & Varnum, M. E. W. (2011). Social class, culture, and cognition. *Social Psychological and Personality Science, 2*, 81–89.

Guetzkow, J. (2010). Beyond deservingness: Congressional discourse on poverty, 1964–1996. *Annals of the American Academy of Political and Social Science, 629*, 173–197.

Hacker, J. S., & Pierson, P. (2010). *Winner-take-all-politics: How Washington made the rich richer – And turned its back on the middle class.* New York, NY: Simon & Schuster.

Hafer, C. L., & Choma, B. L. (2009). Belief in a just world, perceived fairness, and justification of the status quo. In J. T. Jost, A. C. Kay, & H. Thorisdotter (Eds.), *Social and psychological bases of ideology and system justification* (pp. 107–125). New York, NY: Oxford University Press.

Hamilton, G., & Scrivener, S. (2012, March). *Facilitating postsecondary education and training for TANF recipients.* Retrieved from Urban Institute website: http://www.urban.org/url.cfm?ID=412564

Handler, J. F., & Hasenfeld, Y. (2007). *Blame welfare, ignore poverty and inequality.* Cambridge, UK: Cambridge University Press.

Hanson, S. L., & Zogby, J. (2010). The polls – Trends: Attitudes about the American dream. *Political Opinion Quarterly, 74*, 570–584.

Harris, D. A., & Parisi, D. (2005). Gender role ideologies and marriage promotion: State policy choices and suggestions for improvement. *Review of Policy Research, 22*, 841–858.

Hartmann, H., Hegewisch, A., & Lovell, V. (2007, May 24). *An economy that puts families first: Expanding the social contract to include family care* (EPI Briefing Paper #190). Retrieved from Economic Policy Institute website: http://www.gpn.org/bp190/bp190.pdf

Haskins, R., Holzer, H., & Lerman, R. (2009). *Promoting upward mobility by increasing postsecondary education.* Retrieved from Pew Charitable Trusts Economic Mobility Project website: http://www.pewstates.org/research/reports/promoting-economic-mobility-by-increasing-postsecondary-education-85899376351

Hastie, B. (2010). Linking cause and solution: Predicting support for poverty alleviation proposals. *Australian Psychologist, 45,* 16–28.

Hatton, D. C., Kleffel, D., Bennett, S., & Gaffrey, E. A. N. (2001). Homeless women and children's access to health care: A paradox. *Journal of Community Health Nursing, 18,* 25–34.

Haveman, R. (2009). What does it mean to be poor in a rich society? *Focus, 26,* 81–86.

Haveman, R., & Mullikin, M. (1999, April). *Alternatives to the official poverty measure: Perspectives and assessment.* Paper presented at Poverty: Improving the Definition after Thirty Years Conference, Institute for Research on Poverty, Madison, WI. Retrieved from http://www.irp.wisc.edu/research/method.htm

Hayes, J., & Hartmann, H. (2011, September). *Women and men living on the edge: Economic insecurity after the great recession.* Retrieved from The Institute for Women's Policy Research website: http://www.iwpr.org/publications/pubs/women-and-men-living-on-the-edge-economic-insecurity-after-the-great-recession

Hays, S. (2003). *Flat broke with children: Women in the age of welfare reform.* New York, NY: Oxford University Press.

Hennessy, J. (2009). Choosing work and family: Poor and low-income mothers' work-family commitments. *Journal of Poverty, 13,* 152–172.

Henry, P. J., Renya, C., & Weiner, B. (2004). Hate welfare but help the poor: How the attributions of content of stereotypes explains the paradox of reactions to destitute America. *Journal of Applied Social Psychology, 34,* 34–58.

Hertz, N. (2011, November). *Women and banks: Are female customers facing discrimination.* Retrieved from Institute for Public Policy Research website: http://www.ippr.org/publications/55/8186/women-and-banks-are-female-customers-facing-discrimination

Hesse-Biber, S. N., & Leavy, P. L. (Eds.). (2007). *Feminist research practice: A primer.* Thousand Oaks, CA: Sage Publication, Inc.

Hetling, A., McDermott, M. L., & Mapps, M. (2008). Symbolic versus policy learning: Public opinion of the 1996 U.S. welfare reforms. *American Politics Research, 36,* 335–357.

Hildebrandt, E., & Ford, S. L. (2009). Justice and impoverished women: The ethical implications of work-based welfare. *Policy, Politics & Nursing Practice, 10,* 295–302.

Hirschl, T., Rank, M., & Kusi-Appouh, D. (2011). Ideology and the experience of poverty risk: Views about poverty within a focus group design. *Journal of Poverty, 15,* 350–370.

Hochschild, A., & Machung, A. (2003). *The second shift.* New York: Penguin Books.

Hochschild, J. L. (1995). *Facing up to the American dream: Race, class, and the soul of the nation.* Princeton, NJ: Princeton University Press.

Hochschild, J. L. (2006). Ambivalence about equality in the United States or, did Tocqueville get it wrong and why does it matter? *Social Justice Research, 19*, 43–62.

Holcomb, P., Adams, G., Snyder, K., Koralek, R., Martinson, K., Bernstein, S., & Capizzano, J. (2006). *Child care subsidies and TANF: A synthesis of three studies on systems, policies, and parents.* Washington, DC: Urban Institute.

Holzer, H. J., & Stoll, M. A. (2003). Employer demand for welfare recipients by race. *Journal of Labor Economics, 21*, 210–241.

Holzer, H. J., Stoll, M. A., & Wissoker, D. (2004). Job performance and retention among welfare recipients. *Social Service Review, 78*, 343–369.

Hölzl, E., & Kirchler, E. (2005). Causal attribution and hindsight bias for economic developments. *Journal of Applied Psychology, 90*, 167–174.

Huey, L., & Berndt, E. (2008). You've gotta learn how to play the game': Homeless women's use of gender performance as a tool for preventing victimization. *The Sociological Review, 56*, 177–194.

Hunt, M. O. (1996). The individual, society, or both? A comparison of Black, Latino, and white beliefs about the causes of poverty. *Social Forces, 75*, 293–322.

Hunt, M. O. (2004). Race/ethnicity and beliefs about wealth and poverty. *Social Science Quarterly, 85*, 827–853.

Hunt, M. O. (2007). African American, Hispanic, and White beliefs about Black/White inequality, 1977–2004. *American Sociological Review, 72*, 390–415.

Insight. (2008, May). *How much is enough in your county: The 2008 California family economic self-sufficiency standard.* Retrieved from http://www.insightcced.org/uploads/cfes/sss-exec-summ-final-050908.pdf

Institute for Women's Policy Research. (IWPR). (2006). *Resilient and reaching for more: Challenges and benefits of higher education for welfare recipients and their children.* Retrieved from http://www.iwpr.org/publications/pubs/resilient-and-reaching-for-more-challenges-and-benefits-of-higher-education-for-welfare-participants-and-their-children

Institute on Assets and Social Policy (IASP). (2006, December). *Asset opportunity ladder: An example of policies that impact asset building over a lifetime.* Retrieved from http://iasp.brandeis.edu/pdfs/Author/institute-for-assets-and-social-policy/Asset%20Opportunity%20Ladder.pdf

Institute on Assets and Social Policy (IASP). (n.d.). *Why focus on asset building?* Retrieved from http://iasp.brandeis.edu/about/why.html

International Labour Office. (2010). *Global wage report 2010/11: Wage policies in times of crisis.* Retrieved from http://www.ilo.org/global/publications/ilo-bookstore/order-online/books/WCMS_145265/lang–en/index.htm

International Labour Office. (2011). *Special focus discussion: Women's social and economic empowerment and gender equality.* Retrieved from http://www.ilo.org/global/meetings-and-events/regional-meetings/africa/arm-12/reports/WCMS_164291/lang–en/index.htm

Isaacs, J. B. (n.d.). *International comparisons of economic mobility.* Retrieved from Brookings Institution website: http://www.brookings.edu/~/media/research/files/reports/2008/2/economic%20mobility%20sawhill/02_economic_mobility_sawhill_ch3.pdf

Isaacs, J. B., Sawhill, I. V., & Haskins, R. (2008). *Getting ahead or losing ground: Economic mobility in America.* Retrieved from Economic Mobility http://www.pewstates.org/research/reports/getting-ahead-or-losing-ground-85899375818

Iyengar, S. (1991). *Is anyone responsible? How television frames political issues*. Chicago, IL: University of Chicago Press.

Jacob, J. M. (2005). *Factors influencing hiring decisions for welfare recipients* (Unpublished doctoral dissertation, University of Rhode Island, Kingston, RI).

Jacobs, K., Graham-Squire, D., & Luce, S. (2011, April). *Living wage policies and big-box retail: How a higher wage standard would impact Walmart workers and shoppers*. Retrieved from Center for Labor Research and Education website: http://labor center.berkeley.edu/retail/bigbox_livingwage_policies11.pdf

Jankowski, J. (2011). Caregiver credits in France, Germany, and Sweden: Lessons for the United States. *Social Security Bulletin, 71*, 61–76. Retrieved from US Social Security Office of Retirement and Disability Policy website: http://www.ssa.gov/policy/docs/ssb/v71n4/v71n4p61.pdf

Jarrett, R. L. (1996). Welfare stigma among low-income, African American single mothers. *Family Relations, 45*, 368–374.

Jones, E. E., & Nisbett, R. E. (1972). The actor and the observer: Divergent perceptions of the causes of behavior. In E. E. Jones, D. Kanouse, H. Kelley, S. Valins, & B. Weiner (Eds.), *Attribution: Perceiving the causes of behavior* (pp. 79–94). Morristown, NJ: General Learning Press.

Kalil, A. (2001). The role of social science in welfare reform. *Analyses of Social Issues and Public Policy, 1*, 183–185.

Kalil, A., Seefeldt, K. S., & Wang, H. (2002). Sanctions and material hardship under TANF. *The Social Service Review, 76*, 642–662.

Karger, H. J. (2003). No deals on wheels: How and why the poor pay more for basic transportation. *Journal of Poverty, 7*, 93–112.

Katel, P. (2009). Housing the homeless? Is the solution more shelters or affordable housing? *CQ Researcher, 19*, 1053–1076.

Katz, M. B. (1986). *In the shadow of the poorhouse: A social history of welfare in America*. New York, NY: Basic Books.

Katz, M. B. (1989). *The undeserving poor: From the war on poverty to the war on welfare*. New York, NY: Pantheon Books.

Katz, M. B. (2001). *The price of citizenship: Redefining the American welfare state*. New York, NY: Henry Holt and Company.

Keating, C. (2005). Building coalitional consciousness. *NWSA Journal, 17*, 86–103.

Keister, L. A., & Southgate, D. E. (2012). *Inequality: A contemporary approach to race, class, and gender*. New York, NY: Cambridge University Press.

Kelly, C., & Breinlinger, S. (1995). Identity and injustice: Exploring women's participation in collective action. *Journal of Community and Applied Social Psychology, 5*, 41–57.

Kelly, C., & Breinlinger, S. (1996). Social psychological approaches to collective action. In *The social psychology of collective action: Identity, injustice, and gender* (pp. 19–54). Philadelphia, PA: Taylor and Francis.

Kelly, M. (2010). Regulating the reproduction and mothering of poor women: The controlling image of the welfare mother in television news coverage of welfare reform. *Journal of Poverty, 14*, 76–96.

Kendall, D. (2011). *Framing class: Media representations of wealth and poverty in America* (2nd ed.). Lanham, MD: Rowman & Littlefield Publishers.

Kennelly, I. (1999). "That single-mother element": How white employers typify black women. *Gender & Society, 13*, 168–192.

Kenworthy, L. (1999). Do social-welfare policies reduce poverty? A cross-national assessment. *Social Forces, 77,* 1119–1139.

Khadduri, J. (2008, January 29). *Housing vouchers are critical for ending homelessness.* Retrieved from National Alliance to End Homelessness website: http://www.endhomelessness.org/content/article/detail/1875

Kim, C. Y., Losen, D. J., & Hewitt, D. T. (2010). *The school-to-prison pipeline: Structuring legal reform.* Chapel Hill, NC: University of North Carolina School of Law.

King, T. L. (2010). One strike evictions, state space and the production of abject Black female bodies. *Critical Sociology, 36,* 45–64.

Kissane, R. J., & Krebs, R. (2007). Assessing welfare reform, over a decade later. *Sociology Compass, 1,* 789–813.

Kluegel, J. R., & Smith, E. R. (1986). *Beliefs about inequality: Americans' views of what is and what ought to be.* New York, NY: Aldine De Gruyter.

Knecht, T., & Martinez, L. M. (2009). Humanizing the homeless: Does contact erode stereotypes? *Social Science Research, 38,* 521–534.

Kochlar, R., Fry, R., & Taylor, P. (2011, July 26). *Wealth gaps rise to record highs between whites, Blacks, and Hispanics: Twenty-to-one.* Retrieved from Pew Research Center website: http://www.pewsocialtrends.org/2011/07/26/wealth-gaps-rise-to-record-highs-between-whites-blacks-hispanics/

Kocieniewski, D. (2012, January 18). Since the 1980s, the kindest of tax cuts for the rich. *New York Times.* Retrieved from http://www.nytimes.com/2012/01/18/us/politics/for-wealthy-tax-cuts-since-1980s-have-been-gain-gain.html

Korenman, S., Joyce, T., Kaestner, R., & Walper, J. (2006). What did the "illegitimacy bonus" reward? *Topics in Economic Analysis and Policy, 6,* 1–40.

Kornbluh, F. (1998). The goals of the national welfare rights movement: Why we need them thirty years later. *Feminist Studies, 24,* 65–78.

Kozol, J. (1991). *Savage inequalities: Children in America's schools.* New York, NY: Harper Collins.

Kraus, M. W. (2012, July 19). *How the rich are different from the poor I: Choice.* Retrieved from Psychology Today website: http://www.psychologytoday.com/blog/under-the-influence/201207/how-the-rich-are-different-the-poor-i-choice

Kraus, M. W., Piff, P. K., Mendoza-Denton, R., Rheinschmidt, M. L., & Keltner, D. (2012). Social class, solipsism, contextualism: How the rich are different from the poor. *Psychological Review, 119,* 546–572.

Krugman, P. (2012, April 9). The empathy gap [Web log post]. *New York Times.* Retrieved from http://krugman.blogs.nytimes.com/2012/04/09/the-empathy-gap/

Kühhirt, M., & Ludwig, V. (2012). Domestic work and the wage penalty for motherhood in West Germany. *Journal of Marriage and Family, 74,* 186–200.

Kurth, L. (2012, August 20). *Shame, school lunch, and passing* [Web log post]. Retrieved from Class Action website: http://www.classism.org/shame-school-lunch-passing

Latimer, M. (2008). A view from the bottom: Former welfare recipients evaluate the system. *Journal of Poverty, 12,* 77–101.

Leahy, R. L. (2003). *Psychology and the economic mind: Cognitive processes and conceptualization.* New York, NY: Springer Publishing.

Lee, B. A., Tyler, K. A., & Wright, J. D. (2010). The new homelessness revisited. *Annual Review of Sociology, 36,* 501–521.

Legal Momentum. (2009, June). *The bitter fruit of welfare reform: A sharp drop in the percentage of eligible women and children receiving welfare.* Retrieved from http://www.legalmomentum.org/assets/pdfs/lm-tanf-bitter-fruit.pdf

Legal Momentum. (2010a, January, 22). *In the first twenty two months of the recession caseloads increased 35% in food stamps but just 12% in TANF.* Retrieved from http://www.legalmomentum.org/sites/default/files/reports/tanf-rolls -show-slow-growth.pdf

Legal Momentum. (2010b, August 4). *The sanction epidemic in the Temporary Assistance for Needy Families Program.* Retrieved from http://www.legalmomentum.org/ our-work/women-and-poverty/resources–publications/sanction-epidemic-in-tanf.pdf

Legal Momentum. (2011a, June). *Poverty rates for single mothers are higher in the U.S. than in other high income countries.* Retrieved from http://www.legalmomentum.org/ our-work/women-and-poverty/resources–publications/single-mothers-poverty-higher-us.pdf

Legal Momentum. (2011b, September 15). *Single mothers in the United States in 2010.* Retrieved from http://www.legalmomentum.org/our-work/women-and-poverty/ resources–publications/single-mother-poverty-2010.pdf

Legal Momentum. (2012). *Single motherhood in the United States – A snapshot* (2012). Retrieved from http://www.legalmomentum.org/our-work/women-and-poverty/ single-motherhood-in-the.html

Lemieux, A. F., & Pratto, F. (2003). Poverty and prejudice. In S. Carr & T. S. Sloan (Eds.), *Poverty and psychology: From global perspective to local practice* (pp. 147–161). New York, NY: Kluwer Academic/Plenum.

Lens, V. (2003). Examining the role of experts in policy debates: An analysis of expert opinion on welfare reform in The New York Times. *Chicago Policy Review, 7,* 61–76.

Lens, V. (2006). Work sanctions under TANF: Are they helping women achieve self-sufficiency? *Duke Journal of Gender Law and Policy, 13,* 255–284.

Lens, V. (2008). Welfare and work sanctions: Examining discretion on the front lines. *Social Service Review, 82,* 197–222.

Lens, V. (2009). Implementing full and partial work sanctions. The case of Texas. *The American Review of Public Administration, 39,* 286–303.

Lens, V., & Cary, C. (2010). Negotiating the discourse of race within the United States welfare system. *Ethnic and Racial Studies, 33,* 1032–1048.

Lepianka, D., van Oorschot, W., & Gelissen, J. (2009). Popular explanations of poverty: A critical discussion of empirical research. *Journal of Social Policy, 38,* 421–438.

Lewis, O. (1966). *La vida: A Puerto Rican family in the culture of poverty – San Juan and New York.* New York, NY: Random House.

LIFETIME. (n.d.). *Marriage promotion.* Retrieved from http://www.geds-to-phds.org/ welfare_weddings.html

Limbert, W. M., & Bullock, H. E. (2005). "Playing the fool": US welfare policy from a critical race perspective. *Feminism & Psychology, 15,* 253–274.

Limbert, W. M., & Bullock, H. E. (2009). Framing redistributive policies: Tough love for poor women and tax cuts for seniors. *Analyses of Social Issues and Public Policy, 9,* 57–83.

Lind, A. (2004). Legislating the family: Heterosexist bias in social welfare policy. *Journal of Sociology and Social Welfare, 31,* 21–35.

Lindhorst, T., & Leighninger, L. (2003). "Ending welfare as we know it" in 1960: Louisiana's suitable home laws. *Social Service Review, 77,* 564–584.

Lindhorst, T., Oxford, M., & Gillmore, M. R. (2007). Longitudinal effects of domestic violence on employment and welfare outcomes. *Journal of Interpersonal Violence, 22,* 812–828.

Liptak, A. (2011, June 20). Justices rule for Wal-Mart in class-action bias suit. *New York Times.* Retrieved from http://www.nytimes.com/2011/06/21/business/21bizcourt.html?pagewanted=all

Littrell, J., Brooks, F., Ivery, J., & Ohmer, M. L. (2010). Why you should care about the threatened middle class. *Journal of Sociology and Social Welfare, XXXVII,* 87–113.

Loffredo, S. (2001). Poverty law and community activism: Notes from a law school clinic. *University of Pennsylvania Law Review, 150,* 173–204.

Lohman, B. J., Pittman, L. D., Coley, R. L., & Chase-Lansdale, P. L. (2004). Welfare history, sanctions, and developmental outcomes among low-income children and youth. *Social Service Review, 78,* 41–73.

Loprest, P. J. (2011, November). *Disconnected families and TANF.* Retrieved from Urban Institute website: http://www.urban.org/url.cfm?ID=412568

Loprest, P. J. (2012, March 8). *How has the TANF caseload changed over time?* Retrieved from Urban Institute website: http://www.acf.hhs.gov/sites/default/files/opre/change_time_1.pdf

Lott, B. (2001). Low-income parents and the public schools. *Journal of Social Issues, 57,* 247–259.

Lott, B. (2002). Cognitive and behavioral distancing from the poor. *American Psychologist, 57,* 100–110.

Lott, B. (2012). The social psychology of class and classism. *American Psychologist, 67,* 650–658.

Lott, B., & Bullock, H. E. (2007). *Psychology and economic injustice: Personal, professional, and political intersections.* Washington, DC: American Psychological Association.

Lott, B., & Saxon, S. (2002). The influence of ethnicity, social class, and context on judgments about U.S. women. *Journal of Social Psychology, 142,* 481–499.

Lott, B., & Webster, K. (2006). Carry the banner where it can be seen: Small wins for social justice. *Social Justice Research, 19,* 123–134.

Lowe, S. T. (2008). "It's all one big circle": Welfare discourse and the everyday lives of urban adolescents. *Journal of Sociology and Social Welfare, XXXV,* 173–194.

Lower-Basch, E. (2008, March 18). *Education and training for TANF recipients: Opportunities and challenges under the final rule.* Retrieved from Center for Law and Social Policy website: http://www.clasp.org/admin/site/publications/files/0406.pdf

Luna, Y. M. (2009). Single welfare mothers' resistance. *Journal of Poverty, 13,* 441–461.

Major, B., & O'Brien, L. T. (2005). The social psychology of stigma. *Annual Review of Psychology, 56,* 393–421.

Martin, M. C., & Caminada, K. (2011). Welfare reform in the U.S.: A policy overview analysis. *Poverty and Public Policy, 3,* 67–104.

Mason, S. E. (2012). The occupy movement and social justice economics. *Families in Society: The Journal of Contemporary Social Services, 93,* 3–4.

Mazzeo, C., Rab, S., & Eachus, S. (2003). Work-first or work-only: Welfare reform, state policy, and access to postsecondary education. *Annals of the American Academy of Political and Social Science, 586,* 144–171.

McCall, L., & Kenworthy, L. (2009). Americans' social policy preferences in the era of rising inequality. *Perspectives on Politics, 7,* 459–484.

McClelland, S. I., & Fine, M. (2008). Embedded science: Critical analysis of abstinence-only evaluation research. *Cultural Studies ↔ Critical Methodologies, 8,* 50–81.

McCormack, K. (2004). Resisting the welfare mother: The power of welfare discourse and tactics of resistance. *Critical Sociology, 30,* 355–383.

McCormack, K. (2005). Stratified reproduction and poor women's resistance. *Gender and Society, 19,* 660–679.

McCoy, S. K., & Major, B. (2007). Priming meritocracy and the psychological justification of inequality. *Journal of Experimental Social Psychology, 43,* 341–351.

McLanahan, S., & Percheski, C. (2008). Family structure and the reproduction of inequalities. *Annual Review of Sociology, 34,* 257–276.

McNamee, S. J., & Miller, R. K. (2009). *The meritocracy myth* (2nd ed.). Lanham, MD: Rowman & Littlefield Publishers.

McWha, I., & Carr, S. C. (2009). Images of poverty and attributions for poverty: Does higher education moderate the linkage. *International Journal of Nonprofit and Voluntary Sector Marketing, 14,* 101–109.

Merolla, D. M., Hunt, M. O., & Serpe, R. T. (2011). Concentrated disadvantage and beliefs about the causes of poverty: A multi-level analysis. *Sociological Perspectives, 54,* 205–228.

Meschede, T., Chaganti, S., & Mann, A. (2012, February). *Rapid re-housing and short-term rental vouchers for homeless families: Summary report of a pilot.* Retrieved from Institute for Assets and Social Policy website: http://iasp.brandeis.edu/pdfs/Author/chaganti-sara/Rapid%20Re-Housing%20and%20Short-Term%20Rental.pdf

Meschede, T., Cronin, M., Sullivan, L., & Shapiro, T. (2011, October). *Rising economic insecurity among senior single women.* Retrieved from Institute on Assets and Social Policy website: http://iasp.brandeis.edu/pdfs/Author/meschede-tatjana/Rising%20Economic%20Insecurity%20Among%20Senior.pdf

Metzgar, J. (2010, January 11). *America's low-wage future.* Retrieved from Center for Working Class Studies website: http://workingclassstudies.wordpress.com/2010/01/11/america%E2%80%99s-low-wage-future/

Mickelson, K. D., & Williams, S. L. (2008). Perceived stigma of poverty and depression: Examination of interpersonal and intrapersonal mediators. *Journal of Social and Clinical Psychology, 27,* 903–930.

Mink, G. (1998a). The lady and the tramp (II): Feminist welfare politics, poor single mothers, and the challenge of welfare justice. *Feminist Studies, 24,* 55–64.

Mink, G. (1998b). *Welfare's end.* Ithaca, NY: Cornell University Press.

Mink, G. (2001). Violating women: Rights abuses in the welfare police state. *American Academy of Political and Social Science, 577,* 79–93.

Mink, G. (2010). *Women's work, mother's poverty: Are men's wages the best cure for women's insecurity.* Retrieved from New Politics website: http://newpol.org/node/164

Mistry, R. S., Brown, C. S., Chow, K. A., & Collins, G. S. (2012). Increasing the complexity of young adolescents' beliefs about poverty and inequality: Results of an 8th grade social studies curriculum intervention. *Journal of Youth and Adolescence, 41,* 704–716.

Moore, T., & Selkowe, V. (1999). *The impact of welfare reform on Wisconsin's Hmong aid recipients.* Retrieved from http://www.wisconsinsfuture.org/publications_pdfs/past_projects_pdfs/hmong.pdf

Moore, T. S., & Arora, S. S. (2009). The limits of paternalism: A case study of welfare reform in Wisconsin. *Journal of Sociology and Social Welfare, XXXVI*, 107–131.

Moreno, M., Toros, H., Stevens, M., Beardsley, J., Salem, N., Horton, J., & Shaw, L. (2006). *Sanctioned participants and the challenges of meeting welfare-to-work requirements in the era of TANF reauthorization.* Retrieved from http://ceo.lacounty.gov/sib/pdf/RES/Bullet8.pdf

Morin, R. (2011, February 16). *The public renders a split verdict on changes in family structure.* Retrieved from Pew Research Center website: http://www.pewsocial trends.org/2011/02/16/the-public-renders-a-split-verdict-on-changes-in-family-structure/#prc_jump

Murray, S. (2011). Violence against homeless women: Safety and social policy. *Australian Social Work, 64*, 346–360.

Nadasen, P. (2002). Expanding the boundaries of the women's movement: Black women and the struggle for welfare rights. *Feminist Studies, 28*, 270–301.

National Alliance to End Homelessness. (n.d.). *Domestic violence.* Retrieved from http://www.endhomelessness.org/section/issues/domestic_violence

National Coalition for the Homeless. (2009, July). *Who is homeless?* Retrieved from http://www.nationalhomeless.org/factsheets/who.html

National Law Center on Homelessness & Poverty. (2011, March). *U.S. response to U.N. human rights review released: Government supports reducing homelessness as human rights obligation.* Retrieved from http://www.nlchp.org/view_release.cfm?PRID=128

National Low Income Housing Coalition. (2012, February). The shrinking supply of affordable housing. *Housing Spotlight, 2*, 1–6. Retrieved from http://nlihc.org/sites/default/files/HousingSpotlight2-1.pdf

National Women's Law Center (NWLC). (2012, September). *Insecure & unequal: Poverty and income among women and families 2010–2011.* Retrieved from http://www.nwlc.org/sites/default/files/pdfs/nwlc_2012_povertyreport.pdf

Neitzel, C., & Chafel, J. A. (2010). "And no flowers grow there and stuff": Young children's social representations of poverty. In H. B. Johnson (Ed.), *Children and youth speak for themselves* (pp. 33–59). Bingley, UK: Emerald Group Publishing.

Nelson, M. K. (2002). Declaring welfare "reform" a success: The role of applied social science. *Journal of Poverty, 6*, 1–27.

Neubeck, K. J., & Cazenave, N. A. (2001). *Welfare racism: Playing the race card against America's poor.* New York, NY: Routledge.

Newfield, C. (2008). *Unmaking the public university: The forty year assault on the middle class.* Cambridge, MA: Harvard University Press.

Nichols, L., & Cazares, F. (2011). Homelessness and the mobile shelter system: Public transportation as shelter. *Journal of Social Policy, 40*, 333–350.

North Carolina Justice for Sterilization Victims Foundation. (2010, October). *Questions and answers on eugenics in North Carolina.* Retrieved from http://www.document cloud.org/documents/272335-north-carolina-eugenics-informational-brochure.html

NOW Legal Defense and Education Fund. (n.d.). *Why NOW legal defense opposes federal marriage promotion in reauthorization.* Retrieved from http://www.legal momentum.org/assets/pdfs/marriagebackgrounder.pdf

Obama, B. (2004, July 27). *2004 Democratic national convention address.* Retrieved from American Rhetoric website: http://www.americanrhetoric.com/speeches/conven tion2004/barackobama2004dnc.htm

Obama, B. (2007, November 7). *Obama's November 7, 2007, speech on the "American dream."* Retrieved from CNN Politics website: http://edition.cnn.com/2007/POLITICS/12/21/obama.trans.americandream/

Obama, B. (2012, January 25). *The 2012 state of the union.* Retrieved from White House website: http://www.whitehouse.gov/state-of-the-union-2012

Occupy Together. (n.d.). *Occupy Together website.* Retrieved from http://www.occupytogether.org/

O'Connor, A. (2000). Poverty research and policy for the post-welfare era. *Annual Review of Sociology, 26,* 547–562.

O'Connor, A. (2001). *Poverty knowledge: Social science, social policy, and the poor in twentieth-century U.S. history.* Princeton, NJ: Princeton University Press.

Onwuachi-Willig, A. (2005). The return of the ring: Welfare reform's marriage cure as the revival of post-bellum control. *California Law Review, 93,* 1647–1696.

Ooms, T., Bouchet, S., & Parke, M. (2004, April). *Beyond marriage licenses: Efforts in states to strengthen marriage and two-parent families: A state-by-state snapshot.* Retrieved from Center for Law and Social Policy website: http://www.clasp.org/admin/site/publications_archive/files/0158.pdf

Opotow, S. (1990). Moral exclusion and injustice: An introduction. *Journal of Social Issues, 46,* 1–20.

Orth, D. A., & Goggin, M. L. (2003, December). *How states and counties have responded to the family policy goals of welfare reform.* Retrieved from Rockefeller Institute website: http://www.rockinst.org/pdf/workforce_welfare_and_social_services/2003-12-how_states_and_counties_have_responded_to_the_family_policy_goals_of_welfare_reform.pdf

Ostrove, J. M., & Cole, E. R. (2003). Privileging class: Toward a critical psychology of social class in the context of education. *Journal of Social Issues, 59,* 677–692.

Page, B. I., & Jacobs, L. R. (2009). *Class war? What Americans really think about economic inequality.* Chicago, IL: University of Chicago.

Page, T., & Nooe, R. M. (2002). Life experiences and vulnerabilities of homeless women: A comparison of women unaccompanied versus accompanied by minor children, and correlates with children's emotional distress. *Journal of Social Distress and the Homeless, 11,* 215–231.

Pager, D., Western, B., & Bonikowski, B. (2009). Discrimination in a low-wage labor market: A field experiment. *American Sociological Review, 74,* 777–799.

Pandey, S., & Kim, J. (2008). Path to poverty alleviation: Marriage or postsecondary education? *Journal of Family and Economic Issues, 29,* 166–184.

Papp, L. M., Cummings, E. M., & Goeke-Morey, M. C. (2009). For richer, for poorer: Money as a topic of marital conflict in the home. *Family Relations, 58,* 91–103.

Parrott, S. (1998, November 16). *Welfare recipients who find jobs: What do we know about their employment and earnings?* Retrieved from Center on Budget and Policy Priorities website: http://www.cbpp.org/11-16-98wel.htm

Parrott, S., & Sherman, A. (2006, August 17). *TANF at 10: Program results are more mixed than often understood.* Retrieved from Center on Budget and Policy Priorities website: http://www.cbpp.org/files/8-17-06tanf.pdf

Pearce, D. (1978). The feminization of poverty: Women, work, and welfare. *Urban and Social Change Review, 11,* 28–36.

Pearce, D. M., & Moritz, N. (1988). Life changes: A life cycle perspective on women's economic status. *Social Thought, 14,* 4–15.

Pearlmutter, S., & Bartle, E. E. (2003). Participants' perceptions of the childcare subsidy system. *Journal of Sociology and Social Welfare, XXX,* 157–173.

Personal Responsibility and Work Reconciliation Act of 1996. Pub. L. No. 104-193, 110 Stat. 2105 (1997).

Pew Research Center. (2012, June 4). *Trends in American values: 1987–2012: Partisan polarization surges in Bush, Obama years.* Retrieved from http://pewresearch.org/pubs/2277/republicans-democrats-partisanship-partisan-divide-polarization-social-safety-net-environmental-protection-government-regulation-independents

Phelan, J., Link, B. G., Moore, R. E., & Stueve, A. (1997). The stigma of homelessness: The impact of the label "homeless" on attitudes toward poor persons. *Social Psychology Quarterly, 60,* 323–337.

Pierson-Balik, D. (2003). Race, class, and gender in punitive welfare reform: Social eugenics and welfare policy. *Race, Gender & Class, 10,* 11–30.

Piven, F. F. (2001). Globalization, American politics, and welfare policy. *Annals of the American Academy of Political and Social Science, 577,* 26–37.

Piven, F. F., & Cloward, R. (1977). Dilemmas of organization building: The case of welfare rights. *Radical America, 11,* 39–61.

Piven, F. F., & Cloward, R. A. (1993). *Regulating the poor: The functions of public welfare (2nd edition).* New York, NY: Random House.

Ponic, P., Varcoe, C., Davies, L., Ford-Gilboe, M., Wuest, J., & Hammerton, J. (2011). Leaving ≠ moving: Housing patterns of women who have left an abusive partner. *Violence Against Women, 17,* 1576–1600.

Power, C. A., Cole, E. R., & Fredrickson, B. L. (2010). Poor women and the expression of shame and anger: The price of breaking social class feeling rules. *Feminism & Psychology, 21,* 179–197.

Pratto, F., Sidanius, J., Stallworth, L. M., & Malle, B. F. (1994). Social dominance orientation: A personality variable predicting social and political attitudes. *Journal of Personality & Social Psychology, 67,* 741–763.

Preserving the American dream: Predatory practices and home foreclosures: Hearing before the Committee on Banking, Housing, and Urban Affairs of the U.S. Senate. 110th Cong. 1 (2007).

Price, C. (2005). Reforming welfare reform postsecondary education policy: Two state case studies in political culture, organizing, and advocacy. *Journal of Sociology and Social Welfare, XXXII,* 81–106.

Price, J., Desmond, S., & Eoff, T. (1989). Nurses' perceptions regarding health care and the poor. *Psychological Reports, 65,* 1043–1052.

Primeau, L. A. (1992). A woman's place: Unpaid work in the home. *American Journal of Occupational Therapy, 46,* 981–988.

Purvin, D. M. (2007). At the crossroads and in the crosshairs: Social welfare policy and low-income women's vulnerability to domestic violence. *Social Problems, 54,* 188–210.

Rank, M. R., & Hirschl, T. A. (2001). Rags or riches? Estimating the probabilities of poverty and affluence across the American life span. *Social Science Quarterly, 82,* 651–669.

Rank, M. R., Yoon, H. S., & Hirschl, T. A. (2003). American poverty as a structural failing: Evidence and arguments. *Journal of Sociology and Social Welfare, XXX,* 3–29.

Rattner, S. (2012, March 25). *The rich get even richer.* New York Times. Retrieved from: http://www.nytimes.com/2012/03/26/opinion/the-rich-get-even-richer.html

Rector, R. (2010, March 8). *Obama's new poverty measure*. Retrieved from Heritage Foundation website: http://www.heritage.org/research/commentary/2010/03/ obamas-new-poverty-measurement

Rector, R., & Sheffield, R. (2011, July 19). *Air conditioning, cable TV, and an Xbox: What is poverty in the United States today?* Retrieved from Heritage Foundation website: http://www.heritage.org/research/reports/2011/07/what-is-poverty

Redden, J. (2011). Poverty in the news: A framing analysis of coverage in Canada and the UK *Information, Communication & Society, 14*, 820–849.

Reed, M. E., Collinsworth, L. L., & Fitzgerald, L. F. (2005). There's no place like home: Sexual Harassment of low income women in housing. *Psychology, Public Policy, and Law, 11*, 439–462.

Reese, E. (2002). Resisting the workfare state: Mobilizing general relief recipients in Los Angeles. *Race, Gender & Class, 9*, 72–95.

Reese, E. (2007). The causes and consequences of U.S. welfare retrenchment. *Journal of Poverty, 11*, 47–63.

Reese, E., Geidraitis, V. R., & Vega, E. (2005). Mobilization and threat: Campaigns against welfare privatization in four cities. *Sociological Focus, 38*, 287–309.

Reese, E., Geidraitis, V. R., & Vega, E. (2006). Welfare is not for sale: Campaigns against welfare profiteers in Milwaukee. *Social Justice, 33*, 38–53.

Reeser, L. C., & Epstein, I. (1987). Social workers' attitudes toward poverty and social action: 1968–1984. *Social Service Review, 61*, 610–622.

Rehner, T., Ishee, J., Salloum, M., & Velasques, D. (1997). Mississippi social workers' attitudes toward poverty and the poor. *Journal of Social Work Education, 33*, 131–142.

Reid, T. P. (1993). Poor women in psychological research: Shut up and shut out. *Psychology of Women Quarterly, 17*, 133–150.

Reid, T. P. (2011). Revisiting "Poor women: Shut up and shut out." *Psychology of Women Quarterly, 35*, 189–192.

Reimers, F. A. (2007). *Putting it all together: A content analysis and methodological review of the intersections of class, race, and gender in the counseling psychology literature* (Unpublished doctoral dissertation, Texas Woman's University, Denton, TX).

Reingold, D. A., & Liu, H. K. (2009). Do poverty attitudes of social service agency directors influence organizational behavior? *Nonprofit and Voluntary Sector Quarterly, 38*, 307–332.

Renya, C., Henry, P. J., Korfmacher, W., & Tucker, A. (2005). Examining the principles in principled conservatism: The role of responsibility stereotypes as cues for deservingness in racial policy decisions. *Journal of Personality and Social Psychology, 90*, 109–128.

Reskin, B. F., & Hartmann, H. I. (Eds.). (1986). *Women's work, men's work: Sex segregation on the job*. Washington, DC: National Academy Press.

Reutter, L. I., Stewart, M. J., Veenstra, G., Love, R., Raphael, D., & Makwarimba, E. (2009). "Who do they think we are, anyway?": Perceptions of and responses to poverty stigma. *Qualitative Health Research, 19*, 297–311.

Reutter, L. I., Veenstra, G., Stewart, M. J., Raphael, D., Love, R., Makwarimba, E., & McMurray, S. (2005). Lay understandings of the effects of poverty: A Canadian perspective. *Health and Social Care in the Community, 13*, 514–530.

Rice, D. (2011, November 22). *Hardship in America, part 3: Homelessness growing among families with children*. Retrieved from Center on Budget and Policy Priorities website:

http://www.offthechartsblog.org/hardship-in-america-part-3-homelessness-growing-among-families-with-children/

Richards, T. N., Garland, T. S., Bumphus, V. W., & Thompson, R. (2010). Personal and political?: Exploring the feminization of the American homeless population. *Journal of Poverty, 14*, 97–115.

Roberts, D. E. (1995). The only good poor woman: Unconstitutional conditions and welfare. *Denver University Law Review, 72*, 931–938.

Robertson, M. J. (1996). Mental health problems of homeless women and differences across subgroups. *Annual Review of Public Health, 17*, 311–336.

Robinson, G. (2011). The contradictions of caring: Social workers, teachers, and attributions for poverty and welfare reform. *Journal of Applied Social Psychology, 41*, 2374–2404.

Robinson, J. W. (2009). American poverty cause beliefs and structured inequality legitimation. *Sociological Spectrum, 29*, 489–518.

Roesch, J. (2004, November–December). Turning back the clock? Women, work, and family today. *International Socialist Review, 38*. Retrieved from http://www.isreview.org/issues/38/women_family.shtml

Rollins, J., Saris, R., & Johnston-Robledo, I. (2001). Low-income women speak out about housing: A high-stakes game of musical chairs. *Journal of Social Issues, 57*, 277–298.

Romero, D., & Agénor, M. (2009). U.S. fertility prevention as poverty prevention: An empirical question and social justice issue. *Women's Health Issues, 19*, 355–364.

Romich, J. L., Simmelink, J., & Holt, S. D. (2007). When working harder does not pay: Low-income working families, tax liabilities, and benefit reductions. *Families in Society: The Journal of Contemporary Social Services, 88*, 418–426.

Romney, M. (2011, December 19). Romney: What kind of society does America want? *USA Today*. Retrieved from http://www.usatoday.com/news/opinion/forum/story/2011-12-19/romney-us-economy-entitlements/52076252/1

Roschelle, A. R. (2008). Welfare indignities: Homeless women, domestic violence, and welfare reform in San Francisco. *Gender Issues, 25*, 193–209.

Rosenthal, L., Levy, S. R., & Moyer, A. (2011). Protestant work ethic's relation to intergroup and policy attitudes: A meta-analytic review. *European Journal of Social Psychology, 41*, 874–885.

Ross, L. (1977). The intuitive psychologist and his shortcomings: Distortions in the attribution process. In L. Berkowitz (Ed.), *Advances in experimental social psychology* (Vol. 10, pp. 173–220). New York, NY: Academic Press.

Russell, S. (1995, February 17). Doctors tell why they won't treat Medi-Cal patients. *San Francisco Chronicle*. Retrieved from http://www.sfgate.com/news/article/Doctors-Tell-Why-They-Won-t-Treat-Medi-Cal-3044825.php

Sanders, C. K., & Schnabel, M. (2004). *Organizing for economic empowerment of battered women: Women's savings account* (Working Paper No. 04-15). Retrieved from Center for Social Development website: http://csd.wustl.edu/Publications/Documents/WP04-15.pdf

Sanders, M. R., & Mahalingam, R. (2012). Under the radar: The role if invisible discourse in understanding class-based privilege. *The Journal of Social Issues, 68*, 112–127.

Saris, R. N., & Johnston-Robledo, I. (2000). Poor women are still shut out of mainstream psychology. *Psychology of Women Quarterly, 24*, 233–235.

Sawhill, I. V., & Morton, J. E. (2007, May 25). *Economic mobility: Is the American dream alive and well?* Retrieved from Economic Mobility Project website: http://www.pewtrusts.org/our_work_report_detail.aspx?id=24834

Schneider, A. L., & Ingram, H. (1997). *Policy design for democracy.* Lawrence, KS: Kansas University Press.

Schneider, S. K., & Jacoby, W. G. (2005). Elite discourse and American public opinion: The case of welfare spending. *Political Research Quarterly, 58,* 367–379.

Schott, L. (2012). *Policy basics: An introduction to TANF.* Retrieved from Center on Budget and Policy Priorities website: http://www.cbpp.org/cms/?fa=view&id=936

Schott, L., & Finch, I. (2010, October 14). *TANF benefits are low and have not kept pace with inflation: Benefits are not enough to meet families' basic needs.* Retrieved from Center on Budget and Policy Priorities website: http://www.cbpp.org/cms/index.cfm?fa=view&id=3306

Schott, L., & Levinson, Z. (2008, November 24). *TANF benefits are low and have not kept pace with inflation: But most states have increased benefits above a freeze in recent years.* Retrieved from Center on Budget and Policy Priorities website: http://www.cbpp.org/pdf/11-24-08tanf.pdf

Schott, L., & Pavetti, L. (2011, October 3). *Many states cutting TANF benefits harshly despite high unemployment and unprecedented need.* Retrieved from Center on Budget and Policy Priorities website: http://www.cbpp.org/cms/?fa=view&id=3498

Schram, S. F., & Soss, J. (2001). Success stories: Welfare reform, policy discourse, and the politics of research. *Annals of the American Academy of Political and Social Science, 577,* 49–65.

Schram, S. F., Soss, J., Houser, L., & Fording, R. C. (2010). The third level of US welfare reform: Governmentality under neoliberal paternalism. *Citizenship Studies, 14,* 739–754.

Scott, E. K., London, A. S., & Gross, G. (2007). "I try not to depend on anyone but me": Welfare-reliant women's perspectives on self-sufficiency, work, and marriage. *Sociological Inquiry, 77,* 601–625.

Scruggs, L., & Allan, J. P. (2006). The material consequences of welfare states: Benefit generosity and absolute poverty in 16 OECD countries. *Comparative Political Studies, 39,* 880–904.

Seccombe, K. (2011). *"So you think I drive a Cadillac?" Welfare recipients' perspectives on the system and its reform* (3rd ed.). Boston: Allyn & Bacon.

Sechrist, G. B., Swim, J. K., & Stangor, C. (2004). When do the stigmatized make attributions to discrimination occurring to the self and others? The roles of self-presentation and need for control. *Journal of Personality and Social Psychology, 87,* 111–122.

Segal, E. A. (2007). Social empathy: A new paradigm to address poverty. *Journal of Poverty, 11,* 65–81.

Seider, S. (2011). The role of privilege as identity in adolescents' beliefs about homelessness, opportunity, and inequality. *Youth & Society, 43,* 333–364.

Seider, S. C., Gillmor, S. C., & Rabinowicz, S. A. (2011). The impact of community service learning upon the worldview of business majors versus non-business majors at an American university. *Journal of Business Ethics, 98,* 485–503.

Severson, K. (2011, December 9). Thousands sterilized, a state weighs restitution. *New York Times.* Retrieved from http://www.nytimes.com/2011/12/10/us/redress-weighed-for-forced-sterilizations-in-north-carolina.html?pagewanted=all

Shaefer, H. L., & Edin, K. (2012, February). *Extreme poverty in the United States, 1996 to 2011* (Policy Brief #28). Retrieved from National Poverty Center website: http://npc.umich.edu/publications/policy_briefs/brief28/policybrief28.pdf

Shapiro, T. M., Oliver, M. L., & Meschede, T. (2009, November). *The asset security and opportunity index.* Retrieved from tatjana/The%20Asset%20Security%20and%20Opportunity%20Index.pdf

Shaw, H., & Stone, C. (2011, March 7). *Incomes at the top rebounded in first full year of recovery, new analysis of tax data shows: Top 1 percent's share of income starting to rise again.* Retrieved from Center on Budget and Policy Priorities website: http://www.cbpp.org/cms/index.cfm?fa=view&id=3697

Shdaimah, C. (2009). Rescuing children and punishing poor families: Housing related decisions. *Journal of Sociology and Social Welfare, XXXVI,* 33–57.

Shear, M. D., & Barbaro, M. (2012, September 17). In video clip, Romney calls 47% "dependent" and feeling entitled. *New York Times.* Retrieved from http://thecaucus.blogs.nytimes.com/2012/09/17/romney-faults-those-dependent-on-government/?hp

Shen, F., & Edwards, H. H. (2005). Economic individualism, humanitarianism, and welfare reform: A value-based account of framing effects. *Journal of Communication, 55,* 795–809.

Sherman, A. (2011, November 7). *Poverty and financial distress would have been substantially worse in 2010 without government action, new census data show.* Retrieved from Center on Budget and Policy Priorities website: http://www.cbpp.org/cms/?fa=view&id=3610

Sherman, A. (2012, March 5). *Under $2 a day in America, part 1* [Web log post]. Retrieved from Center on Budget and Policy Priorities website: http://www.offthechartsblog.org/under-2-dollars-a-day-in-america-part-1/

Sherman, A., Greenstein, R., & Ruffing, K. (2012, February 10). *Contrary to "entitlement society" rhetoric, over nine-tenths of entitlement benefits go to elderly, disabled, or working households.* Retrieved from Center on Budget and Policy Priorities website: http://www.cbpp.org/cms/index.cfm?fa=view&id=3677

Sherman, A., & Stone, C. (2010, June 25). *Income gaps between very rich and everyone else more than tripled in last three decades, new data show.* Retrieved from Center on Budget and Policy Priorities website: http://www.cbpp.org/cms/?fa=view&id=3220

Shinn, M., & Gillespie, C. (1994). The roles of housing and poverty in the origins of homelessness. *American Behavioral Scientist, 37,* 505–521.

Shpungin, E., & Lyubansky, M. (2006). Navigating social class roles in community research. *American Journal of Community Psychology, 37,* 227–235.

Sidanius, J., Devereux, E., & Pratto, F. (1992). A comparison of symbolic racism theory and social dominance theory as explanations for racial policy attitudes. *Journal of Social Psychology, 132,* 377–395.

Sidel, R. (1998). *Keeping women and children last: America's war on the poor.* New York, NY: Penguin Books.

Sikich, K. W. (2008). Global female homelessness: A multi-faceted problem. *Gender Issues, 25,* 147–156.

Sisson, G. (2012). Finding a way to offer something more: Reframing teen pregnancy prevention. *Sexuality Research and Social Policy, 9,* 57–69.

Skitka, L. J., Mullen, E., Griffin, E., Hutchinson, S., & Chamberlin, B. (2002). Dispositions, scripts, or motivated correction? Understanding ideological differences in explanations for social problems. *Journal of Personality and Social Psychology, 83*, 470–487.

Slack, K. S., Magnuson, K. A., Berger, L. M., Yoo, J., Coley, R. L., Dunifon, R., & Osborne, C. (2007). Family economic well-being following the 1996 welfare reform: Trend data from five non-experimental panel studies. *Children and Youth Services Review, 29*, 698–720.

Smith, A. M. (2007). *Welfare reform and sexual regulation.* New York, NY: Cambridge University Press.

Smith, K. B. (1985). I made it because of me: Beliefs about the causes of wealth and poverty. *Sociological Spectrum, 5*, 255–267.

Smith, K. B., & Stone, L. (1989). Rags, riches, and bootstraps: Beliefs about the causes of wealth and poverty. *The Sociological Quarterly, 30*, 93–107.

Smith, L. (2005). Psychotherapy, classism, and the poor: Conspicuous by their absence. *American Psychologist, 60*, 687–696.

Smith, L. (2010). *Psychology, poverty, and the end of social exclusion: Putting our practice to work.* New York, NY: Teachers College Press.

Smith, L., Allen, A., & Bowen, R. (2010). Expecting the worst: Exploring the associations between poverty and misbehavior. *Journal of Poverty, 14*, 33–54.

Smith, L., Chambers, D. A., & Bratini, L. (2009). When oppression is the pathogen: The participatory development of socially just mental practice. *American Journal of Orthopsychiatry, 79*, 159–168.

Smith, M. B. (1990). Psychology in the public interest: What have we done? What can we do? *American Psychologist, 45*, 530–536.

Smith, R. J. (2006). Family caps in welfare reform: Their coercive effects and damaging consequences. *Harvard Journal of Law and Gender, 29*, 151–200.

Smith, T. W. (1987). That which we call welfare by any other name would smell sweeter: an analysis of the impact of question wording on pattern response. *Public Opinion Quarterly, 51*, 75–83.

Social Security Administration. (2013). *Fact sheet: Social security is important to women.* Retrieved from http://www.socialsecurity.gov/pressoffice/factsheets/women-alt.pdf

Solomon, B. (2007). "Go it alone" poverty in a small city: Pockets of poor housing, the scrutiny of "busybodies," and difficulty accessing support. *Journal of Poverty, 10*, 27–50.

Sommer, B., & Maycroft, J. R. (2008). Influencing public policy: An analysis of published op-eds by academics. *Politics & Policy, 36*, 586–613.

Soss, J. (2005). Making clients and citizens: Welfare policy as a source of status, belief, and action. In A. Schneider & H. Ingram (Eds.), *Deserving and entitled: Social constructions and public policy* (pp. 291–328). Albany, NY: State University of New York Press.

Soss, J., Condon, M., Holleque, M., & Wichowsky, A. (2006). The illusion of technique: How method-driven research leads welfare scholarship astray. *Social Science Quarterly, 87*, 798–807.

Soss, J., Fording, R. C., & Schram, S. F. (2011). *Disciplining the poor: Neoliberal paternalism and the persistent power of race.* Chicago, IL: University of Chicago Press.

Soss, J., Schram, S. F., Vartanian, T. P., & O'Brien, E. (2001). Setting the terms of relief: Explaining state policy choices in the devolution revolution. *American Journal of Political Science, 45*, 378–395.

Steensland, B. (2006). Cultural categories and the American welfare state: The case of guaranteed income policy. *American Journal of Sociology, 111*, 1273–1326.

Steinitz, V., & Mishler, E. G. (2001). Reclaiming SPSSI's radical promise: A critical look at JSI's "Impact of welfare reform" issue. *Analyses of Social Issues and Public Policy, 1*, 163–173.

Stephens, N. M., Fryberg, S. A., & Markus, H. R. (2011). When choice does not equal freedom: A sociocultural analysis of agency in working-class American contexts. *Social Psychological and Personality Science, 2*, 33–41.

Stephens, N. M., Markus, H. R., & Townsend, S. (2007). Choice as an act of meaning: The case of social class. *Journal of Personality and Social Psychology, 93*, 814–830.

Stewart, A., & Gold-Steinberg, S. (1996). Women's abortion experiences as sources of political mobilization. In M. B. Lykes, A. Banuazizi, R. Liem, & M. Morris (Eds.), *Myths about the powerless: Contesting social inequalities* (pp. 275–295). Philadelphia, PA: Temple University Press.

Stewart B. McKinney Act of 1987. Pub. L. No. 100-77, 101 Stat. 482.

Streib, J. (2011). Class reproduction by four year olds. *Qualitative Sociology, 34*, 337–352.

Strier, R. (2008). Client and worker perceptions of poverty: Implications for practice and research. *Families in Society: The Journal of Contemporary Social Services, 89*, 466–475.

Stryker, R., & Wald, P. (2009). Redefining compassion to reform welfare: How supporters of the 1990s US federal welfare reform aimed for the moral high ground. *Social Politics, 16*, 519–557.

Stuber, J., & Kronebusch, K. (2004). Stigma and other determinants of participation in TANF and Medicaid. *Journal of Policy Analysis and Management, 23*, 509–530.

Substance Abuse and Mental Health Services Administration. (2011, July). *Current statistics on the prevalence and characteristics of people experiencing homelessness in the United States.* Retrieved from http://homeless.samhsa.gov/ResourceFiles/hrc_factsheet.pdf

Sullivan, W. M. (2011). Interdependence in American society and commitment to the common good. *Applied Developmental Science, 15*, 73–78.

Supportive Parents Information Network. (2010). *Hunger and the safety net in San Diego County: A participatory action project.* Retrieved from http://www.spinsandiego.org/spin-scans/Hunger-FullReport.pdf

Supportive Parents Information Network. (n.d.). *Mission.* Retrieved from http://www.spinsandiego.org/

Sutter, I. (1996). The construction of poverty and homelessness in US cities. *Annual Review of Anthropology, 25*, 411–435.

Swan, R. S., Shaw, L. L., Cullity, S., Roche, M., Halpern, J., Limbert, W. M., & Humphrey, J. (2008). The untold story of welfare reform. *Journal of Sociology and Social Welfare, XXXV*, 133–151.

Taylor, D. M., & McKirnan, D. J. (1984). A five-stage model of intergroup relations. *British Journal of Social Psychology, 23*, 291–300.

Thomas, A., & Sawhill, I. (2005). For love *and* money? The impact of family structure on family income. *Future of Children, 15*, 57–74.

Thomas, E. F., & Louis, W. R. (2013). Doing democracy: The social psychological mobilization and consequences of collective action. *Social Issues and Policy Review, 7*, 173–200.

Thomas, S. L. (1998). Race, gender, and welfare reform: The antinatalist response. *Journal of Black Studies, 28,* 419–446.

Toure (2012, September 6). How to read political racial code. *Time.* Retrieved from http://ideas.time.com/2012/09/06/how-to-read-political-racial-code/

Triece, M. E. (2011). "Saying it the way we have lived it": Pragmatics and the "impossible position" of ideology critique. *Western Journal of Communication, 75,* 434–439.

Trisi, D., Sherman, A., & Broaddus, M. (2011, September 14). *Poverty rate second-highest in 45 years; Record numbers lacked health insurance, lived in deep poverty.* Retrieved from Center on Budget and Policy Priorities website: http://www.cbpp.org/cms/index.cfm?fa=view&id=3580

Tropman, J. E. (1998). *Does America hate the poor? The other American dilemma: Lessons for the 21st century from the 1960s and the 1970s.* Westport, CT: Praeger Publishers.

Twill, S. E., & Buckheister, N. (2009). A descriptive research study of economic human rights violations in America. *Journal of Poverty, 13,* 365–383.

Uhlmann, E. L., Poehlman, T. A., & Bargh, J. A. (2009). American moral exceptionalism. In J. T. Jost, A. C. Kay, & H. Thorisdottir (Eds.), *Social and psychological bases of ideology and system justification* (pp. 27–52). New York, NY: Oxford University Press.

Unger, R. K. (1982). Advocacy versus scholarship revisited: Issues in the psychology of women. *Psychology of Women Quarterly, 7,* 5–17.

United Nations. (2010). *The world's women 2010: Trends and statistics.* Retrieved from http://unstats.un.org/unsd/demographic/products/Worldswomen/WW2010pub.htm

United Nations Development Programme. (1995). *Human development report 1995: Gender and human development.* Retrieved from http://hdr.undp.org/en/reports/global/hdr1995/chapters/

United Nations Women. (n.d.). *Women, poverty, and economics.* Retrieved from http://www.unifem.org/gender_issues/women_poverty_economics/

Urban Institute. (2006, June). *A decade of welfare reform: Facts and figures.* Retrieved from http://www.urban.org/uploadedPDF/900980_welfarereform.pdf

US Bureau of Labor Statistics. (2010a, May 27). *Employment characteristics of families – 2009.* Retrieved from http://www.bls.gov/news.release/archives/famee_05272010.pdf

US Bureau of Labor Statistics. (2010b, March). *A profile of working poor, 2008* (Report 1022). Retrieved from www.bls.gov/cps/cpswp2008.pdf.

US Bureau of Labor Statistics. (2011a, December). *Consumer spending in 2010.* Retrieved from http://www.bls.gov/opub/focus/volume2_number12/cex_2_12.htm

US Bureau of Labor Statistics. (2011b, July). *Highlights of women's earnings in 2010* (Report 1031). Retrieved from http://www.bls.gov/cps/cpswom2010.pdf

US Census Bureau. (1973, September). *Money income in 1972 of families and persons* (Current Population Reports, P60-90). Retrieved from http://www2.census.gov/prod2/popscan/p60-090.pdf

US Census Bureau. (2004, September 15). *Average number of children per family and per family with children, by state: 2000 census* (Table ST-F1-2000). Retrieved from http://www.census.gov/population/socdemo/hh-fam/tabST-F1-2000.pdf

US Census Bureau. (2011, September). *Income, poverty, and health insurance coverage in the United States: 2010* (P60-239). Retrieved from http://www.census.gov/prod/2011pubs/p60-239.pdf

US Census Bureau. (2012a, September). *Income, poverty, and health insurance coverage in the United States: 2011* (P60-243). Retrieved from http://www.census.gov/prod/2012pubs/p60-243.pdf

US Census Bureau. (2012b, November). *The research supplemental poverty measure: 2011* (P60-244). Retrieved from http://www.census.gov/prod/2012pubs/p60-244.pdf

US Census Bureau. (n.d.). *Poverty thresholds.* Retrieved from http://www.census.gov/hhes/www/poverty/data/threshld/index.html

US Conference of Mayors. (2011, December). *Hunger and homelessness survey: A status report on hunger and homelessness in America's cities, a 29-city survey.* Retrieved from http://usmayors.org/pressreleases/uploads/2011-hhreport.pdf

US Department of Health and Human Services. (2002). *Temporary assistance for needy families: Fourth annual report to Congress.* Retrieved from http://archive.acf.hhs.gov/programs/ofa/data-reports/ar2001/indexar.htm

US Department of Health and Human Services. (2009). *Temporary assistance for needy families: Eighth annual report to Congress.* Retrieved from http://archive.acf.hhs.gov/programs/ofa/data-reports/annualreport8/ar8index.htm

US Department of Health and Human Services. (2012). *Temporary assistance for needy families: Ninth annual report to Congress.* Retrieved from http://www.acf.hhs.gov/programs/ofa/resource/ninth-report-to-congress

US Department of Housing and Urban Development. (2011a). *The 2010 annual homeless assessment report to Congress.* Retrieved from http://www.hudhre.info/documents/2010HomelessAssessmentReport.pdf

US Department of Housing and Urban Development. (2011b, February 9). *Assessing claims of housing discrimination against victims of domestic violence under the Fair Housing Act (FHAct) and the Violence against Women Act (VAWA).* Retrieved from http://www.hud.gov/offices/fheo/library/11-domestic-violence memo-with-attachment.pdf

US Department of Housing and Urban Development. (2012a, November). *The 2011 annual homeless assessment report to Congress.* Retrieved from https://www.onecpd.info/resources/documents/2011AHAR_FinalReport.pdf

US Department of Housing and Urban Development. (2012b, May 15). *Affordable housing.* Retrieved from http://www.hud.gov/offices/cpd/affordablehousing/

US Department of Labor. (1965, March). *The negro family: The case for national action.* Washington, DC: Author.

US Department of Labor. (2011, May 3). *Women's employment during the recovery.* Retrieved from http://www.dol.gov/_sec/media/reports/femalelaborforce/

US Department of Labor. (2012, March). *A profile of the working poor, 2010* (Report 1035). Retrieved from http://www.bls.gov/cps/cpswp2010.pdf

US General Accounting Office (GAO). (1998, January). *Welfare reform: States' efforts to expand child care programs* (GAO/HEHS-98-27). Retrieved from http://www.gao.gov/products/HEHS-98-27

US General Accounting Office (GAO). (1999a, February). *Welfare reform: States' experiences in providing employment assistance to TANF clients* (GAO/HEHS-99-22). Retrieved from http://www.gao.gov/archive/1999/he99022.pdf

US General Accounting Office (GAO). (1999b, April). *Welfare reform: Information on former recipients' status* (GAO/HEHS-99-48). Retrieved from http://www.gpo.gov/fdsys/pkg/GAOREPORTS-HEHS-99-48/pdf/GAOREPORTS-HEHS-99-48.pdf

US General Accounting Office (GAO). (1999c, November). *Education and care: Early childhood programs and services for low-income families* (GAO-HEHS-00-11). Retrieved from http://www.gao.gov/products/HEHS-00-11

US General Accounting Office (GAO). (2000, March). *Welfare reform: State sanction policies and the number of families affected* (GAO/HEHS-00-44). Retrieved from http://www.gao.gov/new.items/he00044.pdf

US General Accounting Office (GAO). (2001, September). *More research needed on TANF family caps and other policies for reducing out-of-wedlock births* (GAO-01-924). Retrieved from http://www.gao.gov/assets/240/232299.pdf

US General Accounting Office (GAO). (2002, July). *Welfare Reform: With TANF flexibility, states vary in how they implement work requirements and time limits* (GAO-02-770). Retrieved from http://www.gao.gov/products/GAO-02-770

US Government Accountability Office (GAO). (2010a, February). *Temporary Assistance for Needy Families: Fewer eligible families have received cash assistance since the 1990s, and the recession's impact on caseloads varies by state* (GAO 10-164). Retrieved from http://www.gao.gov/new.items/d10164.pdf

US Government Accountability Office (GAO). (2010b, May). *Temporary Assistance for Needy Families: Implications of recent legislative and economic changes for state programs and work participation rates* (GAO 10-525). Retrieved from http://www.gao.gov/htext/d10525.html

US Government Accountability Office (GAO). (2010c, September 21). *Temporary Assistance for Needy Families: Implications for caseload and program changes for families and program monitoring* (GAO-10-815T). Retrieved from http://www.gao.gov/products/GAO-10-815T

US Government Accountability Office (GAO). (2011, December 23). *Homeless women veterans: Actions needed to ensure safe and appropriate housing* (GAO-12-182). Retrieved from http://www.gao.gov/products/GAO-12-182

Vobejda, B., & Havemann, J. (1997). Doing the math on the welfare 'family cap.' *Washington Post*, p. A01.

Vojak, C. (2009). Choosing language: Social service framing and social justice. *British Journal of Social Work, 39*, 936–949.

Wagstaff, G. F. (1983). Attitudes to poverty, the Protestant work ethic, and political affiliation: A preliminary investigation. *Social Behavior and Personality: An International Journal, 11*, 45–47.

Wal-Mart wins legal victory in "gender discrimination" case. (2011, June 20). *The Telegraph*. Retrieved from http://www.telegraph.co.uk/finance/jobs/8588182/Wal-Mart-wins-legal-victory-in-gender-discrimination-case.html

Weaver, K. R., Shapiro, R. Y., & Jacobs, L. R. (1995). Trends: Welfare. *Public Opinion Quarterly, 59*, 606–627.

Weber, L. (1998). A conceptual framework for understanding race, class, gender, and sexuality. *Psychology of Women Quarterly, 22*, 13–32.

Weiner, B., Osborne, D., & Rudolph, U. (2010). An attributional analysis of reactions to poverty: The political ideology of the giver and the perceived morality of the receiver. *Personality and Social Psychology Review, 15*, 199–213.

Weinger, S. (1998). Poor children "know their place:" Perceptions of poverty, class, and public messages. *Journal of Sociology and Social Welfare, 25*, 100–118.

Weiss-Gal, I., Benyamini, Y., Ginzburg, K., Savaya, R., & Peled, E. (2009). Social workers' and service users' causal attributions for poverty. *Social Work, 54*, 125–133.

Weitz, R. (1982). Feminist consciousness raising, self-concept, and depression. *Sex Roles*, 8, 231–241.

Welfare Warriors. (2010, December 16). *"CPS is coming for you" song*. Retrieved from [video]: http://www.facebook.com/WelfareWarriors

Wen, C. K., Hudak, P. L., & Hwang, S. W. (2007). Homeless people's perceptions of welcomeness and unwelcomeness in healthcare encounters. *Journal of General Internal Medicine*, 22, 1011–1017.

Wenzel, S., Leake, B. D., & Gelberg, L. (2001). Risk factors for major violence among homeless women. *Journal of Interpersonal Violence*, 16, 739–752.

Wesely, J. K., & Wright, J. D. (2005). The persistence of partners: Examining intersections between women's homelessness and their adult relationships. *American Behavioral Scientist*, 48, 1082–1101.

Western Interstate Commission for Higher Education (WICHE). (1998, August). Welfare reform in the states: Where is higher education? Policy Insights. Retrieved from http://www.wiche.edu/Policy/PolicyInsights/WelfareReform/index.htm

Whitzman, C. (2006). At the intersection of invisibilities: Canadian women, homelessness, and health outside the "big city." *Gender, Place and Culture*, 13, 383–399.

Wilkinson, R., & Pickett, K. (2009). *The spirit level: Why greater equality makes societies stronger*. New York, NY: Bloomsbury Press.

Wilkinson, S. (1998). Focus groups in feminist research: Power, interaction, and the co-construction of meaning. *Women's Studies International Forum*, 21, 111–125.

Williams, W. R. (2009). Struggling with poverty: Implications for theory and policy of increasing research on social class-based stigma. *Analyses of Social Issues and Public Policy*, 9, 37–56.

Willis, J. (2000, February). *How we measure poverty*. Retrieved from Oregon Center for Public Policy website: http://www.ocpp.org/poverty/how/

Wilmoth, G. H. (2001). The "honest broker" role and evaluation research affirmed. *Analyses of Social Issues and Public Policy*, 1, 195–205.

Wing, A. K. (2003). *Critical race feminism: A reader* (2nd ed.). New York, NY: New York University Press.

Winton, R., & DiMassa, C. M. (2006, November 16). L.A. files patient "dumping" charges: Kaiser Permanente is accused of leaving a homeless woman to wander on skid row. *Los Angeles Times*. Retrieved from http://www.latimes.com/news/local/la-me-dumping16nov16,0,3911487.story?coll=la-home-headlines

Women of Color Policy Network. (2011, September). *Income and poverty in communities of color: A reflection on 2010 U.S. Census Bureau data*. New York: NYU Wagner.

Woods, T. A., Kurtz-Costes, B., & Rowley, S. J. (2005). The development of stereotypes about the rich and poor: Age, race, and family income differences in beliefs. *Journal of Youth and Adolescence*, 34, 437–445.

Wright, S. C., & Taylor, D. M. (1998). Responding to tokenism: Individual action in the face of collective injustice. *European Journal of Social Psychology*, 28, 647–667.

Wright, S. C., Taylor, D. M., & Moghaddam, F. M. (1990). Responding to membership in a disadvantaged group: From acceptance to collective protest. *Journal of Personality and Social Psychology*, 58, 994–1003.

Wu, C. F. (2008). Severity, timing, and duration of welfare sanctions and the economic well-being of TANF families with children. *Children and Youth Services Review*, 30, 26–44.

Yoshikawa, H., Aber, J. L., & Beardslee, W. R. (2012). The effects of poverty on mental, emotional, and behavioral health of children and youth: Implications for prevention. *American Psychologist, 67*, 272–284.

Zedlewski, S. (2008, December). *The role of welfare during a recession* (Recession and Recovery, No. 3). Retrieved from Urban Institute website: http://www.urban.org/UploadedPDF/411809_role_of_welfare.pdf

Zlotnick, C., Tam, T., & Bradley, K. (2010). Long-term and chronic homelessness in homeless women and women with children. *Social Work in Public Health, 25*, 470–485.

Zrinyi, M., & Balogh, Z. (2004). Student nurse attitudes toward homeless clients: A challenge for education and practice. *Nursing Ethics, 11*, 334–348.

Zucker, G. S., & Weiner, B. (1993). Conservatism and perceptions of poverty: An attributional analysis. *Journal of Applied Social Psychology, 23*, 925–943.

Zuckerman, D., & Kalil, A. (Eds.). (2000). The impact of welfare reform. *Journal of Social Issues, 56*(4).

Index

Women and Poverty: Psychology, Public Policy, and Social Justice, First Edition. Heather E. Bullock.
© 2013 Heather E. Bullock. Published 2013 by John Wiley and Sons, Ltd.